Founding editor: J. R. MULRYNE
General editors:
JAMES C. BULMAN, CAROL CHILLINGTON RUTTER

Julius Caesar

Manchester University Press

Already published in the series

Geraldine Cousin *King John*
Anthony B. Dawson *Hamlet*
Mary Judith Dunbar *The Winter's Tale*
Jay L. Halio *A Midsummer Night's Dream* (2nd edn)
Michael D. Friedman *Titus Andronicus*
Stuart Hampton-Reeves and Carol Chillington Rutter *The Henry VI plays*
Bernice W. Kliman *Macbeth* (2nd edn)
Alexander Leggatt *King Lear*
James Loehlin *Henry V*
Scott McMillin *Henry IV, Part One*
Lois Potter *Othello*
Hugh M. Richmond *King Henry VIII*
Margaret Shewring *King Richard II*
Virginia Mason Vaughan *The Tempest*

Julius Caesar

ANDREW JAMES HARTLEY

Manchester University Press

Copyright © Andrew James Hartley 2014

The right of Andrew James Hartley to be identified as the author of this work has been asserted by him in accordance with the Copyright, Designs and Patents Act 1988.

Published by Manchester University Press
Altrincham Street, Manchester M1 7JA, UK
www.manchesteruniversitypress.co.uk

British Library Cataloguing-in-Publication Data is available

ISBN 978 0 7190 7919 1 *hardback*
ISBN 978 1 5261 3944 3 *paperback*

First published by Manchester University Press in hardback 2014

This edition first published 2019

The publisher has no responsibility for the persistence or accuracy of URLs for any external or third-party internet websites referred to in this book, and does not guarantee that any content on such websites is, or will remain, accurate or appropriate.

Edited and typeset
by Frances Hackeson Freelance Publishing Services,
Brinscall, Lancs

To my father, who first instilled in me a love of the special magic which is theatre

CONTENTS

	Series editors' preface	page viii
	Acknowledgements	ix
	List of illustrations	x
	Introduction: political theatre	1
Chapter I	**'So are they all, all honourable men':** *Julius Caesar* **before the Second World War**	7
Chapter II	**The rise of European Fascism: Welles at the Mercury Theatre**	36
Chapter III	**(Un)American identities: Mankiewicz (1953)**	56
Chapter IV	**Wise saws and Modern(ist) instances: Anderson, Barton and Nunn**	83
Chapter V	**Glories past: the minor films**	110
Chapter VI	**The Romans in Britain:** *Caesar* **under Thatcher**	134
Chapter VII	**Accents yet unknown: global** *Caesars*	163
Chapter VIII	**'Growing on the South': Georgia Shakespeare 2001 and 2009**	194
Chapter IX	**A strange disposed time:** *Caesar* **at the millennium**	217
	Appendix	245
	Bibliography	249
	Index	253

SERIES EDITORS' PREFACE

Recently, the study of Shakespeare's plays as scripts for performance in the theatre has grown to rival the reading of Shakespeare as literature among university, college and secondary-school teachers and their students. The aim of the present series is to assist this study by describing how certain of Shakespeare's texts have been realised in production.

The series is not concerned to provide theatre history in the traditional sense. Rather, it employs the more contemporary discourses of performance criticism to explore how a multitude of factors work together to determine how a play achieves meaning for a particular audience. Each contributor to the series has selected a number of productions of a given play and analysed them comparatively. These productions – drawn from different periods, countries and media – were chosen not only because they are culturally significant in their own right but also because they represent something of the range and variety of the possible interpretations of the play in hand. They illustrate how the convergence of various material conditions helps to shape a performance: the medium for which the text is adapted; stage-design and theatrical tradition; the acting company itself; the body and abilities of the individual actor; and the historical, political and social contexts which condition audience reception of the play.

We hope that theatregoers, by reading these accounts of Shakespeare in performance, may enlarge their understanding of what a play-text is and begin, too, to appreciate the complex ways in which performance is a collaborative effort. Any study of a Shakespeare text will, of course, reveal only a small proportion of the play's potential meaning; but by engaging issues of how a text is translated in performance, our series encourages a kind of reading that is receptive to the contingencies that make theatre a living art.

J. R. Mulryne, Founding editor
James C. Bulman, Carol Chillington Rutter, General editors

ACKNOWLEDGEMENTS

I would like to thank Jim Bulman for first signing me up for this project and for his attentive editing thereafter, also to Carol Rutter and Matthew Frost for guiding it safely into print. The book has been long in the making and I would like to gratefully acknowledge all those who have kept me sane during its writing, particularly my family, and my friend and colleague Kirk Melnikoff, as well as those who have provided intellectual support over the years – Peter Holland, Barbara Hodgdon, W.B. Worthen, James Vesce and others too numerous to name – who have honed my sense of what theatre is and how we read it.

All Shakespeare quotations are from *The Complete Works of Shakespeare*, ed. David Bevington, 4th edition, HarperCollins, London.

LIST OF ILLUSTRATIONS

1. Norman Lloyd as Cinna the Poet surrounded by the mob in Orson Welles's 1937 production at the Mercury Theatre. *Photofest.* — page 44

2. Marlon Brando as Mark Antony addresses the crowd in Joseph Mankiewicz's 1953 film. *MGM/Photofest.* — 64

3. The assassination scene in Lindsay Anderson's production (1964), with Ian Bannen as Brutus over the prone Caesar. *Lindsay Anderson Archive, University of Stirling.* — 87

4. Cassius and Brutus (Ian Richardson and Barrie Ingram) in John Barton's 1968 production. *Tom Holte Theatre Photographic Collection © Shakespeare Birthplace Trust.* — 96

5. Mark Antony (Richard Johnson) addresses the crowd from the pulpit in Trevor Nunn's 1972 production. *Joe Cocks Studio Collection © Shakespeare Birthplace Trust.* — 102

6. Caesar (Joseph O'Conor) and his senate with rear projection, Brutus (Peter McEnery) bearded on the right, in Ron Daniels's 1983 production. *Joe Cocks Studio Collection © Shakespeare Birthplace Trust.* — 139

7. Robert Stephens as an Imperial Caesar in Steven Pimlott's 1991 production. *Reg Wilson © Royal Shakespeare Company.* — 146

8. The conspirators stand over the dead Caesar, as the audience look on in David Thacker's 1993 production. *Malcolm Davies Collection © Shakespeare Birthplace Trust.* — 153

9. The public, represented by the video images, tear apart Cinna, the poet, played by video artist Björn Melhus who collaborated with Falk Richter on the production (2007). *Photo by Arno Declair, Berlin.* — 174

10. From left to right: Porshia (Mmabatho Mogomotsi), Mark Anthony (Tony Kgoroge) SeZar (Hope Sprinter Sekgobela), Sinna (Siyabonga Twala), Kalphurnia (Keketso Semoko), in Yael Farber's *SeZar* (2001–2). *Photo by Suzy Bernstein.* — 187

11. Bruce Evers as Caesar (left) hectors Decius (Brik Berkes) and Calphurnia (Teresa DeBerry) over breakfast in John Dillon's Georgia Shakespeare production (2001). *Photo by T.W. Meyer.* — 199

12	The closing image of Dillon's 2001 production. Antony (Saxon Palmer) stoops to Brutus' body as Octavius (Gregory Thomas Isaac) levels his pistol. *Photo by Rob Dillard.*	202
13	The conspirators (left to right) Cinna (Eugene H. Russell, IV), Cassius (Joe Knezevich), Casca (Allan Edwards), Brutus (Neal Ghant) and Decius (Brik Berkes) (dir. Richard Garner, 2009). *Photo by Bill DeLoach.*	207
14	A triumphant Caesar (Ian Hogg) greets the crowd after the singing of the rousing republican anthem as Brutus (Greg Hicks) waits upstage centre (dir. Edward Hall, 2001). *Malcolm Davies Collection © Shakespeare Birthplace Trust.*	225
15	Caesar (Jeffery Kissoon) is petitioned before the assassination, with the soothsayer above (dir. Gregory Doran 2012). *Kwame Lestrade © Royal Shakespeare Company.*	240

INTRODUCTION

Political theatre

Julius Caesar opens with a scene in which authority figures struggle to read their audience. That audience, which is celebrating Caesar's triumphal return on the death of Pompey, have dispensed with those signs of their profession which would normally announce their function and status. The carpenter is without his leather apron and ruler, and when the tribunes try to determine who the cobbler is they get puns and double-speak which threaten to derail the hierarchical order of the moment entirely. The tribunes resort to lecturing the people who say nothing, but whether their silence manifests the guilt the tribunes accuse them of – as opposed to boredom, resentment or something more politic – is left open to question.

The scene is a telling one because it establishes right away the play's preoccupation with audience, with reading the outer signs of inner emotion and of shaping performance to generate a desired response in others. When Flavius and Marullus go off to pull the scarves from Caesar's images they are engaging in a counter performance, an *upstaging* if you like, in which they subvert the crowd's prior performance of support for Caesar. This in turn will generate another performance, this time of state power, as they are 'put to silence' for their actions or, to frame the thing theatrically, for their *acting*. That silencing will be read by the conspirators and will itself be part of what generates more action/acting, this time in the form of murder.

The nature of that murder and its aftermath are planned in theatrical terms: the location, the moment, and the announcement to the people all thought through in terms of how they will affect an audience. Caesar dies in the Capitol at the foot of

Pompey's statue, the assassins first orchestrating a moment in which Caesar is coerced to perform his absolute and intractable authority, thereby not just prompting the killing but framing it logically. The killers – sacrificers, not butchers – then process through Rome with their bloody weapons held over their heads, chanting 'Peace, freedom and liberty'. Having thus demonstrated his selfless motives, the chief conspirator then meets with the people to explain what he has done.

That everything goes horribly wrong for Brutus and Cassius cannot be simply attributed to the way Mark Antony speaks to the crowd. The core problem can be glimpsed in that opening scene with the cobbler in which the fundamental instability of theatre is rendered in the simple terms of actor and audience, and the way the semiotics of performance rely upon an exchange which shapes both. Audiences respond to actors, but those responses are also a form of acting which the actor has to respond to as if he were an audience member, modulating his performance accordingly. Thus audiences become actors and vice versa, and the only sure way to fail is to press ahead with a scripted performance regardless. Brutus assumes that if he explains what the blood on his hands means, the audience will applaud him, but he does not consider the way that so dramatic a symbol might take on other associations (butcher, not sacrificer), particularly when inflected by an adversary with a keener sense of the theatrical dynamic. Brutus relies on logic and rhetoric and that most naive of actorly assumptions that motivation is all. Antony learns quickly that passion is catching (on feeling tears start to his eyes when Octavius's servant weeps), that audiences – especially mob audiences – respond more to emotion than ideas, that they have short memories and are swayed most by what happened last, that spectacle – especially bloody spectacle couched in personal terms – trumps all kinds of speech, and that righteously draped self-interest caps everything. These principles guide him through the funeral oration. He speaks after Brutus, he weeps (or pretends to), he produces the violated corpse itself reducing Brutus's abstract rhetoric to the personal and concrete, and he uses Caesar's will to suggest more clearly than Brutus or Flavius ever could which side the people should be on. Beyond the oft commended rhetorical skill of the speech these are theatrical devices, and they speak to the play's core preoccupation with political performance.

This is, of course, only the most obvious and decisive instance of such political theatre. Other smaller examples abound in the play. Time and again the characters use performative means to display their authority, to conceal their purposes and to sway others to their viewpoint at crucial moments. Sometimes these are cat and mouse games between two men – Brutus and Cassius, say, or Casca and Cicero – testing each other's leanings and convictions, each gauging the other before revealing more. Sometimes they are about interpreting signs – omens, portents and dreams, for instance – where the interpretive act is as much a performance as the spectacle it reads, like Decius persuading Caesar to come to the Capitol. Sometimes the performances are not intended as such, being simple events such as skirmishing on the battlefield, but which are then mined for meaning, interpreted or misinterpreted by the key participants. In each case a complex subject is read by an on-stage audience, and the point is not so much that the audience read rightly or wrongly, but that multiple readings are possible, suspended in the special entropy which is the air of performance. Political theatre and theatrical politics cannot force audience reading. They can steer, they can inflect, but precisely how an audience (real or metaphorical) will respond, the performer cannot truly know.

On a crucial level, then, *Julius Caesar* is about theatre and its use on the political stage. But for a play so charged with the theatrical and with ideas of performativity, the play's stage history has been chequered at best, and reviews of strong productions invariably open with a note of surprise. The play tends to be remembered as a classroom text, once considered safe in schools because of its absence of bawdy, and where it was traditionally taught as a meditation on Roman history, on rhetoric and on nobility. Latterly those qualities – coupled with the play's minimal interest in women and none in race – have left it increasingly displaced by more obviously fashionable or topical plays (*Othello*, or *Romeo and Juliet*), and the aura of dust clearly influences audiences and directors. Until the late twentieth century, when it has enjoyed a theatrical resurgence, production of the play has been comparatively scarce, and few stagings have been greeted with real excitement since Orson Welles first pointed squarely at the spectre of European Fascism in his 1937 Mercury Theatre production. However much that first scene might be fascinating as a study in the reading of signs, and therefore as a scene *about* theatre, it is notoriously difficult to stage *in* a theatre, the endlessly punning cobbler often cut beyond recognition, his humour dismissed as deadening archaism. This sense of *Caesar* as shackled by the past and by a lack of inherent theatricality has hung over the play's entire stage history.

Over the last four hundred years of production a series of complaints about the play as the basis for theatrical production has become familiar. First, it is argued, the play climaxes too early. The title character is dead midway through the third act, and after the *coup de theatre* of the funeral orations the play seems to lose its sense of purpose, collapsing into bickering between the various participants and some fragments of combat cribbed from Plutarch. Second, the closest thing to a protagonist in the play is Brutus, a man we never get to know, who has only one real soliloquy revealing surprisingly little, and who never fully takes charge of the play. He is, we are told, a sketch for Hamlet or – more obviously – for Macbeth, but those are infinitely richer roles which are the hearts and minds of their respective plays in ways Brutus is not to *Julius Caesar*. Third, as we move further away from the originating Elizabethan moment, the play seems more old-fashioned in its politics, deriding the public as ignorant and lamenting any assault on the social order as wrongheaded and ultimately doomed. Fourth, two small roles give little scope for actresses, and both directors and audiences find the play's male-dominated world less interesting or acceptable than they once did. Fifth, the play is almost completely devoid of humour.

All these points are, of course, arguable, and many of the productions I will discuss in this book have countered them on stage, but it is striking how often forms of them surface in pejorative reviews, and how frequently these critical chestnuts are used to pelt unsatisfactory productions: they do, in fact, contain truths which have to be grappled with. A survey of the play's stage history reveals, for instance, how few Brutuses have been praised, even when the actors playing other roles are widely applauded. He lacks Cassius's passion or Casca's humour. He is given to moralising and is too quick to believe the praise heaped on him and his family heritage, so he can easily come off as a prig. Most problematically, he is consistently and wilfully responsible for a series of disastrous political and military decisions, so that by the end of the play it is hard to see one thing which he judged correctly, even when overruling the clearer-sighted Cassius. The dominant theatrical interpretation of the twentieth century is close to that played by Orson Welles: Brutus as an ineffective liberal, bookish, principled and clueless about the workings of power. This Brutus, as actors know to their chagrin, rarely pleases.

But pleasure, particularly uncritical pleasure, is not what the play is about, and in recent years audiences have been more willing to find the play interesting – even compelling – because of what used to be considered flaws in the play. From the late twentieth century on there has been a palpable swelling of interest as older concerns with oratory have been replaced by a more complex sense of character, particularly as framed by an urgent sense of the play's political drama. There seem to be more journalists and bloggers applying the most coveted language of the theatre review to *Julius Caesar*: thrilling, surprising, invigorating and, most loaded of all, topical.

Unlike other Shakespeare plays, there has been no seismic shift in *Caesar*'s stage history, no new reading or production innovation which has transformed the play entirely in the theatre. It is not a natural magnet for the identity politics of race and gender which have been at the heart of many radical rethinkings of Shakespeare's other plays, nor has critical opinion of the play's core issues altered especially drastically. Two factors might be identified, however, as marking a shift over the last century and a half. One is the steady movement away from heroic idealism, and the other is the quest for more contemporary political resonance. Welles's 1937 production was astonishingly forward-looking in this latter respect. In pointing up contemporary political issues, his *Caesar* anticipated mainstream production by half a century. In the Mercury *Caesar*'s wake, many companies made use of Welles's Fascist symbolism, but almost none of them achieved his production's urgency, because for them the Nazi threat was already part of history. It was not until the 1990s that major companies like the RSC began looking for similar contemporary resonance, an impulse which was energised by recent political and military events filtered through an awareness of how the media shaped those events for the general public. Few Shakespeare productions have achieved a greater sense of imminent topicality than Deborah Warner's 2005 *Caesar* at the Barbican. If honour and principle were the watchwords for *Caesars* of the nineteenth century, and totalitarianism the core of twentieth, the word which ghosts twenty-first-century productions most clearly is 'spin'.

This book seeks to trace that evolutionary journey, and it is a journey which takes place as much in time as in space, not simply because my study is broadly chronological, but because many of the productions discussed here engage actively with the play's own sense of time. *Julius Caesar* recorded historical events for its original audience, but it did so for a world which has itself become history. When Brutus muses on how many times their actions will be played 'in sport' in the future in 'accents yet unknown', he creates a moment of what I will call temporal vertigo in which the audience experiences a simultaneous layering of past(s), present and future. This vertigo is at the heart of what the play is on stage, the well of its deepest and most stimulating theatrical meanings. It points up not a generic timelessness, but a multiple temporal fixity, different points in time seeming to occur in the same moment, and it is – perhaps more than for any other Shakespeare play in performance – the source of *Caesar's* curious ability to be both historical meditation and urgent contemporary reflection at the same instant.

I have chosen to discuss productions either because they somehow speak to trends and ideas about the play which characterise their period of production, or because they have significant or interesting features in their own right. Though the book is undergirded with a sense of the play's stage history, it seeks to study specific moments in that history rather than trying to retell the larger narrative. I have used an array of means to try to get close to those specific productions, keeping an eye on both practicalities and a sense of critical purpose. In some cases I foreground newspaper reviews as a way of contextualising the production within the larger culture; at other times I have made use of video archives, actor interviews, and my personal experience as an audience member. In each case I have tried to make the manner in which I experienced the production transparent and pertinent to my observations.

CHAPTER I

'So are they all, all honourable men': *Julius Caesar* before the Second World War

The evolution of any Shakespeare play on stage is always in part the story of Shakespeare's standing in society at large, and the trajectory mapped by *Julius Caesar* is a familiar one; a movement away from the eighteenth and nineteenth centuries' interest in spectacle and back towards some of the conditions of the Elizabethan playhouse with increasing value placed on textual purity. The movement in time is also a movement away from populism, the details of which are bound to larger cultural matters of taste, education, and the values with which Shakespeare came to be associated. In the case of *Julius Caesar,* much of that process was marked by a restriction of or resistance to the play's darker political content, and the guiding principles of production grew out of an idealised perspective on its core characters, imposing an overtly moral brand of history on Shakespeare's narrative. This emphasis reflected a larger cultural preoccupation with oratory and classicism: but as the play moved towards the twentieth century, such things were gradually replaced by a version of realism. In the course of that evolution a tension arose between who the core characters were, whose story should be considered dominant. In short, a productive way of considering the play's performance history is by asking whose play it has been perceived to be.

In the twentieth century the title character has occasionally loomed over productions like the colossal statues often relied upon to keep his memory alive in the latter half of the show, and there is some reason – albeit speculative – to think that this was how the play was first seen. Later and most lastingly the play was perceived to be Brutus's story. Though focus shifted fleetingly towards Cassius, Antony became increasingly central. As he did so, the play morphed further and began to be the story of the people of Rome, often reduced to a cipher for a generic and dangerous mob.

Little is known of *Julius Caesar*'s early performance history, so any claims about what it was 'first ... perceived to be' fudges what we mean by 'first'. In terms of traditional stage history, an account of *Julius Caesar* doesn't really begin until almost a century after the play's date of composition, but an impression of audience interest might be gathered from the play's title.

Caesar's play

David Daniel calls the story of the prelude to and aftermath of Julius Caesar's death 'the most famous historical event in the West outside the Bible' (Daniel, 1999: 1), and while we may quibble about such a statement in the twenty-first century, Shakespeare's original audience would probably have concurred. Caesar was central to sixteenth-century English grammar school education as both a writer and a historical personage. Roger Ascham's *Schoolmaster* (1570) lists Caesar with Varro, Sallust and Cicero as one of the four prose writers most to be emulated, and with Varro's works largely non-extant, this core triumverate came to dominate the grammar school curriculum from the 1530s (Baldwin, 1944: 565; Orme, 2006: 124). Ascham praises Caesar as a flawless stylist, so he was particularly well-suited to be a model for study and emulation, but the works for which he was chiefly known – his Commentaries – are historical records of his own time and include the specific political and military circumstances which ultimately led to his death, circumstances which would have been drawn more sharply still by the study of the other core stylists, Sallust and particularly Cicero who were his contemporaries. The story of his death was also studied extensively through the work of historians such as Plutarch, whose *Lives of the Noble Greeks and Romans* was Shakespeare's primary source. Caesar's *Commentaries* were also available to those who had smaller Latin than Shakespeare, being translated into English by Philemon Holland in 1565; and after Thomas North's translation of Plutarch's *Lives* was published in 1579, the account of Caesar's death became part of what Kenneth Charlton calls the period's 'most widely read history book' (Charlton, 1965: 249). The English, moreover, had a particular preoccupation with

Caesar because he had led the first Roman conquest of Britain, and therefore – according to a familiar Elizabethan logic of appropriation – laid the ground work for the founding of a new post-Catholic Roman Empire. Celia cites Caesar's 'thrasonical brag' in *As You Like It*, *Henry V*'s Fluellen is used to lampoon his 'disciplines of the wars', Prince Edward discourses on his wit, achievement and the tradition that he built the Tower of London in *Richard III*, and there are countless other echoes of Caesar's work and personal history percolating through the work of other writers. All of this is enough to suggest the omnipresence of Caesar and his story in the minds of late sixteenth-century culture without the specific associations raised by Steve Sohmer in his *Shakespeare's Mystery Play*.

Sohmer's position, briefly stated, is that *Julius Caesar* was the first play staged at the newly opened Globe Theatre on 12 June 1599, and that through an elaborate system of textual allusion, the play provides commentary and critique of Queen Elizabeth's refusal to reform the old Catholic calendar which had been revised by Pope Gregory XIII in 1579, and which created numerous problems thereafter, particularly in the year of the play. Though I am finally unpersuaded by the argument, the book nicely evokes the way that the historical Caesar (who had reformed the calendar and named a month after himself) could serve to focus issues of power and dissent of a strictly Elizabethan kind. Rather than reducing Caesar to a morally binary study of tyranny in which the present monarch is surreptitiously evoked for her high-handed religious direction of the country, however, I prefer to see in Caesar a complex and shifting locus of cultural authority that permeated Elizabethan culture to its very marrow, but which had multiple valences and associations. As Maria Wyke has recently demonstrated, Caesar's story morphed into various distinct incarnations with different instructive and entertainment purposes, some of them fabular (such as the medieval tradition that no one but Caesar could ride his horse, which was often depicted as a fantastic beast resembling a unicorn), some foregrounding his adventurism and courage, some his cruelty and military acumen, some his exploits in love and lust. He also became a matrix for ideas about government, liberty and tyranny, particularly in the circumstances of his death. Sometimes he was a hero whose assassins were forever damned like Dante's Brutus and Cassius, linked by their crimes to none other than Judas Iscariot himself, despite a medieval tradition which had made his name synonymous not just with the abuse of secular power but with the Antichrist (Wyke, 2008: 155, 247). Machiavelli rejected Caesar's form of government as something to be followed by Renaissance princes, but humanist scholars drew distinctions among Caesar's various personae so that his literary and military talents were unsullied by his restriction of republican liberties (155).

The point is a simple one but crucial for this study: Caesar could mean many things, as could his murder, and though Brutus and Cassius are sometimes mocked for anticipating the way their actions would be repeated 'in states unborn and accents yet unknown', their most significant mistake was in failing to recognise that Caesar's assassination would retain an element of semantic ambiguity, not that they had simply misread the future. In other words, Caesar's death was the stuff of theatre from the outset: something to which audiences responded depending on their prior mindset and – literally and metaphorically – their line of sight. More to the point, and in this I agree with Sohmer, the ambiguity inherent in what Caesar's death *meant* was always finally political, and though I will not speculate on how the diverse audience of an Elizabethan theatre processed what they were seeing in terms of their own political climate, it seems impossible to deny the play a topical resonance for that original audience. Elizabeth had grown old and inflexible, had tightened her grip on all aspects of English politics, had stirred opposition among religious proponents of various stripes, had caused fears of civil war on her heirless death, and had been the focus of plots and rebellions domestic and foreign. Ireland was in chaos, and the Essex rebellion was waiting in the wings. However the antiquity of the subject matter might have protected the company against charges of direct topicality, there can be no question that *Julius Caesar* touched something of the contemporary zeitgeist.

The play did not appear in print until the First Folio of 1623, though it was probably written in 1599. It is not listed in Francis Meres' 1598 *Palladis Tamia*, but seems to be recalled by John Weever in his *The Mirror of Martyrs* (1601) which refers to the 'many headed multitude' listening to 'Brutus' speech that Caesar was ambitious', and then to 'eloquent Mark Antony'. Though it is possible that he has a similar play by someone other than Shakespeare in mind, Weever's direct quotation – 'Caesar was ambitious'(3.2.80) – seems more than coincidental. Weever's book was probably written within the previous two years, which coincides with an account by one Thomas Platter, a visitor from Switzerland, who – on 21 October 1599 – saw 'the tragedy of the first emperor Julius Caesar' in a thatched theatre on the south bank of the Thames. No known Caesar play was owned by the Admiral's men at the Rose, and the Swan was not then operating regularly, so the 'strewn roof-house' in question is almost certainly the newly erected Globe, home of Shakespeare and the Chamberlain's Men. Some scholars hear echoes of Antony's 'O judgment! Thou art fled to brutish beasts, / And men have lost their reason!' (3.2.106–7) in lines from Ben Jonson's *Every Man Out of his Humour* (also 1599) and the anonymous *The Wisdom of Doctor Dodypoll* (1600), though these repeat the sentiment rather than the wording and may suggest that the exclamation was proverbial.

Platter's account, though brief, presents a few telling details. He says that the performance had 'at least fifteen characters' and was 'very well acted'. At the end of what he calls a 'comedy,' the cast 'danced according to their custom with extreme elegance.' The jig seems to have involved only four of the players, since Platter concludes: 'Two in men's clothes and two in women's gave this performance, in wonderful combination with each other' (Chambers, 1923,Vol II: 365).

Leonard Digges' prefatory verse printed in the First Folio cites 'half-Sword parlaying Romans', a phrase which reappears in the 1640 edition, now made more specifically referent to *Julius Caesar*:

> So have I seen, when Caesar would appear,
> And on the Stage at half-sword parlay were,
> *Brutus and Cassius*: oh how the Audience,
> Were ravish'd, with what wonder they went thence ...

Poems lauding the quality of what they preface must, of course, be taken with caution, but Digges affirms a memory of the playhouse atmosphere itself, and one which holds on – seventeen years later – to that image of the parlaying half-sword Romans.

What is striking about all these early references is how visual and theatrical they are. Even the verbal echoes in Weever and possible parodies in Jonson – all from Mark Antony's funeral oration – echo not dialogue, but its more performative cousin, oratory.

Indeed, I find it suggestive that Weever's reference to what Brutus said about Caesar is actually phrased in Mark Antony's terms, as if the memory of the words has been shaped by the experience of an audience member who is finally swayed by the 'eloquent Mark Antony'.

Maddening though it is that Platter's remarks about the play are so brief, it is worth noting that he gives such weight to an element of the production which has no textual traces: the dance at the end. Together with the remark that the production was 'very well acted', his comments on the dance emphasise the performers and the scale of the spectacle ('*at least* fifteen characters' [added emphasis]).

Even Digges' verses designed to set off the Folio text recall an expressly visual version of the play. The audience were ravished 'when Caesar would *appear* [added emphasis]', and though it's unclear if this refers to the star actor's first entrance or his later ghostly apparition, the emphasis is on the visual.[1] The reference to Brutus and Cassius parlaying is also a visual memory of the 4.3 (or possibly 5.1) argument whose key detail is drawn from a piece of stage business, their being at 'half-sword'.[2] Whatever has happened to the play since, it began as a theatrical event driven by a striking visual dimension, by the bodies of actors in conflict, by spectacle and by dance.

We know of several performances for royalty, one for the marriage festivities of Princess Elizabeth in the winter of 1612–13 at Whitehall, then two for King Charles I, one at St James's in January 1636 and another at the Cockpit in November 1638. It is difficult to identify the specific appeal of the play for these audiences, though it is tempting to see an official Stuart reading of the play as a morality against tyrannicide. Such a general idea – complicated as it would have been by Caesar's non-Christian status if analogue were pushed into allegory – may have drawn more topical specificity from James's overt self-association with the peace-making Augustus, which the pragmatic Octavius would become. As with the topical associations of *Macbeth* and its ties to James through Fleance, only a persistently blinkered reading of the play which irons out or ignores all its ambiguities and contradictions can make the play simply a paean to the Stuart monarchy, but the pressures of governmental orthodoxy and vanity may have rendered such a reading plausible, even self-evident.

The play reappears on Drury Lane after the interregnum in 1663, performed by the King's Company with Charles Hart as Brutus and Michael Mohun as Cassius, both of whom had been actors before the Civil War and saw military service during it. By 1670 the frequently revived play also featured the young star Edward Kynaston as Mark Antony, who stayed on in the role after Hart and Mohun were replaced by Thomas Betterton and William Smith respectively in 1682 when the King's Company merged with The Duke's Company. Little is known of the early Restoration stagings beyond the assumption that Mohun and Hart would have brought vestiges of a Caroline sensibility to their brand of performance, but the audience must in the new royalist climate have seen echoes of the execution of Charles I and the Civil War in the play's subject matter. If so, one might expect productions to have foregrounded Caesar and the wrongness of the conspirators.

Kynaston's casting as Antony is intriguing. In his youth, Kynaston was renowned for his performance of women, and in the 1660s he often played both male and female parts, sometimes in the same play, in spite of the fact that women were now permitted on stage.[3] Kynaston was famously androgynous of appearance and – some said – lifestyle, Pepys calling him both 'the prettiest woman' and 'the handsomest man' in the theatre while Colley Cibber mentions in his memoirs Kynaston's penchant for slipping away from the theatre in drag and in the company of court ladies (Cook, 2007: 67; Cibber, 2000: 71). In a play so preoccupied with male values and rivalries, the casting of Kynaston may reveal a notion of Antony's emotional nature, the text's depth of personal feeling and tendency to (unfeigned) tears in accord with period ideas about femininity. Kynaston's reported ties to George Villiers, second Duke of Buckingham, may even have suggested a frisson of the homoerotic in his connection to Caesar, though such associations – if they were ever there – had surely faded away by the time Kynaston played the role with Betterton and Smith. Such an interpretation does not banish the possibility of a calculating, political Antony, but it does suggest that any such deliberation probably proceeded from both a genuine sense of closeness to Caesar and a passionate commitment to revenge his memory. This is, of course, highly speculative, though after the formation of the United Company more information about productions of *Caesar* becomes available, partly due to the reprinting of the play at least six times between 1684 and 1691 (Ripley, 1980: 17).

Brutus's play

The printed text of the 1684 edition, largely a reproduction of the Folio without significant cutting or prompt-book insertions, claims that it is printed 'As it is now acted at the Theatre Royal', and the cast list includes characters such as Cinna the Poet who was often cut in later productions. Marellus is replaced with Casca, and Cicero with Trebonius, surely a theatrical detail, but the idea that the acting text of the day was effectively the same as the Folio is unlikely. The 1684 text contains the errors of the Folio which would surely have been corrected in performance, and there are inconsistencies introduced by the elimination of Marellus and Cicero because the change has been made only at the level of speech prefixes.[4] The implication is that the printer made alterations to the speech prefixes only to square with the appended cast list, thereby justifying his claim to topicality ('As it is now acted ... '). What actual cuts and changes were made to the lines themselves, we cannot possibly say. It may be tempting to see the eighteenth and nineteenth centuries' adaptive hand as a later incursion into what was originally a far purer approach to the letter of Shakespearean text, but this is problematically wishful thinking of a post-lapsarian kind.[5]

The insertion of Casca for Marellus (different printings vary in their spelling of the name, some making it Marullus or Marallus, as is now more common) might be seen as creating a tonally and psychologically fractured character, though this substitution (as with that of Trebonius for Cicero) became the rule for the eighteenth and nineteenth centuries. But that sense of fracture or character inconsistency may be a twentieth-century construct, premised on ideas about character continuity which grew out of nineteenth-century fiction. It might also be said that a sense of inconsistency in parts rolled together is largely a readerly phenomenon, lacking as it does the perception of unity automatically created by the persistent body of the actor, and recent productions have actually reverted to these kinds of character conflation with productive results (See Chapter VIII). Perhaps the replacement of Marellus with Casca enacts a specifically theatrical memory of earlier doubling in which the audience experience of the parts in performance barely drew distinction between the two roles, personated as they were by a single actor. In any case, the rolling of Casca and Marellus into a single role, rather than being obviously absurd as is sometimes asserted (Ripley, 1980: 26), makes good theatrical sense and does not necessarily disrupt or corrupt the play.

Betterton continued to play Brutus until January 1707/8, treating the role as that of a dignified, patriotic and thoughtful hero, establishing a sense that he was the play's tragic hero.[6] Cassius became his irascible foil, and 'the quarrel scene' (4.3) became the play's high point, its appeal seeming to lie in the modulation of Brutus's restraint, particularly in transitioning from the fury of the argument to the revelation of Portia's death. Mark Antony pursued Brutus with respect, a patriot avenging the death of a dear friend, an interpretation which would culminate more than a century later in the cutting of the 'proscription scene' (4.1) in Kemble's 1812 production, thereby emphasising Antony's Roman equanimity and removing any sense of ruthlessness and opportunism.

The view of a Roman heroic ideal which had shaped the staging of Brutus, and Betterton's approach to the part in particular, hardened and clarified in the eighteenth century. With the ascendancy of Walpole and the Whigs and the steady reduction of monarchical powers first under Queen Anne – whose Tory leanings were manifest – and then under George I who was deeply unpopular and considered (probably unfairly) both unintelligent and unconcerned with England, the political climate changed. If Caesar had been a victim for much of the seventeenth century, he became a villain to the eighteenth, and the overt patriotism of productions fastened squarely on Brutus. He was seen as modelling a Whiggish aristocratic republicanism, fiercely opposed to absolute monarchy, selfless and devoted solely to the good of his country, in the face of over-reaching monarchical meddling at odds with the public interest.

This is clear from the Dryden–Davenant performance text of 1719 which persisted, with occasional tweaks, for almost a century thereafter as the core theatrical script.[7] This text cut only 160 lines and added 28, continued the tradition of combining roles (Artemidorus and the Sooth Sayer, for instance), reduced speaking parts and minimised references to the supernatural which the rationalist eighteenth century found embarrassing. Most conspicuously, however, it simplified character in moral terms, and Brutus was the principal beneficiary. He became morally clearer, more elevated in mind and utterance, references to his impatience or intemperance stripped from his exchange with Portia and from the quarrel scene. In his encounter with the ghost he was allowed to restate his anti-tyrannical motives, calling Caesar 'ungrateful' for wanting to 'enthral' Rome. Most strikingly, his suicide speech was given greater dignity and patriotic purpose:

> Scorning to view his Country's Misery,
> Thus Brutus always strikes for Liberty.
>   [Stabs himself]
> Poor slavish Rome, Farewel, Caesar now be still,
> I kill'd not thee with half so good a will.
> (Ripley, 1980: 29)

This sense of Rome as 'slavish', an ideal corrupted by the actuality of its ignoble people, was entirely in keeping with the Whigs' aristocratic base, and the abstract nature of Brutus's Roman republic was achieved in production at the expense of the actual Roman populace who were effectively banished from the stage. Crowd scenes were heavily abbreviated, all responses to the funeral orations were eliminated entirely, and the death of Cinna the Poet – the darkly comic study of mob violence which is often the core of modern productions – was cut. Caesar himself was personally vilified as a tyrant who curbed the liberties of his people. He was depicted without grandeur or anything that might render him impressive, but his corruption was not permitted to extend to the other principals who remained idealised.

So completely did the Whiggish anti-royalist position dominate theatrical interpretation of the play that a counter was sought in a heavily adaptive pair of plays – neither of which was staged – by Edmund Sheffield, second Duke of Buckingham, in 1722. The first of these (*The Tragedy of Julius Caesar, Altered*) took Shakespeare's play – rewritten heavily and with choric speeches between the acts – as far as the murder of Caesar itself, and the second (*The Tragedy of Marcus Brutus*) picked up the story immediately before the battle of Philippi.[8] The former, tellingly, includes some of the now familiar combining of roles (Casca for Marellus, Trebonius for Favius), and rethinks Brutus's orchard soliloquy in ways conspicuously suggesting Macbeth contemplating Duncan's virtues. The speech is worth considering for the lengths to which it goes to push what many modern readers would consider an already problematic speech into still more morally dubious territory:

> But my own words reproach me; can I call
> Myself his friend, and yet consent to kill him?
> By heav'n, no less than plain ingratitude!
> That heavy load presses my tender mind;
> I cannot bear it. Nay, this Caesar also
> Is humbly brave and gentle in his greatness;
> Apt for converse, and easy of access;
> Skill'd in all arts, matchless in eloquence;
> In war and business indefatigable.
> Bounteous as nature, merciful as Heav'n;
> In all, sublime, high and unparrallel'd.
> Yet oft is humility but the ladder,
> By which the ambitious climber gets so high;
> But when he once attains the utmost round,
> Then strait he throws the useless engine down,
> Looks in the clouds, and scorns the low degrees
> By which he did ascend.
>   (Sheffield, 1722: 155)

The play concludes after Antony's (very lightly amended) funeral oration with a couplet tacked onto 'Mischief, thou art afoot': 'Ambition, when unbounded, deserves a curse / But an assassination deserves a worse' (202). It is hardly surprising that this adaptation was critically ridiculed and never performed, but the desperate tang of its royalist rhetoric perhaps throws some light on just how Whiggish contemporary productions seemed to their political rivals. Further, it suggests that Shakespeare's version of Brutus's soliloquy, which was unaltered in the Dryden–Davenant acting text, was – in spite of its pragmatic moral ambivalence – considered compatible with the heroic, principled and self-sacrificing anti-royalist Brutus of the theatrical day.

The productions would probably have seemed stiff and declamatory to a modern audience, the performances overly artful, as is suggested by the critical praise actors received for their vocal musicality, elegance, nobility, propriety and sensibility (Ripley, 1980: 44–8). Unsurprisingly, what was valued was the extent to which actors modelled a version of Rome mediated by the ideals of eighteenth-century England. Similarly rigid and restrictive were the conventionally 'realist' scenic flats and the costuming: generic, unhistorical Roman cuirasses, skirts and close-fitting breeches. The stars wore the best attire, even if disproportionate to their roles, so that Caesar himself – played as a stock tyrant devoid of personality or magnificence – was sartorially outshone by Brutus. Women wore contemporary dress, reinforcing a sense that this version of Rome was male, the female actors very much limited by the mores of their own culture (41). Performances seem to have been briskly paced, at least by the standards of the subsequent century, a century which would also dispense with the relative immediacy of the apron stage and confine the action inside the proscenium.

The play was extensively produced throughout the first half of the eighteenth century when English political sensibilities, classicism and nationalism combined with the performances of renowned actors – notably Barton Booth (Brutus) and Robert Wilks (Antony) – to keep the play among the most often produced of Shakespeare's plays on stage. This period coincided with the rise of Shakespeare as national poet, and *Caesar* figured prominently in that process since it was seen to reinforce the nationalist values for which Shakespeare had been newly canonised. Indeed, *Julius Caesar* was the first Shakespeare play to become part of secondary school education, appearing at Westminster school in 1728 (see Dobson, 1995: 61). Pope's edition of Shakespeare (freely 'corrected' to meet the tastes of the day) appeared in 1725. The fundraising committee for the monument to Shakespeare in Westminster Abbey mounted a benefit performance of *Julius Caesar* at Drury Lane in 1738, in which the Whiggish reading was made explicit in a specially written prologue and epilogue. The former nicely dovetails the pro-Republican and pro-British stance:

> While Brutus bleeds for liberty and Rome
> Let Britains crowd to deck his Poet's tomb.
> > (Dobson, 1995: 23)

And the epilogue pounds the Whig manifesto home:

> When Rome's firm Patriots on the stage were shewn
> With pride we trace the Patriots of our own;

From bondage sav'd when that bold state we see,
We glow to think that Britain is as free.
(Dobson, 1995: 23)

But Whig power faltered at the mid point of the century, and it is a telling instance of both the political shift and the primacy of *Caesar* in the period that the first known political cartoon to reference Shakespeare is a depiction of Walpole as Caesar, with his opposing politician (William Pultenay) identified as Brutus (21). By the late 1750s Whig control had collapsed, and 'farmer' George III (so called for his interest in mundane subjects and an unwillingness to employ the majestic pageantry which had characterised the style of his predecessors) took over a throne whose powers were significantly circumscribed. The new monarch became – at least at home – a generally popular king. Partly as a result, *Caesar* lost its topical appeal, and as the process of Bardolatry escalated, Shakespeare tended to be lifted outside the specifics of contemporary politics, viewed increasingly as an abstract repository of more general virtue and truth. The reluctance of a theatrical giant like David Garrick to tackle the play seems to have had more to do with the demands of the wing and drop scenery as with the play's politics;[9] the play was staged infrequently after 1751, and not at all from 1781 to 1812.

In America, *Julius Caesar* was played infrequently around the time of the Revolutionary War, and for all the classicism and republican fervour of the period, the play did not rise to theatrical prominence until the nineteenth century when Shakespeare's own star was close to its zenith.[10] Thomas Abthorpe Cooper played all three major roles between 1802 and 1837 in Boston, Philadelphia and New York, most famously as Mark Antony. Thomas Hamblin was particularly renowned for his Brutus in the 1830s and 1840s, and Edward Loomis Davenport persisted in the role from 1853 to 1870.[11] All the productions seem cut from the same basic cloth, a sketch of high-minded Roman heroism characterised by even, patriotic virtue and elocutionary polish. In these productions (and the now familiar carping among newspaper critics as to whether or not a given player had the suitably noble physical stature for the role), we see the form of the play into which its theatrical essence had crystallised, particularly in the subordination of character to an oratory resembling the civic life of the period. The play's ubiquity and the consistent approach taken by companies are partly explained by Richard Halpern, who provides this window onto nineteenth-century America:

> Even after its decay [in the 1860s], oratorical culture survived as 'public speaking' in American high school education, and with it the almost universal experience of being made to read *Julius Caesar*, whose pre-eminence in the secondary school curriculum is a topic too little remarked on. The play's depiction of classical oratory and politics clearly fit it for a system in which 'civics' was, until not too long ago, still a taught subject. The play's Roman setting, moreover, made it suitable for the kind of pseudoclassical philological training embodied in G.L. Craik's notorious *The English of Shakespeare: Illustrated in a Philological Commentary on his Julius Caesar*, whose American edition by W.J. Rolfe was endlessly recirculated in high schools during the second half of the nineteenth and the early twentieth centuries. Finally, the play's plot, in which rebellion against imperial rule is suitably defeated and punished, no doubt supplied a welcome lesson in the politics of the authoritarian classroom. (Halpern, 1997: 75)

Julius Caesar's popularity on stage reached new heights between 1871 and 1891 when it was staged thousands of times and boasted two extraordinarily long New York runs, first with Edwin Booth as Brutus and – effectively – director at his own theatre, then revived in 1875 by Jarrett and Palmer with Davenport again as Brutus. Booth's production was striking in that it romanticised Brutus, a decision (one of few) to deviate from concurrent British models, and though his performance was generally well received, it was Lawrence Barrett's slightly manic Cassius who garnered particular praise. Yet Booth's Brutus is intriguing in its movement away from a heroic Brutus and into someone smaller, more well-meaning and introspective; and though this is usually ascribed to the actor's consciousness of his own physical appearance and abilities (he was only five foot seven and slightly built), it might be worth considering the choice in the context of recent political history. After all, after 1865, it became harder to see in Caesar simply a symbol of an abstract will to kingship and tyranny.

Edwin Booth had last appeared on stage with his brothers Junius Brutus and John Wilkes in 1864 in a production of *Julius Caesar* at the Winter Garden in New York, which, like the Drury

Lane performance of 1738, was a benefit for a Shakespeare memorial, this time the statue in Central Park. A few months later John Wilkes (who played Mark Antony) assassinated President Lincoln and cried (supposedly after the historical Brutus) '*Sic semper tyrannis*' ('Always thus to tyrants'). After the assassination, Edwin disowned his brother and reputedly would not allow his name to be spoken in his house, but after a period of absence from the stage he returned as a highly successful Hamlet before returning to Brutus. It is tempting to see that 1864 production as a watershed moment in American culture, a moment in which *Julius Caesar* ceased to be about general principle and civic virtue (the stuff of commemorative statues) and became anchored to a specific and damning moment of American history; but if this happened, it was brief and soon over-written by Booth himself.

There can be no question that his brother's crime hung over Edwin's career and that he found it both professionally and psychologically damaging, so to play the part of history's most famous assassin had both built-in market appeal and considerable perils. A heroic Brutus might seem to endorse what his brother had done, something which would have incurred the wrath of a nation much of which viewed Lincoln as a martyr and the country's greatest president. So Booth brought his own sensibility to the part, finding in Brutus a thoughtfulness and sincerity which drew distinctly on his experience as Hamlet. This was a different brand of ideal, one more in the romantic than the heroic tradition. Critics complained about its sentimentality, its lack of grandeur and moral clarity, but the production was a popular success, running for 85 performances, and in focusing on Brutus's inner life – rather than celebrating his actions – Booth was able to side-step the valorising of his brother's topically infamous act.[12] Thus the play retained its general patina of republican idealism without succumbing to the darker specifics of recent history.

Rome's play

Back in London, John Philip Kemble's 1812 production at Covent Garden significantly extended the overall trajectory of previous productions and was rewarded with massive commercial success. Inspired by his friend Sir Joshua Reynolds, principal advocate for the *beau ideal* school of painting which aspired to a quasi-Platonic notion of art wherein the painter should depict life in a heightened, more clearly admirable state, Kemble and his sister, Mrs. Siddons, brought 'the grand style' to *Julius Caesar*. Every aspect of the production was shaped to drive home a sense of perfection, unity and grandeur. The text was rigorously adapted, cut by 450 lines and fourteen speaking roles, a decision designed to focus and unify the action and to further purge the play of discordant notes moral, historical, and philosophical. There were thirteen complete set changes, vast and impressive versions of a historical Rome (Imperial rather than Republican), and broad landscapes for the concluding battles.[13] Costuming was meticulously historical – or was touted to be so – involving togas and draperies derived from ancient statuary, and the supernumeraries exponentially multiplied. From the shuffling gaggle of comedians that had been the crowd of the eighteenth century, the stage was suddenly packed with about a hundred extras whose primary job was to stand silently in statuesque clusters. What had been a play about heroic individuals was now a vast tableau centred on the city itself – or rather an idealised version of it.

The focus on the pictorial and spectacular was carried over to the acting, which was large, declamatory and grandiose, even down to a ponderously stately manner of walking. All inconsistency of character was banished, and the selfless, dignified Stoics glimpsed by the eighteenth century were honed and shaped still further. Some critics complained that the result was unnatural, but the beau idealist in Kemble was not especially interested in the natural, and his position seems to have mirrored the tastes of the moment. While the staging of the solemn, but histrionically drawn-out assassination scene gave a new prominence to the play's central event, focus remained on Brutus, and Kemble played the part as man of passionate conviction but ruled by Stoicism. Only on the revelation of Portia's death did he show any emotion, even then revealing it as through a window of control, and this restraint seems to have successfully grounded the stylised ideal of his performance. It was a counterpoint to Charles Mayne Young's more restless and volatile Cassius and to the youthfully effusive emotion and excitability of their Mark Antony, played by Kemble's younger brother Charles. Daniel Egerton's Caesar was less well received, though this seems to be the unhappy result of the part's lacklustre stage tradition colliding with the beau ideal's refusal to expose Caesar's frailties. The result was a posturing, stalking hollow man who, even in such an inflated landscape, could not be mistaken for a human being.

Kemble's version of the play was slightly renovated by William Charles Macready, particularly at Drury Lane and Covent Garden in the 1830s and 1840s. Macready played Brutus as a less uniformly consistent character than had become the norm, finding in him a domestic quality to temper the heroic dignity, and this less lavishly unified notion of the role was echoed in Samuel Phelps's Cassius.[14] His approach sought to infuse Kemble's pictorial style with something like the breath of actual life (his acting style has been called a hybrid of Kemble and Edwin Booth), something particularly evident in his use of supers, whose number he increased still further (Ripley, 1980: 89–90). Instead of the statuesque groupings favoured by Kemble, the supers were allowed to move and were even encouraged to complement the main action by spreading their energy through the whole stage, except when Macready himself was on stage, when they were told to keep still and not steal focus. The sheer number of supers milling about lent a kind of realism, but they were still largely window dressing; seventy soldiers brought static atmosphere to Mark Antony's final eulogy but did not participate in the battle scenes at all. The murder of Cinna the poet was still excluded, so the Roman populace were never permitted to turn into the lethal mob of Shakespeare's play, since that too would – at very least – steal focus from the production's brand of idealised history. Macready's most innovative move, however, was to include in the assassination a vast array – over seventy – of supers (senators, priests, soldiers and citizens) who remained on stage to witness the murder itself, a murder executed with brief and savage realism quite unlike the slow and stately ballet of Kemble's production. The panicked and horrified exit of the supers after the killing fed directly into the forum scene where – for the first time in at least 150 years, perhaps for the first time ever – the crowd became real arbiters and participants in the funeral orations which followed.

Back in 1601, John Weever's recollection of the play in performance hinged on the 'many headed multitude' listening to 'Brutus' speech that Caesar was ambitious' and then to 'eloquent Mark Antony'. In the subsequent two-and-a-half centuries, the crowd listening to the oratory had virtually – and in some cases literally – disappeared, all emphasis falling on the speakers of that oratory: Brutus and Mark Antony. In those later productions, the compelling scene had become – surprisingly, from a modern perspective – the Quarrel scene (4.3), because it manifested the Stoic dignity of Brutus in the face of Cassius's anger; and it was not until Macready brought life to the forum crowd, energised by the horror of witnessing the murder itself, that the play's large-scale politics emerged on the stage. Weever's early remarks may suggest that the crowd was indeed an active part in the earliest productions, and it is tempting to think that the few scripted roles for the crowd in the funeral scene might have been given to actors who were positioned in the house itself. In the daylit space of the Globe where actor and audience met each other's gaze head-on, those who paid to attend the performance may well have been encouraged by those salted in their midst to respond vocally to what Brutus and Antony said. It is, of course, dangerous to speculate about what the dynamic of the early modern playhouse might have been, doubly so with no evidence of such placement of actors in the audience; but surviving accounts of audience behaviour, coupled with the intimate and engaging nature of theatre construction in amphitheatres like the Globe, suggest that this kind of audience participation may have been more readily achieved than in the more distant proscenium theatres of later periods.[15] However cautiously we say it, there is a clear logic to the emergence of the Quarrel scene in the more restrained theatrical culture of the eighteenth century, and an analogous logic to a scene encouraging audience participation in the early years of the Globe, an audience which – as Weever seems to recall – had an active hand in the story of Julius Caesar as told by the Chamberlain's Men.[16]

Macready's strategy was, of course, different, in that he created an on-stage audience instead of goading the audience already present in the house as *may* have happened at the Globe. His theatre was of a different age and its audiences were more separated from the action. They wept and applauded, but they did so in the dark, behind the proscenium's invisible fourth wall. They did not come to the theatre to be part of its action. The effect must have been different from being part of that original Globe audience, but it must also have invited association with that on-stage audience, refocusing the action of the play from the doings (and musings and speechifyings) of noble, long-dead Romans, to an impression of the play in which those Romans were part of a larger community which ultimately determined their fate. With an actual crowd to sway, Mark Antony's funeral oration acquires a new urgency and can no longer be a set piece calmly admired for its elegance and sophistication. Instead the moment embraces the particular semiotic energy of the theatre.

The result of creating an engaged crowd for the principals was a reduction of their own colossal scale, feeding that sense of 'humanity' which made them more recognisable as actual people rather than ideals. Brutus's death thus did not stand as a monument to patriotism or heroic dignity, but – if reviewers can be taken as representative – drew from the audience a melancholy and understanding sense of a good man's failure (Ripley, 1980: 93).

The shift from star roles and isolated set piece scenes to an ensemble playing a larger Roman unity continued with the German language production by George II, Duke of Saxe-Meiningen performed at Drury Lane in May 1881. The forum scene emerged even more clearly as the climax of the production, with Antony having to fight for the attentions and sympathies of a large and well-rehearsed crowd, the supers being encouraged to think of their roles as rounded and crucial to the whole.[17] While critics complained about the distracting and unhistorical presence of women and children during the assassination scene, they applauded the power which the crowd had on the dynamic of the forum sequence. Brander Matthews' remarkably detailed account of the 1883 New York version asserts that Ludwig Barnay's Antony was 'making it up as he went along', struggling with a crowd 'who were not only hostile, they were hopelessly indifferent', talking amongst themselves, drawn in only by curiosity about the contents of the will with which Antony teased them (Ripley, 1980: 149–50). The production may have too clearly subordinated the lead roles to the ensemble, and the production seems to have stalled after the forum scene, but it made a particular impression, drove home the importance of the crowds, and went some way towards shaping what would be the last and best received production of the century.

Antony's play

If the production history of *Julius Caesar* had been oscillating between privileging the visual over the auditory, Beerbohm Tree's production at Her Majesty's in January 1898 went furthest in turning its audience into spectators. The result was a massive critical success, ran for over a hundred performances, and was frequently revived over the subsequent eighteen years. In a star-driven theatre which had lately discovered the power of large-scale crowds in the play, it was perhaps inevitable that at this point in the play's theatrical history an English actor-manager chose, for the first time, to play the role of Mark Antony and structured his production accordingly. Tellingly, Tree wrote to his wife: 'I like Brutus best – he is so much deeper – but I still feel that Antony has the colour – the glamour of the play, don't you?'[18] To make this work, Tree produced the play in three acts, each concluding with a curtain moment devoted to Antony: the first and longest included everything up to the assassination itself (the climax being Antony's vengeful promise of what was to come), the second and grandest was the forum scene, and the third was a curtailed compilation of Shakespeare's Acts four and five, ending with Antony's speech over the dead Brutus.

The text was cut by about 550 lines, the edits falling most heavily on anything that might detract from Antony's heroism – including, of course, the death of Cinna the poet (which might be seen as the indirect product of Antony's rhetoric) and the proscription scene (4.1) – and from what kept him off stage in the final third of the production. The once climactic Quarrel scene was significantly pared back, and the sparring before the battle cut short the moment Antony left the stage. The result gave Antony centre stage ('the colour – the glamour of the play'), but also deprived him of the 'depth' Tree saw in Brutus. With 4.1 and his duplicitous promise to Brutus before the forum scene gone, Antony became two-dimensional, all sense of thought behind what he articulated – *contrary* to what he articulated – gone. Antony in Shakespeare's play does not lack depth, but those depths are not ruminatory as Brutus's are, and they were still too dark in 1898 to withstand the persistent legacy of a theatrical tradition bent on seeing Roman ideals and ideal Romans.

Speaking roles were, as usual, reduced, this time by fifteen: some speakers had their lines cut outright (Lepidus, Cicero, Cinna the Poet, the Camp Poet and young Cato), while others (Flavius, Marullus, Titinius, Messala, Lucilius, Volumnius, Clitus, Strato and Dardanius) had their lines given to other characters. Since the mid-point of the century, interpolation of non-Shakespearean lines and scenes had fallen from favour as the Bard's cultural star rose, so Brutus's extended suicide speech was cut; but a tremendous amount of stage business was added in order to give new life to that character which had been edging into the footlights since 1812: Rome.

The curtain rose on a city bustling with life and energy. There were boys playing, girls dancing to the music of a piper, fruit-sellers moving through the crowd, a girl filling a jug at the fountain downstage of the holiday-trimmed statue of Caesar. Lictors cleared paths through the people, runners sprinted to a finish line just off stage, and a patrician family with a black servant crossed as one of the citizens cuffs the boys off. All of this occurred before Flavius and Marullus's entrance (here made by Trebonius and Metellus).[19] The scene set the tone for a production which was to be both picturesque and realistic, at least in scope. The large-scale, lavish sets designed by the Academic painter Lawrence Alma-Tadema were meticulously archaeological, to such an extent that when some were criticised as being of a slightly later period, the theatre issued a formal communiqué apologising for the inaccuracy but explaining it in quasi-historicist terms. The authority of the production was, at least in part, grounded in its claim to historical authenticity, and the bustling streets – though clearly in some ways a transposition of a quaint version of London – were part of that claim. The spectators were invited to see the production as a kind of window into the past, and though the production revolved around the forum scene, Antony's oration to a massive *on-stage* audience reinforced the solidity of the invisible fourth wall.

The forum scene was set under the colossal shadow of temple fronts and the reactive crowd were initially so opposed to Antony that one menaced him with a sledgehammer and was only quelled by Tree's still and steely glare. But no staring contest would win the struggle to be heard, and Antony had to importune several of the citizens silently to entreat their fellows to listen to him. The jeering and laughter persisted through his first lines and only the apologetic 'I come to bury Caesar not to praise him' brought the noise level down to where he was clearly audible. From that point on, the crowd followed the movements of the speech as might be expected, though the first sarcastic repetition of 'honourable man' was risky and produced a new hostility from the crowd. By refocusing on Caesar's body and on the will, Antony took the crowd with him, worked them into a frenzy, but the concluding curtain moment was triumphant rather than malicious.

Even more than the conclusion of the play with Antony's speech over Brutus's body, the funeral oration was the production's high point.

A more naturalistic approach had by this time found its way into Shakespearean performance, but the Roman 'set piece' nature of *Julius Caesar* on stage meant that Tree's production was the first to subvert the oratorical style of acting in this play, though, while this shift was largely championed by the critics of the day (a few – including George Bernard Shaw – lamented the absence of Shakespearean 'music' in the delivery), it was a difference in degree rather than kind (Daniel, 1999: 141). Existing recordings of Tree's 'O, pardon me, thou bleeding piece of earth' sound, to a modern ear, almost as ponderous and elocutionary as anything he could have been supplanting. Tree's Antony at the start of the production was a little more rakish than in the past, so his transition into the grim avenger after the assassination, though sentimentally motivated, was particularly striking, and the naturalness with which he won over the crowd in the forum scene was almost universally applauded. With the exception of Charles Fulton's refreshingly dignified Caesar, few of the other performers attracted much attention; *Julius Caesar* was now Antony's play, and the Roman crowd was at least as important as those honourable men who cut the title character down.

Tree was not the only actor-manager heavily influenced by the Meiningen production and ensemble method. F.R. Benson sought similar results, but without the massive and sumptuous sets and heavy textual adaptation which he felt had come to stifle Shakespeare in performance. Benson's company toured extensively from 1883, but his recurring presence at the Memorial Theatre in Stratford made the strongest impact on theatrical culture where Shakespeare was concerned, and his *Julius Caesar* was staged at the festivals there eleven times between 1892 and 1915, with Benson as Antony.

In his sense of Antony's centrality Benson followed Tree, and despite his purist rhetoric, he emulated the production at Her Majesty's in other ways too: at least some of his antipathy to grand, realist sets was about budget and portability, and he continued to blue-pencil the text extensively, eliminating the usual phalanx of speaking roles and reducing the text by almost exactly the same amount as Tree, albeit for slightly different reasons. Benson continued to seek untarnished heroism in the Kemble tradition, and in the name of classical structure he simplified character, structure and theme. In doing so (and in evading the kind of laborious scene changes that kept the audience at Her Majesty's waiting), he gave the play a new and relentless pace, though paradoxically critics often found the result tedious. Some audience members found the flattened and simplified script, delivered – it seems – at something like a full-throated shout,[20] exhausting, even if subsequent critics and theatre historians have come to regard his re-emphasis on the verbal dimension of the play as triumphant and trail-blazing. While other actors were approaching Shakespeare from a more naturalistic perspective, Benson sought majesty in deportment and an impressive 'bell-like' clarity in his verse-speaking which to many ears sounded old fashioned and overdone.

'Shakespeare's' play

From 1919 to 1934, Benson was succeeded in Stratford by William Bridges-Adams, a director (rather than actor-manager) strongly influenced by Harley Granville-Barker and William Poel, the latter being the chief advocate for quasi-Elizabethan stage practice in the production of Shakespeare. What Poel's approach meant for Bridges-Adams was a return to the forestage of the proscenium theatre (there being no apron at the Memorial Theatre), a further stripping back of scenic elements – though not to the bare stage Poel preferred – and, most important, a speeding-up of delivery in order to accommodate a largely uncut Shakespearean text. All of these gestures towards the 'Elizabethan' need qualifying. Though Bridges-Adams did away with footlights where possible, the stage lighting bore no resemblance to anything Shakespeare would have seen at the theatres of his own day, costumes were generically Roman (togas and breastplates), women's parts were played by women (not boys), and though scenic elements were flexible and a far cry from Tree's massive structures, they were intended to evoke a strong sense of place, even if they were too simple and generic to be called realist. In short, the productions were really only 'Elizabethan' in comparison to what had been going on elsewhere lately, but the largely restored script was certainly a substantial innovation, and one which put new demands and opportunities before the cast.

As part of his 'Elizabethanism', Bridges-Adams strove for an ensemble effect at odds with the star vehicles of the old system, much of which was very much alive and well in the 1920s and 1930s. But suitably trained actors were in short supply and rehearsal periods were painfully short: in some cases, a mere week. Unsurprisingly, performances were uneven, but the largely uncut script (though Cinna the Poet and the attendant scene of mob violence still made no appearance)[21] disrupted the familiar nobility of the cast, and the reinsertion of the proscription scene (4.1) radically altered Mark Antony, bringing a crafty and callous deliberation to the role which had not been seen in three hundred years.

Critical response at the time was largely positive, though it is difficult to fully evaluate Bridges-Adams's production because so much theatre history is written by Shakespeareans who view him as a kind of white knight championing an expressly textual core to the theatrical event (see for instance, Ripley, 1980: 202). However much the 'Elizabethan' tag was used to authorise the methods and limitations of the production, the emphasis here was not so much historical as verbal. The actor-manager's starring role was taken by Shakespeare himself, and the spectators became audiences, action and visual elements reduced to serve a 'function' which seems to have been the airing of the words themselves. Ripley calls Bridges-Adams's production a 'landmark' because it redressed 'two centuries of mistreatment textual and scenic', thereby offering 'ample cause for rejoicing' (213–14). But he goes on to bewail the drought of actors then and since who were capable of performing the play's 'heroic' content, at least in part because of the advent of a naturalism he sees at odds with the verbal grandeur of the play (214).

In all this, naturally, Shakespeare's own status in the larger culture looms large. The performance history of any long-lasting play must be a history of the tastes of the period spanned, successful productions being a part of the life of the community. It is not an accident that the reversion (if indeed it is one) to a largely full text began not in London or New York but in Stratford at the newly created festival devoted to the play's author and staged at the significantly titled *Memorial* Theatre. Bridges-Adams's first production was staged the year after the end of the Great War, a time of massive social and political upheaval, a time of cultural and economic devastation which had not yet given birth to the roaring twenties, a time scarred by world events which would inevitably confine the notions of heroism Ripley sees as the heart of the play to an antique past. Nothing in the contemporary response to Bridges-Adams's productions suggests any kind of conscious echo of those times. Rather, and perhaps understandably, his productions harken back to a pre-lapsarian past, part-Roman, part-Elizabethan, grounded in the Memorial to Shakespeare, English monolith, cultural and educational bastion of all we once knew and loved.[22]

Stratford became a site of pilgrimage, and pilgrims are not looking for the ordinary things of life. Significantly removed from the thriving playhouses of London, Stratford theatre was pointedly not Drury Lane or Covent Garden. It wasn't music hall or cinema. It was a version of the past grounded in what was most clearly valuable: the words themselves. The Victorians had idolised Shakespeare, but Stratford memorialized him, elevated him in different ways, ways which crucially attempted to lever his plays out of the theatrical world of stars, lavish scenery and general audiences, in order to enshrine them as text.

The Festival productions of Bridges-Adams and, to a lesser extent, Benson were in some ways innovative, but that innovation was paradoxically conservative, by which I mean that the productions set out to *conserve* a particular cultural heritage. In this case, what was to be conserved had first to be constructed, the immediate theatrical legacy having falling short of the original ideal. Never before, or not since the first performances, had so much Shakespeare been audible on stage, but the impulse to make that happen is complicated by factors having at least as much to do with Shakespeare as encountered in books, particularly in school books, as with an idea of Shakespeare as immediate theatrical communication. Whatever these Poel-inflected productions discovered in terms of real theatrical value in the foregrounding of actors over scenery, the comparative immediacy of their relationship with the audience, and a newly recognised irregularity of character and play structure, Bridges-Adams's version of *Julius Caesar* struggled to find the enthusiasm with which audiences greeted Kemble and Tree. It would take an aggressively contemporary approach to rescue the play's topical politics and excite twentieth-century audiences, and such a rescue would take place on the other side of the Atlantic in the hands of a twenty-two-year-old director.

Notes

1 The suggestion that Caesar appeared while Brutus and Cassius were at half-sword parlay is hard to reconcile with the text we have, Cassius having left the tent thirty lines before the ghost appears in 4.3, and there being no other scene in the play when Caesar enters with the conspirators at half-sword. It is possible that early theatre-goers saw a scene in which the ghost of Caesar appeared to both Brutus and Cassius, but it seems more likely that Digges' verse has merely conflated two separate theatrical moments.

2 I take the reference to being at 'half sword' to suggest being in close and hostile proximity – at cross swords – rather than a reference to the kinds of swords themselves, the short Roman *gladius* which figured so prominently in later more authentically antiquarian productions. Whether the reference comes from the tent scene – suggesting that both men faced off, armed – or from the argument between Octavius, Antony and the conspirators before Philippi I can't say, the specific reference to Brutus and Cassius suggesting the tent scene but the word 'parlay' suggesting 5.1.

3 In Jonson's *Epicoene* and the collaborative *Rollo Duke of Normandy*, for instance.

4 Casca uses the Folio's 'O Cicero, I have seen Tempests ...' while addressing Trebonius (1.3.4–5) and Trebonius's exit 35 lines later is marked by the Folio's 'Exit Trebonius'.

5 John Ripley's study of *Julius Caesar* on stage is a masterpiece of research and documentation, and my own study is indebted to it in numerous ways. It is detailed, specific, insightful and thorough. It hinges, however, on a particular reading of the play and how that play should be manifested on stage, a fact which turns the book into a kind of lament – occasionally lightened by enthusiasm and optimism – for what Ripley considers the failure of the play's potential brought about by a combination of inadequate performers and a long line of arrogant directors and actor-managers who have tinkered with the script. For all its strengths as a history, Ripley's study is curiously antitheatrical in that it persistently sees deviation from the letter of the Folio as failure, as if the task of the stage is merely to broadcast the words of the text. With few exceptions, his praise or blame of a given production can be aligned specifically with how full a text the production used, and he begins his tale of decline in the eighteenth century, and assumes – problematically, to my mind – that the earliest productions used a full, Folio-style text. This is not the place to rehash the ongoing scholarly debate about the relationship between text and performance in the early modern period, but it should be said that there are significant reasons to think that the Folio represents the most *writerly* incarnation of Shakespeare's plays, an incarnation that may be at some remove from the way they were first staged.

Ripley is right to point out that the Restoration included Cinna the Poet in ways later productions did not, but this says little about textual purity. He points out that many of the minor characters (Lucilius, Young Cato, Volumnius, Varro, Clitus, Claudius, Strato, Lucius and Dardanius) are not assigned actors in the 1684 cast list, and speculates that these were considered too minor to merit listing or that their lines were redistributed. The omission could suggest more radical cutting, however; and if we are to put so much faith in the implications of Cinna's still being in the play, what are we to make of the absence of these others? The Cinna scene is, after all, easily imagined as a brutal and vivid moment of theatre. It is potentially funny and viscerally upsetting. It needs no claim to a textually purist agenda on the part of the company to justify its presence in a production. Indeed, one might argue that its subsequent disappearance from the stage has more to do with a valorising of text than it does with theatrical contingency or directorial flight of fancy, since the scene contains no great speeches or quotable lines. The later cutting of Cinna the Poet was probably tied to eighteenth- and nineteenth-century notions of decorum, moral elevation and dramatic aesthetics. Allowing the scene to be played, whether in modern productions or in the seventeenth century, speaks to the scene's theatrical power in a culture which can tolerate the kinds of random violence and political discomfiture that other periods could not. We cannot use the assignment of an actor's name to Cinna the Poet in seventeenth-century copies of the Folio text as evidence for a 'pure', uncut script honoured more in the breach than the observance thereafter. If we concede that the printed text of 1684 represents the stage version only in so far as two characters have been cut and their lines redistributed without regard to content, then we must abandon the idea that early performances used the Folio 'in something like its entirety' (Ripley, 1980: 19). What changes and cuts were made at the level of individual utterance we simply cannot say.

6   That he originated this tradition is, of course, impossible to verify. He may well have been drawing on a long-established theatrical tradition originating in earlier, less well documented, productions.
7   The Covent Garden prompt book of 1766 and Bell's edition of 1773 follow and expand upon the alteration and cutting logic of the Dryden–Davenant script.
8   Michael Dobson discusses Sheffield's plays in detail, focusing particularly on the gendering of the Portia/Brutus scene and on the plays' part in an ongoing debate about the applicability of Shakespeare to contemporary politics which shifted towards a more transcendent Bardolotry around the middle of the century.
9   David Daniel's introduction to the Arden third series cites a letter from Garrick to this effect (1999: 103).

10   Shakespeare in eighteenth-century America continued to be dogged by charges of immorality and associations of Englishness, but this perspective altered radically over the next hundred years due to extensive publication of Shakespeare's works, popular lecture tours, and the steady disassociation of Shakespeare from his homeland, particularly as a source of sententiae and rhetoric. By 1882, the German visitor Karl Knortz was able to remark that 'there is no land on the whole earth in which Shakespeare and the Bible are held in such high esteem' (1882: 60). As will become clear in Chapter VII, such a statement from a German carries considerable weight. Incidents such as the Astor Place riots of 1849 foreground the extent to which Shakespeare had become a conduit for issues of identity and nationalism, with Americans laying claim to an authentic version of the Bard who belonged to them. This was particularly the case on the stage where, as Edwin Forrest maintained, Shakespeare should be played by actors who understood their audience – not by British interlopers like Macready – thereby recreating the theatrical dynamic Shakespeare had originally enjoyed. (Vaughan, 2007: 24).

11   The dominant acting script was one based largely on Kemble's (see page 22).

12   Ripley provides thorough coverage of the production's specifics and its critical reception (1980: 115–39).

13   Some of this visual spectacle was replicated or at least emulated in the American productions of the 1870s and 1880s.

14   Phelps continued many of Macready's innovations at the Sadler's Wells theatre between 1846 and 1862 in what were the only major English revivals of the play between the end of Macready's career in 1851 and Beerbohm Tree's 1898 production.

15   It may be argued, of course, that the house of amphitheatres like the Globe would have been too volatile an environment for the safe placement of actors who might risk more than the undermining of their performances. But if Tony Dawson's liturgical analogy to early modern theatre is correct, there must surely have been some sense of communal activity which helped to contain the audience's potential belligerence.

16   As stated earlier (see note 2), Digges' prefatory verses to the Folio may reference the tent scene, though they may also refer to 5.1, and might already reflect later theatrical practice.

17   Ripley speculates that the crowd – the 80-member cast augmented by 'hundreds' of German-speaking supers recruited in London by the stage manager – may have been the largest number of people ever to appear on a London stage (1980: 148).

18   Summer, 1896. Cited in Ripley, 1980: 151.

19   The recasting of Flavius and Marullus as characters who were present in the latter parts of the play gives them clearer identities but significantly reduces one of the play's few pieces of hard evidence against Caesar's regime: their being 'put to silence'.

20 Benson thought that the old school of declamatory delivery as practiced by veterans of the mid-nineteenth century was much underrated (Ripley, 1980: 176).
21 Bridges-Adams professed a desire to keep the Cinna episode, but cut it, ostensibly because he feared his available supers would not be able to pull it off effectively (Ripley, 1980: 200). Whether Stratford audiences would have been receptive to this most troublesome scene is a matter of conjecture.
22 Michael Anderegg puts this down (citing Lawrence Levine: *High Brow/Lowbrow: The Emergence of Cultural Hierarchy in America* and Gary Taylor's *Reinventing Shakespeare*) to the decline of oratory, the rise of naturalism and romanticism (which made Shakespeare a poet, not a dramatist), and an increase in class difference. 'Shakespeare, in the nineteenth century, had been simultaneously popular and elite ... [but] by the early years of the twentieth century he had become more and more associated with elite culture and less and less with popular culture' (Anderegg, 1999: 7).

CHAPTER II

The rise of European Fascism: Welles at the Mercury Theatre

In November 1937, Orson Welles's production of *Julius Caesar*, staged at New York's Mercury Theatre on Broadway, opened to immediate adulation and controversy. The production, famously, was decked out with all the trappings and scenic theatricality of contemporary European Fascism and renamed *Caesar: Death of a Dictator*. However much scholars have sometimes questioned just how original the production really was, the production's legacy is clear, as is its claim to being the most important single production in the play's performance history. Under Welles's bold and innovative direction, the Mercury company found in the play's political dimension a new and urgent topicality, the resultant production becoming iconic, a bold and strident landmark which dominated staged *Caesar*s for decades to come.

More has been written about this production than about any other staging of *Julius Caesar*, much of it focused on the actor/impresario who steered it into the headlines and who came to loom over the second half of the twentieth century as a cultural icon with a troubled history of negotiating the gap between high and low culture.[1] As is to be expected, much of that writing focuses on the measurable and extant product of Welles's particular genius: his recordings, films (including his Shakespeare adaptations *Othello*, *Macbeth* and *Falstaff/Chimes at Midnight*),[2] books, and television appearances from *I Love Lucy* to TV commercials for Paul Masson wines and Carlsberg beer. But the Mercury production, with its singularly specific engagement with contemporary world politics, cannot be reduced to a study of the director and actor despite his centrality to the project, though his experience certainly facilitated its heightened awareness of world events.

[36]

Contexts: historical, personal and technological

1937 was a long year, one which did not so much lay the groundwork of the Second World War as begin it, save for the fact that the nations which would lead the fight against the Axis forces – Britain, France, the USSR and the United States – had managed thus far to be refused to be drawn in. By the time the Mercury production had opened in November, the Japanese had invaded China, Himmler's Gestapo had stepped up their programme of arrests and were now operating outside traditional law,[3] the German air force's Condor legion had bombed Guernica in support of the Spanish dictator Franco, and Mussolini – also a supporter of Franco – had invaded Ethiopia. Hitler, whose Nazi party had been in control of Germany for three-and-a-half years, continued to hold the massive political rallies he had inaugurated in 1925 in Nuremberg, and privately drafted the Hossbach Memorandum which made the case for an expansion of Germany's borders. Despite the protestations of Neville Chamberlain, who became Britain's prime minister at the end of May, many saw global conflict as inevitable, though others – particularly in the United States – were doing everything they could to stay out of it. In October in Welles's home town of Chicago, only a month before *Caesar* opened, Franklin Delano Roosevelt delivered his powerful plea for an end to American neutrality and isolationism in the so-called Quarantine speech, in which he suggested the use of economic pressures on what would shortly become the Axis powers. Public response was mixed, much of it polarised, but it would be almost another four years before the United States committed military forces to the war which began in Europe in 1939.[4]

Enter Welles. He was only 22 when he directed the Mercury's *Caesar*, but he had had a remarkable career already and had become a media darling, so much so that his actual calendar age is, in some ways, misleading. By this time he had performed at The Gate Theatre in Dublin in *Jew Suss* and *Hamlet*, garnering rave reviews from newspapers including the *New York Times*, despite – staggeringly – being only 16. He had performed in *Twelfth Night* for his former school players in Chicago, in an Off-Broadway production of *Romeo and Juliet*, in Archibald MacLeish's Marxist verse play *Panic*, and in various radio productions (notably in *The Shadow* series). He had also directed the *Voodoo Macbeth* for the Federal Theatre Project (1936), the premier of Aaron Copeland's *The Second Hurricane*, the absurdist play *Horse Eats Hat*, Marlowe's *Doctor Faustus*, and Marc Blitzstein's expressly socialist *The Cradle Will Rock*. All this despite the privations forced onto the theatrical community by the Great Depression. He had also co-authored with Roger Hill *Everybody's Shakespeare*, a popular introduction to the plays which stayed in wide circulation in schools for forty years (Callow, 1995: 185). Though it had taken him a couple of years to parlay the status of prodigy which he had built in Dublin into regular work in New York, Welles was already something of a celebrity, visible, well-connected, and recognised as a real talent. Much of this was coloured by his youth, and some critics were cautiously waiting to see if his obvious gifts, his charisma and drive, would survive into his maturity, when age would make him less of a phenomenon; but the company of people like Copeland and MacLeish, along with his remarkable breadth of learning and experience, gave him an undeniable gravitas.

Welles had personal experience of many of the countries embroiled in the pre-war events of 1937. Within the previous decade he had taken walking tours of Bavaria and had visited England and France from his base in Ireland, where he spent most of 1932. He had first-hand knowledge of countries such as China and Japan, Spain and parts of North Africa, all of which had become hotspots by 1937. It is impossible to think that he was unaware of the political conditions in these places during his travels, however much his letters tend to focus on their romantic and exotic aspects; and the prominent leftist intellectuals who became his friends and artistic collaborators in New York must have honed that awareness. Welles was no mere tourist. Compared to most people in this period, and in spite of his youth, he knew an astonishing amount of the world beyond the borders of the United States, and his *Caesar* was a conscious sally into the politics which threatened that world.

Caesar was the Mercury's Theatre's inaugural production, brought to the stage only a few months after the increasingly financially precarious outfit – headed by Welles and John Houseman, who had worked together at the Federal Theatre – came into being. More clearly and aggressively than any of the productions mentioned so far, this was a staging which embraced its historical moment, and by that I don't simply mean its sharp silhouettes of social forces which would lead to the Second World War only two years later. Its mindset, its technology, its politics, even its style of acting and of Shakespeare were defined by 1937, which is not to say that these were simply modern. Rather, they were on the cusp of various kinds of change, and much of what the Mercury *Caesar* did was of a hybrid and liminal nature. But for all its contemporary trappings, the production was also an actor-manager's star vehicle in the finest eighteenth- and nineteenth-century tradition, and Welles's pursuit of that tradition was not confined to grabbing the plum role. His textual editing – butchery, to some – reshaped the play with different purpose than his predecessors but with the same sense that the authority of the theatrical moment took precedence over reverence for Shakespeare's text. Welles knew of the so-called 'uncut' productions being staged in England by Poel and Bridges-Adams; but though he took from them certain ideas about ensemble acting and a bare 'Elizabethan' stage, he did so not out of a sense of historical authenticity, but because he saw them as theatrically effective. Bridges-Adams had found the bare stage to be flexible and actor-centred, but at least some of his impulse was to get back to the authenticity of the Elizabethan; Welles, by contrast, saw a method which would work in the present if expressly unshackled from Shakespeare's past.

The stage itself was bare, a series of three platforms, the highest of which was a little over six feet higher than the main acting area and accessed from a broad upstage ramp. Behind that, serving as a backdrop for the whole production, was a wall painted a dark red, something between dried blood and the bricks so rarely seen among the elegant Roman stone and plaster of other productions. Costumes were contemporary: street clothes for the crowds, near-contemporary 'blackshirt' uniforms for Caesar and the military. Marc Blitzstein (of *The Cradle Will Rock*) wrote the music which, performed on horns, drums and a Hammond organ, used anthemic military marches to foreground – as did the other design elements – a distinctly current and European Fascism. Caesar was a strutting Mussolini and a ranting Hitler, a visual analogy made particularly striking by the use of thirteen 500-watt up-lights set into the floor of the second level: the so-called 'Nuremberg effect'. This bold pictorial style grew in part out of Welles's training as a painter. His capacity to mimic the newsreel footage images, however, had been learned at The Gate in Dublin, whose designer – Micheal Mac Liammoir – had learned the new aesthetic and technological innovations in lighting at the

Berlin theatres in the early 1930s, the very theatres whose effects had been commandeered for Hitler's spectacular rallies. At the Federal Theatre, Welles was fortunate enough to meet and work with Jean Rosenthal, a former student of the seminal lighting designer Stanley McCandless, and Rosenthal was able to realise the impressions and ideas Welles had glimpsed in Ireland. Welles's *Faustus*, which had opened in January of the same year, had similarly been defined by its use of light, albeit without the topical overtones which characterised *Caesar*.

Welles's dispensing with the flats and wings of nineteenth-century theatre was probably as much an economic as an aesthetic decision, and it is notable that the *New York Times*'s end of year assessment of the state of theatre holds up the Mercury *Caesar* as a sign of a more frugal direction for the theatre of the Depression. The production also made use of a technology – modern electrical stage lighting – which had really only been around in theatres for a decade or so, emerging most prominently in the great American musicals of the 1930s. The cultural force of such technology was felt not merely at the theatrically overblown Fascist/Nazi rallies in Europe, but in the newsreel footage which brought them to the United States, and indeed in all the movies which had become so central to American life and whose production depended upon the manipulation of light. What is striking about the images of Welles's *Caesar* is how cinematic they seem in comparison with the staginess of what was going on in London and Stratford, and much of the difference results from the use of light and shadow. Welles, always the showman with an eye for what would connect a contemporary audience to a dusty classic, tapped directly into the style and semantic conventions of movie melodrama in his use of light and sound. It should be remembered that theatre was struggling to make its way in a ruined economy, and productions had to catch something of the public's imagination if they were to be successful. It was partly because of this that Welles had moved away from the European notion of director as interpreter of the play into something more clearly resembling an auteur, and some theatre historians credit his *Voodoo Macbeth* (1936) as the first major 'concept' production (Callow, 1995: 215).

It could be, depending upon one's definition, that 'concept' productions require the technological trappings of a modern theatre; but even without the scenic bells and whistles available to Welles, his must be considered the first 'concept' production in *Caesar*'s history. However much his attitude to text may superficially resemble the cut-and-paste approach of former ages, his purpose was quite different. He was not driven by issues of decency, antiquarianism, or idealism, nor was he simply shaping the text as a star vehicle. The playing text (now available from Routledge) reads with the brevity, focus and thematic unity of a contemporary screen or radio play, and like a screen play, it tells its story in broad strokes, not without nuance, but with a clarity of purpose designed to make the main plot accessible to an audience increasingly unfamiliar with Shakespeare's language. The production was built around an idea – a reading extrapolated from the text but magnified by the exclusion of other competing readings, a 'take' on the play which then informed a production. That production then used all the semiotic apparatus of the stage to foreground the resulting 'concept'. The story within that concept was no longer about the nobility of ancient Romans, but about the ineptitude of liberal-minded thinkers confronting a ruthless and manipulative dictator and those savvy enough to ride his coattails.

This story focuses on Brutus, Caesar and – at least for the forum scene, on Mark Antony. Cassius is significantly trimmed back, Portia's scene with the soothsayer is cut, the washing of the conspirators' hands in Caesar's blood and the dialogue with Mark Antony's servant are gone entirely. All scenes are heavily pruned, but the most striking cuts occur after the forum scene. Famously, the mob's murder of Cinna the Poet was included (though it was almost left out) and became the highlight of the production. After that moment, however, Shakespeare's fourth and fifth acts (approximately 763 lines) are reduced to only about 280 lines.[5] Much of what remains is an abbreviated version of the quarrel scene, a significant memory of the former focus of actor managers. The ghost and the proscription scene, which had lately found new depths of calculation in British Antonies, were excised. Also cut was all of act five, save for Antony's final lines over Brutus's body, the battles themselves skipped entirely, the production moving via a cobbled transition from the end of the quarrel in which Brutus and Cassius say their farewells in anticipation of defeat to Antony's final speech.

Welles's elimination of the battle scenes was, he said, because he found their effect invariably reductive, even absurd, on stage.

Film would later allow for large-scale combat, but in essentially realist productions, unlike those of the seventeenth century, the alarums and excursions of the end must always verge on the ridiculous, forcing directors to suggest that the action we are seeing is either in the wings of the battle (and therefore is not the focus we probably want) or is an inadequate representation of that military focus (a handful of horseless men, with ragged foils standing in for the thousands that did affright the air at Philippi). The nineteenth century, for all its love of supers, had never tried to show anything like real battle on stage in *Julius Caesar* for a couple of reasons. First, the supers were insufficiently trained for fight choreography, and any attempt to orchestrate large conflict on stage was thus expensive and dangerous. Second, the conception of the play as a study of noble and mighty men would be significantly undermined by the crucial events being determined by a mass of nameless soldiers. It was one thing to have rediscovered the power of the crowd in the forum, where they could still be the instruments of an Antony, but it is something quite different to give them centre stage and let them determine the course of history while the play's heroes stand by and watch to see what happens. Battles on stage would function like the Cinna the Poet scene: they would project a larger view of the world than most productions were prepared to tackle and diffuse the nobler sentiments of the play and its philosophical mood with the excitement, chaos and terror of large-scale combat. In cutting them, Welles – for all his modernity of setting – maintained an ancient tradition that kept the audience's attention trained on the core statuesque heroes.

The battles also raise a particular problem for modern dress productions. While it is acceptable – just – to have a modern dictator struck down by men with daggers, the battles already breaking out all over the globe as the Second World War came to a boil were being fought with rifles, grenades, aircraft, machine guns and tanks. Apart from taxing the resources of all but the largest theatres, modern weapons risk a greater disjunction from the text than do mere uniforms, even if the script is adjusted. They demand a new conceptual vocabulary for war, as well as strategies, tactics and protocols unprovided by a Renaissance play. While such things can be made to work, they change the tenor of a production radically, if only because they alter the combat dynamic; the battlefields of the contemporary Spanish

Civil War, for instance, where the Nazis were then testing out the hardware that would lead their Blitzkrieg through Europe – shells bursting all around and bullets screaming seemingly randomly in the air – bear little resemblance to the battlefields of a period (or a heroic version of that period) in which a general would march into the enemy lines, sword and shield in hand. The reductive chaos of the play's final scenes had long been a problem for directors of realist productions, and Welles's modern dress choice exacerbated that problem.

The crowd, and the murder of Cinna the Poet

That the battles should go but Cinna the Poet should be allowed back in says a lot about Welles's conception of the production. Battles are fought by soldiers, and for all the emphasis given to military uniforms, *Caesar* was not finally a military production at all. Rather, it focused on the people who created the circumstances for large-scale conflict, the leaders and the people who allowed themselves to be led. Although the Second World War would be fought largely by amateur soldiers – conscripts – it would be fought with as much *professionalism* as could be mustered. Welles wanted to explore the root political causes of war, not its military consequences, and in so doing he kept the amateur status of the crowd, its essential ordinariness, firmly at the forefront of the production. Instead of seeing a militarised Other taking control of the play's events, the audience saw itself – street clothes and all – in what was (given the cutting) the show's last great scene and ominously resounding note.

The importance of reintroducing of Cinna the Poet to the stage after an absence of at least 250 years cannot be overstated. For the first time, the crowd's potential and power, glimpsed in the forum scene, was allowed its brutal culmination, brought (quite literally at the Mercury) out of the shadows from where they had cheered on Mark Antony and into the light. In productions prior to Welles's, the power of the mob had been an abstraction, an idea, one which had been firmly kept in check and – at least in the eighteenth century – utterly subordinated to the power of the principal actors. Now the people of Rome were revealed not merely as changeable and dangerously potent, but as vividly callous, arbitrary and cruel. The scene became the emblem of the production, though it almost didn't get into the show at all.

1   Norman Lloyd as Cinna the Poet surrounded by the mob in Orson Welles's 1937 production at the Mercury Theatre.

The killing of Cinna the Poet had been a core conceptual element of the production from the outset, underscoring as it does the power of the thoughtless facilitators and agents of dictatorships. But if such concerns were largely considered foreign to the American audience, the Cinna scene presented something a good deal closer to home. The Depression had seen a great many strikes and labour-related actions. Welles had seen them firsthand in the Federal Theatre, which was a government-funded project to find work for unemployed theatre workers. More pointedly, the divided nature of American labour had involved him directly only a few months earlier during his work on *The Cradle Will Rock*, in which the Works Progress Administration's solution to a breach of union law was to send a pick-axe team to smash up the company's expensive sets. Bickering between the collective smaller entities of the steel industry ('Little Steel') and the American Communist Party had stoked *Cradle*'s politicised audiences, and a show of solidarity for the Little Steel strikers in Chicago led to the Memorial Day Massacre of 30 May. Prostrike demonstrators had clashed with police who fired on the crowd, injuring thirty and killing ten outright. Welles's sprinkling of paramilitary blackshirts in his mob tends to get the most critical attention because it squares with the larger concept so tidily, but the flat caps and fedoras which fill out the crowd suggest something quite different. Norman Lloyd's tousle-haired Cinna was an effete intellectual surrounded by working-class thugs and agitprop paramilitaries. This, far from an inconceivably foreign scene, felt a lot like home to Americans in 1937, where an economically stressed society, fractured along lines of class sympathy and mode of employment, was perpetually in danger of turning in on itself with deadly consequences. The issue at the heart of the Cinna scene might have been any of the polarising issues of the day, be it economics, domestic politics, or – the hot button subject of the moment – isolationism.

Welles's cutting of the script refocused the production on the title character and on the mob which facilitated his rise to power and took vengeance for his death. Though Welles imported some lines from *Coriolanus* to give the workers more to say, they formed a particular type of mob: humourless, malleable and bloodthirsty, so almost all of the initial banter with Flavius and Marullus which might suggest wry, independent intelligence, was deleted. Interestingly, the crowd were all given the names of the actors who played them (and this is how they appear in the prompt script), and though those names were never spoken, the device suggests a Stanislavskian take on the Meinenger ensemble approach. The actors were invited to think and feel as if they themselves, as individuals, were the audience of Caesar, Brutus and Antony, even if the audience experienced the crowd as a unit. They were, moreover, positioned for the forum scene in near darkness below the carefully lit faces of the orators above, and as such, their restlessly increasing, lethal energy seemed as though it came from the theatre audience itself. That the on-stage crowd shared a sightline with the theatre audience was an innovation of the Welles production, since even crowd-heavy stagings of the past had contained the mob within the fourth wall, sometimes with Antony delivering his lines in pictorial profile.[6] Macready had shown a crowd that was a crucial determining factor in the events, but it was the Mercury production, with its contemporary clothing and restrictive lighting, that made the crowd an extension of the audience.

To bewail Welles's lack of interest in the wit and intelligence of his crowd in a production subtitled 'death of a dictator' is to complain about a cat for not barking. The production was not interested in the crowd as an intelligent force. It wanted to show crowds as the dangerously powerful tool of men who knew how to manipulate them. This may not be a full account of the crowd as Shakespeare wrote it, but Welles's obligation was not to Shakespeare's text but to the theatrical moment in 1937, the audience who would attend that moment and to the larger 'concept'.

The problem with the Cinna scene was that it was rehearsed in classic Welles fashion and based on ideas about theatre which dominated this and other Welles productions. In all scenes, the director sought a particular visual image, what Norman Lloyd who played Cinna called 'the shot'. The phrase obviously reflects the director's cinematic influences, the way his visual sensibility was shaped by the iconography of film melodrama long before he launched his career as a film maker, but it also suggests the extent to which character was subordinated to image. Welles did not direct his actors in the contemporary sense, working with them to find choices at the level of utterance and gesture grounded in psychological realism. He left that to them. He was interested in choreographing the whole, laying out the stage pictures in their entirety, a style again aligning him with the actor managers of the past (think of Kemble's artful statue-groupings of supers) as much as with the directorial wave of the future. Welles was the star of the show not so much because he played Brutus, with the text heavily cut to make his centrality unmistakable, but because he was the director. Astonishingly, he relied on a stand-in for Brutus throughout the rehearsal period so that he could watch the show from the house, only inserting his own inadequately rehearsed Brutus into the play at the last moment.

This was understandably frustrating to his fellow actors, who were sufficiently modern in their sense of their craft that they depended upon building scenes organically through relationships with the other actors on stage. To have the lead actor slotted into scenes which had been rehearsed with someone else made nonsense of their process and created a tense, uncertain environment in which it was difficult to be creative and committed. Welles – as both a traditionalist who adored Shakespeare's lines and an actor who knew that much of his power lay in his own deep, resonant 'mid-Atlantic' voice – had no great interest in layers of psychological complexity in the Stanislavskian tradition; and if the other actors needed to build such layers, he expected them to do so silently, unaided, and in their own time. As Simon Callow shrewdly observes, for Welles, 'every rehearsal was a technical rehearsal' (Callow, 1995: 330).

Welles's cavalier attitude to characterisation took its toll with the actors, and not just those who had to share the stage with Brutus. Discontent came to a head over the Cinna scene. Norman Lloyd felt that the scene had never been properly rehearsed despite the amount of rehearsal time which had been allotted to it but which had been taken up, in Lloyd's view, with technical details of the lighting and rhythmic musical underscoring and large-scale choreography. There had been no work on acting, on character, on motivation; as opening loomed, Lloyd refused to play the scene. It was cut, replaced in the first preview by another lighting device which shone directly into the audience's eyes.

The preview was a fiasco. The sound system didn't work, and at the end of the show the audience simply got up and left without a single round of applause, a response which almost led to a fist fight between Welles and the press officer (Henry Senber) back stage. In the damage-control rehearsals that followed (while other previews were suspended), the Cinna scene was reinstated, reworked according to Lloyd's actorly impulses and given the director's visual signature. The result made Cinna temperamentally something like Welles's Brutus in miniature: another liberal, according to Lloyd, incapable of 'Tak[ing] a position' (Callow, 1995: 328). The scene began in comedy, Cinna playing the witty buffoon for the amusement of the audience onstage and off – a Poet Laureate who thinks he's been recognised as a celebrity (335) – but the crowd turned (slowly, thanks to some interpolated lines from *Coriolanus*), closing on him one by one, hyena-like, a tightening, menacing circle of men around him. Finally the mob surged forward through the red light which suffused the scene, overwhelmed him, and rushed him to 'black oblivion'.[7] Interestingly, it was the comic aspect rather than the much discussed horror of what followed that was foregrounded in the *New York Times* review, Brooks Atkinson referring to the scene as 'the one humorous episode'.[8] Atkinson, however, clearly got the point, referring to the 'witless, savage, demoniac mob' in a second piece two weeks later.[9]

Brutus, Welles and the great dictator

Welles's effective absence from rehearsal as an actor led to a performance which was often hesitant about such basics as physical placement, blocking and script. Some of this he was able to cover (he was famous for his iambic improvisation), and in this role the hesitation may even have fed the audience's sense of a character who was – in Welles's conception – *supposed* to be hesitant, uncertain, 'the eternal, impotent, ineffectual, fumbling liberal'.[10] But there is no doubt that this approach to Brutus did not sit well with Welles's strengths as an actor, and therefore with the expectations of his audience. Welles was renowned for the scale of his performances, for their charismatically effulgent sense of personality and a boldness which flirted with ham. This Brutus was too small, too uncertain for so over-sized a performer. Welles both for his conception of the play and his attitude as a director, might have been better as Caesar. As he wrote in *Everybody's Shakespeare* three years earlier: 'Commentators say the play is misnamed. *Brutus* should be its title ... I disagree ... the personality of Caesar is the focal point of every line of the play' (Callow, 1995: 184).

Such a view informed Welles's Brutus who was the play's protagonist but not, paradoxically, its most important figure. While the first night review references this Brutus's 'reverie and calm introspection; it is all kindness, reluctance and remorse', Atkinson's subsequent piece makes the play (not simply the production) 'the story of an idealist who fails as a man of action because he is not cynically clever and cannot stomach the enormity of the bloody forces with which he finds himself allied'. This is over-deterministic as a reading of the play and seems to echo Welles's rhetoric of the 'ineffectual, fumbling liberal' in the face of Fascism, an echo which, if not derived from *The Mercury* bulletin, may have come from the man himself, an interview with whom appears (conducted by John Hutchens) in *The Times* on the same day. But the performance of Brutus as fumbling liberal was effected, like the other elements of the production, by directorial manipulation, not simply actor performance, and the script was trimmed of those moments where Brutus might seem deliberate, even conniving, most notably in the orchard scene's soliloquy beginning 'It must be by his death'. In the Mercury version, Portia enters after 'Then, lest he may, prevent' (2.1.28), thereby eliminating the following:

> And since the quarrel
> Will bear no color for the thing he is,
> Fashion it thus: that what he is, augmented,
> Would run to these and these extremities.
> And therefore think him as a serpent's egg
> Which, hatched, would, as his kind, grow mischievous;
> And kill him in the shell.
>
> (28–34)

The imprecision of the argument might have suited Welles's Brutus, but the scheming, the plans to justify their actions by 'fashioning' a plausible case, did not. The Mercury's Brutus may have been ineffective, but the virtue of his intent was unimpeachable.

The *Times* interview is part-biographical sketch, part-discussion of the production and the future of the Mercury, and all panegyric. Indeed, with its gleeful citation of the mere $6,000 *Caesar* had cost to mount in comparison with the ruinous expenses incurred by other productions (the Atkinson piece makes the same comparison, citing a $100,000 *Antony and Cleopatra* which had flopped spectacularly), the *Times* piece amounts to a coronation.[11] The old theatre is dead, it seems to say, and the light of modernity has dawned in the person of this slightly odd-looking wunderkind. The article (tellingly entitled 'Mr. Orson Welles says it was like this', and continued on subsequent pages as 'Mr. Welles explains') puts Welles front and centre, but saves its greatest flights of admiration for the star's self-deprecating humility and work-ethic. It concludes:

> He got up from the table in the bar where all this talk had been going on, adjusted what he called his low comedy scarf and walked down the street – very deliberately, like an old-time actor – toward the Mercury Theatre ... [H]e would be going on in an hour or so as Brutus. He did not particularly look like the youngest actor-director-manager who has arrived in a very long time.

If the paper was trying to crown Welles, it seemed that he was putting it by (with the back of his hand – thus) but retaining, even emphasising, that which made them want to crown him. Houseman, who was almost as integral to the company's inception, however much he let Welles rule the roost artistically, did not get a mention.

Discussion of the Mercury production always effects this strange conflation of Welles with both Brutus and Caesar. He was, naturally, the star actor in a production cut to keep him central, and he was, just as naturally, the directorial orchestrator of the whole, the face of the company, the showman with whom the Mercury and its work would always be associated. As a director, he was Caesar, and a Caesar of a cloth cut from his own production. Jean Rosenthal, the lighting designer, put it this way: 'Welles dictated very clearly and exactly the kind of look he wanted the production to have, a very simple look, based on the Nazi rallies at Nuremberg' (Callow, 1995: 325). Her use of the word 'dictated' in the context of this particular production (and that particular sentence) is unavoidably suggestive. Most of those involved in the production describe Welles's dictatorial direction, his dismissal of whatever didn't come from him directly, and the slick heartiness with which he bullied and intimidated to get his way. Rehearsals were driven by his whim, actors were badgered, designers were left with nothing to do but execute Welles's orders, and the newspapers cheered him on.

But however much the centrality of Welles to the production and his dictatorial approach to running it clarify things in one way, they don't help to turn the 'concept' production into a 'message' production. Indeed, the political waters of the play which seemed to have been so impressively straightened and made navigable by the director also became distinctly muddy. Under all the applause was a persistent question about what it all meant. Caesar was Mussolini, apparently, or Hitler (reviewers were unsure which) and Welles's Brutus was the hero, but he was a hero out of touch with reality, stuck in his own contemplation and reduced to a corpse only minutes after the grand funeral orations. Which suggested what? That Fascism couldn't be opposed? That it shouldn't be? Or that the solution was to out-Caesar Caesar à la Mark Antony who, as a grand, manipulative orator, was a clearer stand-in for a Mussolini than was the relatively easy target who gave his name to the show. In *The Mercury* bulletin, Welles retreated from his initial claims about the specificity of the production by suggesting that it wasn't so much a direct parallel to modern Europe as a refreshing context which allowed Shakespeare's lines to resonate more immediately, and generally the press seemed satisfied by this. If nothing else, the production brought Shakespeare's play directly into engagement with the political issues of the day and the debate over isolationism, and even if it did not finally and unequivocally take a side in that debate, it staged the perilous attraction of Fascist spectacle as a tool for militarising the populace, and this surely was the sounding of an alarm.

It seems reasonable to add – having already drawn parallels between the title character and Welles's own dictatorial approach – that the production further mirrored the play's content in enacting a kind of rebellion against the monstrously expensive, oversized stagings of Shakespeare which were still the rule in twentieth-century United States. But revolutionary though it certainly was, the *Caesar* mounted by the Mercury – for all its Fascist trappings – retained more of Booth and Tree's approach than is usually credited. As in the play where the final political landscape emphasises *real politique* over idealism, insurrection leads only so far: the King is dead, long live the King. Welles shook the remnants of Victorianism to its core, ousting not just Booth and Tree but Bridges Adams and Poel in the process, but in doing so he created not a new theatrical democracy but a new version of the all-powerful director. Welles acted the conspirator but played the dictator as director, and it is no accident that in the later audio recording, he played not Brutus but Cassius, Mark Antony (differentiated with a slightly higher voice) *and* the Narrator. It is hardly surprising that so much of the talk about this production then and now is really talk about Welles himself: he dominated every aspect of the show, not as the colossal Imperial statues dominated earlier productions but as if everything on stage, every scenic unit, every actor, somehow *was* Welles himself, and that their shadows flickering under the Nuremberg lights were his. Concept productions are, after all, conceived, driven and executed by auteurs.

Subsequent critics – particularly Shakespeareans, whose investment is primarily in the original text – have sometimes tended to belittle Welles's production as diminishing the richness and complexity of the play, in the political refocusing as much as in the cutting. Michael Anderegg tracks some textual editors' attempts to downplay any 'liberal' leanings in the play at all in their pursuit of a kinder, gentler – or at least more admirable – Caesar (Anderegg, 2005). Moreover, while it is difficult from our perspective to see the Fascist setting as anything other than morally black and white, the original performative moment was, of course, quite different. Before the full horrors of the Nazi ideology had imposed themselves upon the national consciousness, figures like Mussolini inspired admiration as well as fear, and the Mercury's jackbooted Caesar was thus a divisive figure, not simply the strutting villain that history has made him. It is striking that a leftist publication like *The Daily Worker* saw the production as itself essentially fascist because of its negative representation of the masses.

Placing the Mercury production on a timeline of *Julius Caesar*s and evaluating its place therein is tricky, because both its originality and its influence on subsequent productions are difficult to assess. Welles had seen Frank Benson's touring productions in Dublin as a teenager and had surely seen other Shakespeare in England. though we can't say for sure what; and whatever he rejected from such productions, he clearly owed some of his sense of theatrical space and ensemble performance to the legacy of Poel and Bridges-Adams.[12] He knew of modern dress Shakespeare at the Birmingham Repertory Theatre where *Macbeth* and *Hamlet* had been directed by Barry Jackson, but also knew enough of the nineteenth-century actor-manager traditions to use them for his own benefit.

Though it is the most famous, Welles's was not the first twentieth-century production of *Caesar* to engage contemporary politics. Though not well-known outside Poland, and certainly unseen by Welles, one wonderfully visual and stylised production by Leon Schiller at the Polski in Warsaw in 1928, designed by the Pronaszvko brothers, had targeted the de facto dictatorship of Marshal Josef Pilsudski. This was not a modern dress production, and it concealed its political agenda inside a familiar and respectable notion of Shakespeare. Instead of individuating the mob, Schiller – an ardent communist – strove for a less realist and more aestheticised crowd who moved *en masse*, becoming a kind of visual chorus which waved and undulated in response to action. The people formed an organic unit, and what Schiller called 'the game of the crowd' was both an aesthetic effect and a political statement about how power-hungry individuals manipulate society.

Nearly a decade later in 1936, a Czech production, though in traditional dress, took similar aim at the dictatorships risen all too close at hand, with the result that the Prague company was shut down after right-wing protests in the press. There is even evidence of a production titled *Julius Caesar in Modern Clothes* done with Fascist trappings only a few months before Welles's at the Delaware Federal Theatre, which the *Newark Post* read as a species of satire. Clothing aside, this production seems to have been conceived along nineteenth-century lines and generated little excitement beyond the relative novelty of being in modern dress. Scholars debate whether Welles knew of this production (Anderegg thinks he must have (1999: 27), Callow doubts that word of the show had reached New York (1995: 322)), but it is clear that the idea had been independently suggested to Welles and Houseman by Hallie Flanagan and the playwright Sidney Howard. Ideas, however, are impossible to sell or copyright. Execution is all. Given what was happening in Europe, it seems impossible that educated people working on this particular play did not note some possible linkage; but Welles's particular genius was to take something which might easily have grown out of the cultural zeitgeist and turn it into what Anderegg calls 'an event' (20). His *Julius Caesar* was a colossal risk, aesthetically and even financially. For all the journalistic talk about how cheap it was to mount, the company was haemorrhaging money they simply didn't have. Failure would have shut them down. What damage failure would have done to Welles's credibility is harder to say, but the stakes were high, and to reduce them with carping about just how original his production was is petty at very least.

However indirect the legacy of the Mercury *Caesar*, it altered the future of the play on stage at least as radically as anything before it, breaking the shackles of the past in ways comparable to – say – Brook's *Midsummer Night's Dream* thirty-three years later. Part of that legacy was that American directors became wary of the play for some time, but that only attests to the extent to which the production had caught the mood of the present moment. Something of that legacy is anticipated by the *New York Times* review's slightly surprised subheading: 'A Story of Action'. The eighteenth- and nineteenth-century tradition had made the play a story of discussion, of rhetoric and abstract values. At the Mercury, even with Welles's reflective and impotent Brutus, the story became swift and driven, much of which needs to be attributed to the muscular cutting of the script and to the turning of its characters from distant idealised figures from a lost (and largely imaginary) world into contemporaries of the audience. In the process, the play blew off its schoolroom dust. In the words of one of the production's most ardent supporters, John Mason Brown of the *New York Post*,

> Shakespeare ceases at The Mercury to be the darling of the College Board of Examiners. Unfettered and with all the vigor that was his when he spoke to the groundlings of his own day, he becomes the contemporary of all of us who are Undergroundlings.[13]

That last word punningly hits the spot. This was a production recognisably of the present moment and place (theatrical groundlings who used the New York underground), which linked the audience both to the conspirators and to the crowd for better and worse. That a play so steeped in tradition could suddenly feel so spontaneous, so urgent, speaks volumes about the production's success.

As is to be expected, not everyone liked the production. While some complaints stemmed from a desire for an older version of staged Shakespeare, other complaints targeted the acting as well as the streamlined script and the conceptual frame. Welles himself drew the most fire; he was accused of mumbling, of being overly hesitant and generally boring. Such an effect may have been at least partly intentional as a take on the character, but the critique may also register problems with Welles's approach to rehearsal, with his relative lack of interest in the role itself, and with his limitations as a performer who tended to rely on his voice. It is suggestive that in the subsequent radio broadcast, he gave Brutus to George Coulouris. But the negative criticism – much of it deliberately flying the flag of different notions of Shakespeare or – indeed – of Fascism, was drowned out by the applause.

There is much the production didn't do, things it wasn't interested in, elements of the text it underplayed or omitted, but that is the nature of theatre, and Welles had the intellectual honesty to announce as much by addressing his adaptive approach in the very title: *Caesar: Death of a Dictator*, not '*Julius Caesar* by William Shakespeare'. Adaptation is at the heart of the theatrical process, and the purpose of a production is not to provide a definitive account of the play as text. Each performance can exist only as the manifestation of something which is both a version of something pre-existent (the text) and a new art object which has never been seen before. Subsequent productions of the play will make different choices and have different effects on their audiences, but it seems unlikely that any will so radically alter the way people see the play as did Welles's.

Notes

1 Michael Anderegg's excellent *Orson Welles, Shakespeare and Popular Culture* (1999) does a particularly good job of mapping the man's uneasy straddling of these increasingly separate worlds.
2 *Falstaff* was the title used in the UK.
3 In July, for instance, they arrested the prominent (and controversial) Lutheran pastor Martin Niemöller for crimes against the state.
4 Lend Lease, the programme by which the United States supplied Britain with materials before entering the war itself in March 1941, eighteen months after the war in Europe had begun.
5 The prompt script does not always maintain verse form in matters such as shared lines, so the precise number is unclear.
6 See for instance Jean Chothia (2003: 120).
7 Sidney Whipple writing for the *World Telegram*, New York, 15 November 1937.
8 'THE PLAY: Mercury Theatre Opens with a Version of "Julius Caesar" in Modern Dress', 12 November 1937.
9 'Mercury Theatre', *New York Times*, 28 November 1937.
10 Welles in *The Mercury, a Weekly Bulletin of Information Concerning the Mercury Theatre*. Undated.
11 The *Antony and Cleopatra* was a Tallulah Bankhead vehicle. It should also be said that for the cash-strapped Mercury, $6,000 was a good deal of money.
12 For details of Welles's theatre-going in Dublin, see Callow (1995: 83). While in London he may have seen Edith Evans as Viola in *Twelfth Night*, Robert Speight or Robert Harris as *Hamlet* at the Old Vic or Sadlers Wells and – if he made a trip to the newly opened Memorial Theatre in Stratford – may have seen Bridges-Adams *Henry IV, As You Like It, Midsummer Night's Dream* and *Julius Caesar*. There he may also have seen a revolutionary *King Lear* by Theodre Komisarjevsky. There were also numerous Shakespeare offerings in the West End (112–13).
13 *New York Post*, 12 November 1937.

CHAPTER III

(Un)American identities: Mankiewicz (1953)

Though the Mercury Theatre *Caesar* created ripples through the play's subsequent performance history which are difficult to map precisely, it played a more direct hand in generating what is generally acknowledged to be the play's best filmic incarnation. The links between the two productions are arguable and have sometimes been overstated, but they have one clear point of contact in John Houseman. Houseman had continued to work with Welles after *Caesar*, notably on the *War of the Worlds* radio broadcast (1938), but they quarrelled repeatedly over Welles's cinematic masterpiece, *Citizen Kane* (1941). Houseman (who himself made uncredited contributions to the script) believed that Herman Mankiewicz should have been considered the primary writer, instead of sharing writing credits with Welles as appeared in the billing. The resulting argument ended their friendship and they never worked together again.

Houseman went on to direct in his own right, but was best known as a producer for Paramount, Universal and MGM, with whom he worked on eighteen films between 1945 and 1962. One of the MGM pictures paired him with Herman Mankiewicz's younger brother Joseph as director, and returned him to Shakespeare's *Caesar*. The film hit screens in 1953 to almost universal praise. It went on to win an Oscar (for best set decoration) and garnered four other Academy Award nominations (best picture, best leading actor (Brando), best cinematography and best music). It won BAFTAs for best actor (Gielgud) and best foreign actor (Brando), and a National Board of Review best actor award (Mason), as well as receiving a nomination for Outstanding Directorial Achievement in Motion Pictures (Mankiewicz) from the Screen

Directors Guild (later known as the Directors Guild of America). Critical response in the press was likewise largely very positive.

From a twenty-first century perspective, the film may seem ponderous, talky, and limited in its visual scope, but the precedent set by Hollywood Shakespeare had been fairly inauspicious, and whatever else it has, Mankiewicz's film positively crackles with great performances. As argued here, moreover, I think the film's political dimension has been significantly underplayed by scholars and critics, the production actually growing partially out of the McCarthyist zeitgeist of the period and a particular chain of events centring on Mankiewicz himself which began two years prior to filming. Viewed in light of these formative elements, the film might be considered a fascinating and probing investigation of contemporary American political identity, and in this the film might be considered an extension of Welles's Mercury production, retooled for the post-war age.

At the heart of that political identity is fear: fear of mob rule, fear of communists, but also a fear of informants and the eyes of the thought-police. Shakespeare's play becomes a forum for a consideration of an ethics of American identity, and the film maps a moment in history after the triumphs – military and economic – of the previous decade, when men uniquely connected to the popular zeitgeist could feel the culture changing. These changes were reflected in the film industry, which was striving to find a new identity to suit the latter part of the century, but they also suggested more pressing social and philosophical concerns about individual freedom and the manipulation of power. The film is a 'message picture' disguised as respectable classicism, using the Shakespearean dimension of that classicism to give authority and cultural force to a subversive position. The 'message' is anti-fascist, but not in Welles's largely Eurocentric terms. This is a Fascism much closer to home, and it is figured less in Caesar than it is in Antony, the cynical manipulator of a gullible populace primed to see the conspirators as subversive not to an individual political figure but to a way of life. James Mason's Brutus and John Gielgud's Cassius are the foreign communist intellectuals, while Marlon Brando's Antony – who styles himself the home-grown, plain-dealing patriot – is the new face of McCarthyist Fascism. To get to such issues we have to begin, as the film's audiences and critics began, with the stars of the movie, and a contest over audience sympathies, acting styles and their implications for the national ownership of Shakespeare.

'In our stars': owning Shakespeare through celebrity performance

As the awards suggest, there were three stars: two Englishmen and an American. Of the Englishmen, only one was known to American movie audiences, James Mason, who had made a career in Britain playing suave, romantic rogues in films such as *The Seventh Veil* (1945), before coming to Hollywood to star in such pictures as *The Desert Fox* (as Rommel, 1951) *Five Fingers* and *The Prisoner of Zenda* (1952), expanding his repertoire for urbane and appealing villains. He is an interesting choice for Brutus because while he has a suitable intellectual gravitas and fine facility with language, his prior roles must surely have kept audiences wary of identifying with him. Lacking John Gielgud's passion and more insistently musical delivery, Mason is bookish and restrained, an approach which cannot entirely efface the cold and sophisticated separateness for which he was famous. Gielgud remarked of Mason that there 'is something a bit murderous about him, and [Brutus] should be the last one you'd think [to be a murderer]' (Geist, 1978: 227). Intentionally or otherwise, this Brutus became a patrician; aloof, dignified and intellectual, someone who gave little thought to the ordinary people or what part they might play in the aftermath of the assassination. For all his sophistication there is a shortsightedness about the raw power and magnetism that Antony would command, and a complete blindness to the ruthlessness with which that power would be deployed.

Even before his first conversation with Cassius (Gielgud), Mason defines Brutus by having him studying a little book (the book which will return in the ghost scene before Philippi). This is a man who avoids company and events, a private intellectual who would rather be left to his own thoughts. He seems most comfortable alone, and his most intimate moment with his wife is when he looks in on her while she is sleeping. During the 'It must be by his death' soliloquy (done as all soliloquies in the film are done, as speech, not voice-over) Brutus walks around, thinking it through, though the thought seems abstract, without anguish or soul-searching: an intellectual exercise like a skilled debater walking through his points. For all their large scale, Gielgud's soliloquies look more like actual thought, and though Brutus talks of his sleeplessness and mental turmoil ('the state of man like to a little kingdom suffer[ing] then the nature of an insurrection') there is no sign of his being in any way disordered or unsettled. Indeed, the smoothness and lack of passion some critics complained about in Mason seem to me quite appropriate for Brutus – or for a version of him. His high-minded abstraction and bloodlessness lay the ground for his downfall: he doesn't think with his gut and doesn't realise that others do.

Gielgud was unknown in the United States, recruited for the role on the basis of his stirring stage performance in Stratford in 1950 directed by Anthony Quayle and Michael Langham, in which he had been praised not only for his nobility and fine verse-speaking, but as the 'coiled spring which vitalize[d] the tragedy' (Ripley, 1980: 247). His was a complex Cassius, intellectual but also impetuous and emotional, awed by Brutus's moral superiority but exasperated by his tactical errors, passionate but prone to self-doubt. This performance survives largely intact in the film, and the critics were delighted by the discovery of a fully fledged Shakespearean talent, though his transition to screen acting was a difficult one. He tended to freeze up when the camera came in tight, so even his close-ups had to be filmed at some distance, perhaps feeding a tendency to address the back wall, in spite of various attempts to scale back his delivery, to make him 'just *say* it' or even 'just *think* it' (Geist, 1978: 228). That said, Gielgud's Cassius has subtlety and passion, and however large his voice, it is always nuanced (in contrast, say, with Flavius's [Michael Pate] more stagey declamation). In his first exchange with Brutus, Cassius circles him, his eyes steady, biting off the words, spitting them. When he gazes up at the bust of Caesar (who has 'now become a god') there's a fiery contempt at their predicament and his place in it. Mason in contrast is smooth, almost bland, and one can see why this fiery Cassius needs this polished Brutus to modulate his cause.

Still, the deference the conspirators show Brutus, emphasised as it is by camera angles which elevate him over them and by choices such as Casca's pointing his sword at him during his speech about where the sun arises, becomes more problematic as the film progresses. Mason's Brutus stabs Caesar almost as a last resort, the wounded (but still quite mobile) general not giving him a lot of choice, and it strains credibility when Brutus then confidently dictates what they should do next.

Cassius is violently opposed to letting Antony speak at the funeral, and the rightness of his opinion seems to merit a clearer sense of why Brutus continues to dominate strategic discussions, particularly in the tent scene. That Mason does not convey the requisite strength of character further strains the logic of the power dynamic between the conspirators. Cassius is furious, but Brutus never rises to the emotive challenge, so that lines like Cassius's 'Must I endure all this' seem barely merited: there's not enough coming from Mason to feed Gielgud's outrage, an outrage that twice makes his hand stray to the hilt of his sword. Gielgud finds a real range of emotions in this scene, for all his passion (his 'did I say better?', for instance, is nicely uncertain, and directed at himself), and though Mason is clearly meant to be the mature, cool head, his part feels underplayed, undeserving of Cassius's 'I did not think you could have been so angry.' The moment is reminiscent of Portia's earlier account of Brutus's furious stamping of his feet and waving her away, actions it is almost impossible to imagine this Brutus doing.

As fits his private sense of the man, Mason's strongest work is probably his response to Portia's death, which is touchingly natural and foregrounds the stoic control which makes perfect sense in the moment. Here it is Gielgud who seems stiff, and stagey, suggesting that the larger problem may spring from trying to meld differing acting styles into a coherent whole.

The loss of Portia seems to linger into the preface to the appearance of the ghost through the boy Lucius's song, an interpolated adaptation of a John Dowland (1562–1626) madrigal. The words are:

> Now, O now, I needs must part
> Joy once fled cannot return
> If that parting be offence
> It is she which does offend.[1]

The song, following Brutus's parting from Cassius, seems to focus his attention on thoughts of separation and loss, though the pronoun in the last line suggests he may specifically be thinking about Portia, to whom the boy Lucius provides a visual link, having been seen before only at Brutus's house. Brutus seems affected by the song, reflective, revealing the thoughts his stoic performance had earlier suppressed, before brushing them off ('this is a sleepy tune'). The melody becomes the faint underscoring as Brutus puts Lucius to bed, and though he returns to his reading, he seems distracted – even overwrought – before falling asleep. This Brutus is a private man, a family man (even his attitude to Lucius is paternal), a man out of his depth in political and military affairs.

Caveats about Mason's Brutus notwithstanding, both British actors are functioning at the top of their respective traditions, and both give compelling performances full of nuance and ease. They enact a kind of *sprezzatura* which their American co-stars don't quite have, partly because what defined acting in 1950s America had less to do with Shakespeare, with verse-speaking and with theatre, than it did with film, with contemporary drama and, most importantly, with the approach to acting known as the Method.

Brando – who studied with Stella Adler (the only American actor to have been trained by Stanislavski) and the Actors' Studio – came out of that tradition, even defined it. His background in emotional realism had made him a casting choice which generated a great deal of comment, much of it sceptical. He had been praised as the mumbling but potent Stanley Kowalksi of the 1951 *A Streetcar Named Desire*, for which he got an Academy Award nomination, but most critics assumed Shakespeare was beyond him. Though he listened to recordings of John Barrymore and Laurence Olivier in preparation for the role (Geist, 1978: 225), his instincts were expressly rooted in his training and contrary not just to Barrymore, who was popularly seen as the end of a quasi-Victorian tradition as far back as 1940, but to Welles, whose sonorous delivery had recently been considered the new voice of Shakespeare.[2] Terrified of the part, he was extensively coached by both the director and Gielgud; and while Bosley Crowther's *New York Times* review gives the palm to Gielgud, it sees Brando's Antony as 'the delight and surprise of the film', concluding, 'in him a major talent has emerged' (Canby, 1999: 444).

The surprise was genuine. As Kenneth Geist points out, for weeks before the film's release, comedians had been getting a lot of mileage out of Stanley Kowalski doing 'Friends, Romans, Countrymen, lend me your ears'.[3] In fact the film's Antony might not be Brando at his mumbling, naturalistic best, but the clarity coached into him in no way turns him into a Gielgud clone. What the press applauded in his Antony was a middle ground, and an American middle ground at that, suspended between media and acting traditions; and in some ways the act of casting him over more obvious choices such as Richard Burton, who was unavailable, or Paul Schofield, who was testing for the part when approval from Brando came down from the studio, was Mankiewicz's most radical stroke. The film announced that Shakespeare could be as much American as he was British, and in many respects Brando was seen to have out-performed Mason and Gielgud just as Antony had outdone Brutus and Cassius.

Brando chooses his operatives sparingly, an approach which creates fewer semantic punches per line than Gielgud's rhythmically more aware delivery, and which both simplifies and clarifies utterance:

> Friends, Romans, countrymen LEND me your ears.
> I come to BURY Caesar not to praise him
> The evil that men do lives after them
> The good is OFT interred with their bones
> So let it be with Caesar.
> The noble Brutus hath told you Caesar was ambitious
> If it were so it was a GRIEVOUS FAULT
> And grievously hath Caesar answered it.

This approach, awkward or baffling though it sometimes is, foregrounds the actor in the process of character construction as the British tradition tends to foreground the text. Brando's approach also places fewer demands on the ear of the attentive audience, presenting a choice so emphatic that other possibilities are suppressed. Gielgud's reliance on the stress patterns of the iambic line, by contrast, make emphasis a subtler matter which manages to keep various options open to the ear even as the line is delivered. Gielgud's approach benefits from a greater familiarity with the text on the part of the audience, conjuring its myriad possibilities even in the delivery. Brando's articulation, on the other hand, insists upon a single reading, naturalising the act of speech by hitting the word which bears most weight for the actor, often – predictably, given his training – the verbs which suggest action.

The choices in the above passage and elsewhere ('Shall I descend and will you give me LEAVE?') are sometimes counterintuitive, surprising the ear, with an emphasis that presents a strong sense of will, a controlling of the line which fuses actor and role as the complex is pared down. What gets foregrounded in the process is not always clear or unified but it does suggest personhood rather than elocution, passion rather than dignity, and commitment to a single thought, even if the origin or nature of that thought remains opaque.

As a thinking presence, Brando's Antony is hard to read because there are so many moments where his passion is shown to be performative and therefore potentially insincere, but his first entry to Caesar's body, ignoring Brutus's greeting, shows a singularity of purpose and a real connection to the dead man which seems to give rise to his subsequent machinations. His response, however, is outrage rather than desolation, and when Cassius cuts him off at 'to close / In terms of friendship with thine enemies' he does so to clarify the direction of Antony's anger, not his distress. Antony's explanation that what he says is but 'cold modesty' is similarly charged, and even after the long silence when he is left alone with the corpse, his mood is earnest and vengeful. There are no tears in his 'O pardon me, thou bleeding piece of earth' and the speech builds naturally to his cry of 'havoc'. He may kennel the dogs of war until he has the people on his side, but he was always going to let them slip.

For all his passion there, and his clever fakery in the funeral oration, Brando's great scene is – surprisingly – 4.1, the proscription scene so frequently cut from all but the most recent productions, and one he would not have been able to hear performed on record by Barrymore. Here, without an audience to perform to, he is at his Method-driven best, tossing off lines like a man flicking ash from a cigarette, his character revealed in the self-regarding slouch as much as in the casual cynicism with which he marks others for death. Nothing reveals his character better than the way he turns the bust of Caesar to face him and then settles languidly into the imperial seat to peruse his handiwork thus far. Indeed much of Brando's interpretive genius is shown less in the delivery of Shakespeare's more famous lines than in the space around them.

In the forum scene, for instance, the clues to who he is and what he is doing lie in his silence, in the way he surreptitiously listens to the crowd, feeling its mood, assessing what kind of progress he has made so far, particularly when he turns from them

2   Marlon Brando as Mark Antony addresses the crowd in Joseph Mankiewicz's 1953 film.

to 'weep'. At the end of the speech, as the crowd start to rampage, his 'Now let it work' speech is cut, replaced – like other asides presumably considered too theatrical for film – with a grim, private and calculating smile. It is shocking, because for all his manipulation of the audience, he did seem to be talking to them rather than orating at them, as used to be the case in this part of the play. After Mason's polished speech, Brando's finds moments of real fervour, but a good deal of its strength is less in choices or what may have been directed and more in a notion of acting unique in the film, something organic, spontaneous and human. Brando may have begun his acting career famous for his animal sexuality and may have concluded it as something of a caricature, but few actors could so completely inhabit a role that he seems to be improvising his lines as he goes. His approach is perhaps not well suited to Shakespeare, whose mode is a long way from simple naturalism even when the thoughts and sentiments uttered are at their most real; but he connects with Antony and with sharing the scene with him in ways which are, for most audiences, impressive. As such, Brando represents a new direction for the cinema, one which dramatised the triumph of the United States over its colonial forebears in that most British of endeavours: the production of Shakespeare.

Hollywood Shakespeare had hitherto failed to garner anything like the critical reception for Olivier's *Henry V* and *Hamlet* films, so the success of Mankiewicz's *Caesar* was a special cause for celebration, doubly so in that it did not rely on the things associated with American film: large-scale visuals and technological innovation, particularly in the use of colour. In recent years the film has been criticised for being stagey and dialogue-driven, even its monochrome look suggesting a staid classicism, but it might be said that this was a deliberate attempt to do 'authentic' Shakespeare on English terms. As well as saving money on a film with a tight budget, the choice to shoot in black and white was made, according to Mankiewicz, less to play that classicism up than to engage the play's dramatic dimension and downplay the sensationalism of, say, a *Quo Vadis* (1951), from which *Caesar* borrowed both sets and actor Deborah Kerr.[4] The film seems concerned to present the play in ways that cannot be dismissed as light or showy, but that do assert an American ownership of Shakespeare. The result is a savvy, wise-guy Cassius, played by Edward O'Brien, and a coiffed, iconic Calpurnia in Greer Garson, who had been recently naturalised as a US citizen. Caesar was played by former matinée idol Louis Calhern, late of *The Prisoner of Zenda* (with Mason), *The Asphalt Jungle* and *Annie Get Your Gun*. Though dubious of the Hollywood epic modelled by directors like Cecil B. DeMille, Mankiewicz was still making a Hollywood picture, and he assembled a cast of bankable stars to do it. The film's American affect was further emphasised by moments like the battle scenes, which were filmed to resemble contemporary Westerns and shot on location at Bronson Canyon, which had been used in such films as *Riders of the Purple Sage* (1926), *The Lone Ranger Rides Again* (1939) and *Silver River* (1948), as well as sci-fi movies such as *The Adventures of Captain Marvel* (1941), *Atom Man versus Superman* (1948) and *Robot Monster* (1953). But if the film embodies an American Shakespeare, it also raises real questions about what it is to be American in ways that go far beyond the issue of acting styles.

Roman politics

What constitutes American and – for that matter – unAmerican identity was a burning question in the 1950s, tied to political anxieties about the redrawing of the global map after the Second World War and to the rise of communism. As I shall argue, Mankiewicz's *Caesar* engages those anxieties more fully than is usually credited, and it does so by first defying augury and other elements of the supernatural. The film shies away from the cinematic appeal of the ghosts, visions and portents with which the text is saturated in order to focus on the human and political dimension of the story. The storm, though dramatically initiated by Cassius's lines about shaking Caesar, is finally just a storm, whatever people *say* about whelping lions and servants with flaming hands. Similarly, the audience sees Calpurnia dreaming, but nothing of the dream itself, and Caesar's impulse to dismiss her concerns is understandable, even intelligent given the political situation. The soothsayer's warnings about the Ides of March seem more likely to be political foresight than divine inspiration (he touches Brutus's face and, recognising him, shrinks away), so what sounds like prophesy plays more like an instinct akin to Caesar's concern about the lean and hungry Cassius.

The mood of the film suggests that something is in the air, something less about omens and the heavens than it is about whispering and political danger. The guards in the marketplace are looking for troublemakers like Flavius, and Caesar's remark about Cassius comes after catching him exchanging significant nods with Casca. When Cicero responds to Casca's talk of the prodigious storm by inquiring if Caesar will be coming to the Capital in the morning, the query is charged, knowing, and both Casca and Cassius – who is eavesdropping – recognise it as such. In this paranoid atmosphere, Popilius Lena's wish that Cassius's enterprise (the assassination) might thrive gives further weight to the idea that everyone suspects something is coming, and that Calpurnia's dreams are the psycho-symbolic manifestation of conscious anxieties. Even Casca's panic at the strangeness of the storm is stripped of its supernatural overtones by Cicero and Cassius, reduced to what the sports reporters call 'big match nerves'. Casca is over-reading, seeing spectres of a higher power where there is only political intrigue.

Caesar's ghost appears to Brutus once. It is translucent and vanishes when Brutus tries to stab it. But the film is careful to include Brutus's subsequent demands if the guards saw the spectre, and their negative responses suggest that what we saw may have been in Brutus's mind. It does not return. Similarly, Cassius's birthday speech before the battle achieves a certain pathos, but his lines about the departing eagles are cut, and the moment is thus stripped of its intimations of fated disaster. Throughout, what could have been charged with a sense that the actions of the characters had reverberations in the natural and supernatural world is muted, even undercut, and those who believe in such stuff – Calpurnia, say, or even Casca who is revealed in the storm as a gullible child – are shown to lack weight and seriousness, even when the outcome of the story confirms their instincts. In such a reading, it might be said that Brutus's glimpse of Caesar's ghost, rather than showing the long arm of the dead and a kind of cosmic justice or vengeance, reveals only how far he has fallen, how slack his grip on hard political and military reality has become. Seeing ghosts before battle is, the film suggests, a symptom of failure and defeat, not their cause.[5]

The suppression of the supernatural seems to ground the story in a familiar reality marked by faction and machinations of an expressly human kind. Indeed, the politics of the film, much to the chagrin of critics seeking something like the Mercury Theatre's sketch of Fascism, avoid the grand sweep of ideological posturing and remain at the level of the personal. Mankiewicz was famously and unapologetically apolitical in terms of party affiliation and causes, and this has surely fuelled the assumption that *Caesar* is an apolitical film, problematically so for some.[6] Such a reading is understandable, not only from the vantage point of the twenty-first century but also in the context of the reviews that greeted the film's initial release, none of which seem to perceive a strong political agenda. Subsequent reviewers and critics have battled over the film's merits in terms of its cinematic aesthetic, its treatment of Shakespeare, and the quality of its individual performances, but its politics have largely been ignored or assumed to be nonexistent. Houseman claims that the director proved 'the most conservative among us' in his refusal to foreground ideas, create transitional scenes, or otherwise reinvent the play as a movie (Houseman, 1953: 25), and the fascist associations of Houseman's last *Caesar* production survived only in the slenderest echoes of imposing architecture, Roman eagles, and the black and white of newsreel footage. But it is a mistake to assume that the absence of Nazi banners makes the film politically shallow. Indeed, while an anti-Fascist production was on the cutting edge in 1937, such a staging would have been a good deal less radical in 1953 when European Fascism had already been vanquished. I accept that political resonances have to be seen to have effect, and that Mankiewicz's film is subtle – perhaps to a fault; but it targets contemporary American political culture, and that makes it more intriguing and potentially dangerous than any shots of goose-stepping, swastika-adorned armies would have been.

I want to scrutinise the film's political dimension in the light of two factors: one general, the other specific. The general one is simply put and widely acknowledged: Hollywood has long used classicism as a stalking horse for politically dangerous ideas and issues. As Pierre Sorlin says, history in film 'is a mere framework, serving as a basis or a counterpoint for a political thesis. History is no more than a useful device to speak of the present time' (Sorlin, 1980: 208).[7] Setting a film in Rome need not dull its political edge as commentary on the present-day United States, though it might insulate the film against the clumsiest kinds of censorship and the outrage of those whose position comes under fire.

The second, more specific factor I want to consider in assessing the film's politics centres on events which took place eighteen months before shooting began. Let me say from the outset that I am not looking to reduce the film to personal or political allegory; rather, I am reflecting upon the way the film blends those personal and political elements as the play does, producing not the broad brush strokes of ideological cartoon (*à la* Welles/ Houseman) but something more nuanced and slippery to the point of contradiction. I want to consider the film as growing out of the particulars of a battle over American identity which centred on Joe Mankiewicz and which very nearly ended his career before a frame of *Caesar* was in the can.

'Their names are pricked': Cecil B. DeMille and the Loyalty Oath

MGM had dominated the 1930s box office but had struggled to draw audiences after the war as television kept people at home. The studio countered by increasing the numbers of large-scale (and expensive) musicals which other studios were moving away from, and tended to rely on series and less challenging or innovative material, also developing few new stars. Something had to be done. In 1948 MGM hired Dore Schary, a writer/producer to replace the box-office genius Irving Thalberg. Schary soon clashed with Mayer over the substance of the films they would produce, Mayer preferring safer fare than the gritty 'message pictures' which Schary had developed while working at rival studio RKO Pictures. RKO had come under the scrutiny of the House Committee on Un-American Activities (HUAC), and two of its top talents (producer Adrian Scott and director Edward Dmytryk) had been members of the so-called Hollywood Ten: ten writers, directors and producers who had refused to give information to HUAC, prompting the Motion Picture Association of America to suspend them without pay until they were cleared of Contempt of Court charges and swore a loyalty oath disavowing communist affiliations. They refused to do so, and the blacklist was born.

The blacklist grew out of post-war anxieties about a pervasive communist presence in the entertainment industry coupled with the activities of right-wing organisations in Washington, generating a good deal of nationalist paranoia within the film industry. Disney, for instance, produced a pamphlet cautioning against the smearing of industry and capitalism, or the glorifying of the 'common man' and collective identity (see Schwartz, 1999). By 1950, the Hollywood Ten had begun serving prison sentences, and the blacklist had expanded significantly, adding another dozen names including Paul Robeson, Richard Wright, and most of the 151 other writers, producers and artists whose names appeared in the Red Channels pamphlet of June 1950. It was Schary, who had witnessed the beginning of these events up close at RKO, who championed Mankiewicz's *Julius Caesar* as MGM's chief of production. In 1950 he produced the left-leaning 'message pictures' *The Next Voice You Hear* and *Asphalt Jungle*, the latter directed by John Huston and starring Sterling Hayden, both members of the Committee for the First Amendment which opposed the blacklisting of alleged communists.

In that same year – the year Senator Joseph McCarthy first claimed to have a list of communist sympathisers bent on undermining the United States – Joseph Mankiewicz became president of the Screen Directors Guild (SDG). He was elected on a liberal intellectual platform which opposed the open balloting then standard in the guild and the mandatory signing of a loyalty oath which disavowed any communist affiliations. The SDG board of directors was then dominated by the director and producer Cecil B. DeMille and his cronies. DeMille was the principal conservative ideologue within the industry at the time, and his cinematic taste for populist (even vulgar) spectacle of massive proportions was about as far from Mankiewicz's as his politics; thus the liberal campaign which had got Mankiewicz elected SDG president did not sit well with DeMille. He set out to get a loyalty oath passed for the guild before Mankiewicz had a chance to consolidate his position, and to have him ousted from the presidency.

While Mankiewicz was out of town in August, DeMille used the opportunity to ram the loyalty oath through the membership, exploiting the fact that the ballots were not secret and that most members were afraid to be seen questioning any display of patriotism in front of the well-connected board. DeMille then launched a smear campaign against Mankiewicz, leaking unfounded allegations of his alleged communist sympathies, and claiming (disingenuously) to find agitprop and subversion in his films, notably *All About Eve* and *Philadelphia Story*. He fed to the trade magazines stories which suggested Mankiewicz had not signed the oath, while in fact he had had to sign it as an officer at election, and suggested that he was a 'pinko' and a 'fellow traveler' (derogatory terms of the day suggesting communist sympathies). On Mankiewicz's return to Hollywood, DeMille engineered another open ballot calling for his dismissal, a ballot permitting only a 'yes' verdict, which was forcibly hand-delivered by motorcycle couriers during the night to the entire membership.[8]

Mankiewicz became a rallying point for left-leaning directors including John Huston, Billy Wilder and Joseph Losey, who hastily gathered the twenty-five signatures required to summon a general meeting of the guild and begin what Mankiewicz subsequently called the most dramatic evening of his life. The meeting took place on 22 October 1950 at the Beverly Hills Hotel and lasted an extraordinary six-and-a-half hours. Mankiewicz made a careful, hour-long speech outlining his position, his principles and the details of the DeMille faction's campaign against him. He ended by attacking the 'Politburo quality' of that campaign – a crucial implication of Soviet tactics in support of a supposedly anticommunist agenda – a strategy 'foreign to everything I have ever known or learned or thought as an American' (Geist, 1978: 192). By the time DeMille himself stood up to speak the mood was becoming incendiary, since the facts of the case as Mankiewicz saw them had not been made clear to the rest of the membership till this point, and many were outraged by the tactics of what Geist calls 'the key triumverate': DeMille, Albert S. Rogell and George Marshall (190). DeMille – bathed in the baby-pink spotlight he had insisted upon – proceeded to make an extraordinary rhetorical gesture, a gesture which was to shape Mankiewicz's *Caesar* two years later.

DeMille's speech began with the statement that he came 'neither to praise Caesar, nor to bury him'. The lengthy oration which followed used close, deliberate and obvious parallels to Mark Antony's funeral oration. In an attempt to turn the crowd against Mankiewicz and his supporters, he took a passive-aggressive tack designed to bolster his own nationalist principle at the expense of Mankiewicz and the other 'honorable, good Americans' who stood with him. His persistent and ironic use of 'honorable' was weighted not just *like* Antony's but partly *because* of it, the play's famed device making DeMille's agenda flagrantly clear. He did not wish to come out and say so directly because, as Antony was beholden to Brutus in being allowed to speak, he professed himself beholden to Mankiewicz as SDG president, but he wanted to make it very clear that Mankiewicz was 'UnAmerican' in his sympathies and was thus dangerous not just to the guild but also to the country and its values. He made hay out of an account of American soldiers ('boys') who had been executed by communists in Korea, indirectly suggesting that support for Mankiewicz was support for the perpetrators of such atrocities. He pretended to suggest personal disinterest and implied the beneficence of the board in offering the membership a vote on Mankiewicz's recall, suggesting (like Antony with Caesar's will) that he was merely serving their best interest, and dodging the specifics and implications of an open ballot which did not permit a negative vote. He concluded that everything he had done had been above board and in the service of his country.

The smugness and injustice of his rhetorical strategy had the opposite effect on his audience, inflaming them. When heckled for his claim to have done everything above board, he proceeded to read a list of Red Front organisations to which some of Mankiewicz's supporters had been linked in a HUAC report. He concluded these insinuating observations by stating that while 'troubled waters attract strange specimens', he was making 'no accusations against anybody, least of all Mr. Mankiewicz' who was, after all an 'honorable American'. The crowd now became openly hostile, hissing and booing, turning particularly nasty when DeMille laid the fault at the feet of 'foreign born' elements whose patriotism was not all it should be. He ended by making more dark suggestions about the delight which would be taken by the Communist newspapers the *Daily Worker* and *Pravda* about the work of Mankiewicz's supporters, again framing the attack with a faux disinterest worthy of Antony: 'I am simply bringing to light the coincidence that the group opposed to the recall happened to be so heavily loaded with the elements that have been repudiated by this Guild in election after election and vote after vote' (Geist, 1978: 194).

A series of nonpartisan directors spoke up in Mankiewicz's favour, angered by what they had heard, and it was the conservative director of Westerns John Ford (whom Mankiewicz had feared could go either way) who delivered the *coup de grâce*, demanding that in addition to Mankiewicz receiving a full show of support from the membership, DeMille, his triumverate, and indeed the entire board of directors should resign in acknowledgement of the gap between their position and that of the membership. DeMille, who had been outmanoeuvred and had grossly over-estimated his capacity for manipulation and intimidation, was forced to concur, and the board resigned.

Remarkably, no critic I can find – including those who documented DeMille's pastiche of Mark Antony's funeral oration before going on to comment on Mankiewicz's *Caesar* film, have connected the SDG events of late 1950 with the *Julius Caesar* Mankiewicz began working on a year-and-a-half later. Instead they have seen DeMille's defeat represented filmically in Mankiewicz's 1951 *People Will Talk* (particularly in the image of the villain Elwell sloping off in defeat with his briefcase). Critics have found in the angry white mob of his *No Way Out* (1950) an implicit critique of HUAC which echoed other films of the period (Losey's *The Lawless*, Cy Endfield's *The Sound and the Fury*, and Russell Rouse and Leo Popkins's *The Well*, all released 1950–51) 'as manifestations of the fascist tendency that liberals saw as dominating American political life at the time' (Krutnik, 2007: 106). But if one looks past this *Julius Caesar*'s classicism, past its status as respectable drama, past even the focus on virtuoso performances, we might see Mankiewicz's film as a complex reflection on the political moment and the manipulative power of insinuation. The film is a nightmare version of an alternative October meeting in which DeMille triumphed, and – by extension – it is a meditation on the dangers of the new American nationalism. The bloody vengeance of the mob was finally cut by Dore Schary from the film, much to the fury of Mankiewicz, who had filmed the crowd like massed hyenas dragging down a hapless Cinna; but the omission does not strip the film of its HUAC critique. Rather, it shows itself more interested in the men who drive the mob than in the tendencies of the mob itself.

A new kind of Antony

Comparison is often made between Mankiewicz's film and Welles's Mercury production, tied as they are by the presence of Houseman, and both productions have suggestive omissions as discussed earlier in this chapter. The final cut of the Mankiewicz film loses the murder of Cinna, but it retains what is perhaps the most loaded and directorially clear moment in the movie which Welles (and most of his directorial forebears) had eliminated: the proscription scene. Because Welles was interested in the spectre of Fascism as a cultural force, he was drawn to Nazi symbolism and to the embrace of its attendant violence by the mob. For Mankiewicz, the fault was less in the people than in those who – cynically, ideologically, or both – drove them. This is why Brando's Antony so dominates the forum scene with his careful, deliberate plotting, his thoughtful listening, and that telling smile of triumph at the end. This Antony can speak not as a hectoring Fascist orator but as a 'plain, blunt man' to his 'countrymen' as did DeMille the populist and nationalist, but the film was able to add what had never been seen explicitly before: Antony's cynical motivation, his detachment. Past Antonys had been noble and passionate, and recent Antonys had been politically shrewd, but never had an audience seen an Antony who so lived by fakery and mock outrage. This Antony listened dispassionately to the crowd as they discussed his noble tears, and his private smile as they begin to riot exposes his villainy.[9]

The play had been staged many times with many kinds of Antonys, several who moved from the tradition of noble outrage to demagoguery, but this is the first whose cynicism makes him the villain of the play. Unlike Welles's Antony, Brando did not step into the trappings of Fascist spectacle established for Caesar, delivering his speech from the dramatic glare of the Nuremberg lights. Brando's villainy is smaller, but its coolness and deliberation go beyond dictatorial manipulation of the masses and foreground the schemer himself. This is a cinematic effect, something achieved by means of the camera's ability to reveal what a stage audience cannot see: the 'upstage' face listening, calculating, the secret smile. Even in those recent productions which had turned the play into a study of Antony as demagogue, the audience's viewpoint had been shaped by the effect of his public persona except in a few framing, solitary moments ('now let it work'); but Mankiewicz uses the reversed camera angle to take the audience inside Antony's performance *as* he is creating it, showing the wheels turning in his head even as the crowd respond to what they think they are seeing. However impressive Antony's oratorical display, then, the film audience, unlike the on-screen audience, is never entirely taken in. They always know it's a show because they get to glimpse the backstage preparation, and this novel and privileged insight confirms his villainy.

The fact that Antony is also appealing, charismatic and personated by someone so significantly American merely troubles the nature of that villainy. In the frequently cut proscription scene, his ruthlessness is revealed not simply as political contingency, desperate times calling for desperate measures, but Machiavellian ambition and narcissism. In addition to the ordered executions, the script keeps Antony's injunction to trim Caesar's will of its legacies. More specifically, the scene invokes the poisonous climate of the HUAC tribunals in which entertainers were cajoled into offering up the identities of others who might have 'UnAmerican' leanings. In the diction of the day, Antony, Octavius and Lepidus 'name names'. With casual disregard for the consequences of the documents they produce, they damn friends and relatives as did informers who gave up those with alleged communist sympathies. Brando's Antony seems amused that Lepidus might try to forestall the execution of his brother by insisting on the death of Antony's nephew, something which clearly means nothing to him. Throughout the scene he eats and drinks, showing casual disdain for the scale of the triumverate's actions. Once alone and reclining in the regal seat before the bust of Caesar, his reconsideration of the list of names reaffirms both the flippancy and paradoxical purposefulness of his actions. In this context, the death of Cicero reported during the tent scene (a moment sometimes cut along with Cicero's whole character) shows not just the scale, but the indiscriminate nature of the reprisals, echoing current events where simply being named at a hearing could end your career. As Thomas Doherty says of the so-called 'graylist',

> [O]n March 21, 1951, the name of the actor Lionel Stander was uttered by the actor Larry Parks during testimony before HUAC. "Do you know Lionel Stander?" committee counsel Frank S. Tavenner inquired. Parks replied he knew the man, but had no knowledge of his political affiliations. No more was said about Stander either by Parks or the committee – no accusation, no insinuation. Yet Stander's phone stopped ringing. Prior to Parks's testimony, Stander had worked on ten television shows in the previous 100 days. Afterwards, nothing. (Doherty, 2003: 31)

For Antony, as for HUAC, guilt was by the most tenuous of associations.

If Antony's was the most lauded of performances, at least in the United States, it was, as I have already implied, a kind of American triumph. Hollywood had bested the English in the most English of arenas: Shakespeare. But what did this loaded casting suggest about the version of America which was triumphant? Antony was the victor, but he was also – more clearly than in any other film and more than he had been in Welles's production – the villain. Indeed, might it not be argued that Brando's Antony had, like DeMille, wrapped himself in the flag and preyed on the suspicions of his audience about 'foreign born' actors such as Gielgud and Mason, the latter a familiar movie villain? To see the film in these terms demands a certain ironic distance, one which recognises that the film was doing consciously, even pointedly, what Antony and DeMille both did, feeding popular prejudice and suspicion, fanning flames of a lethally destructive nationalism. As it had been for DeMille – a man Mankiewicz said had his finger *up* the pulse of the public (Dauth, 2008: 157), the question of honour was really one of private intent, of motivation. DeMille had failed in his bid to oust Mankiewicz from the SDG presidency, but the larger impulse he represented lived on in the expanding blacklist and in the atmosphere of distrust and paranoia that ran on through the decade. Consequently, the film reimagines that moment in October 1950 as DeMille's triumph, Mankiewicz easily fitting into the role of a liberal intellectual Brutus who clings to a notion of reasoned debate and private integrity as he is steadily outmanouevred by ideologically clearer and more ruthless forces. Though some have said that the usually villainous Mason was miscast as Brutus, there is a logic to the decision to make him less viscerally appealing while casting a charismatic but morally flawed Antony. This was the United States as Mankiewicz saw it, easy populism and glamour masking corruption and self-interest while the rational and public-spirited were dismissed as lacking sufficient appeal or being insufficiently patriotic.

Even the infamous box canyon 'Philippi' makes sense in this context. The classic Western location, underscored by 'native' drums, creates a filmic echo, a 'movie cliché', an indefensible 'ludicrous chestnut' of a scene (Geist, 1978: 230).[10] But in light of the film's preoccupation with national identity, the battle may be seen to emphasise the expressly American framework within which politics and culture operate in film. Mankiewicz invokes the (ultimately racist) ethno-morality of the Western in terms movie-goers should understand; Antony's Indian-style ambush shows his characteristic cynicism in contrast to the soldiers of his ingenuous enemy who march about in full view. The agonising pause before he orders his archers to open fire hints at the same deliberate ruthlessness evident in the proscription scene. The battle which follows is a slaughter, brief and one-sided. There is no mercy, no chivalry, just the studied mechanics necessary for absolute victory.

Antony is pointedly a giver of orders, not a combatant, and is therefore deprived of the kind of heroism to be afforded other film Antonys. In a sense he becomes the director of the action not just militarily but in a filmic sense, orchestrating armies like DeMille directing one of his epics, without actually getting bloody himself. DeMille had – in the furious words of Second World War combat veteran George Stevens – been too busy 'raking in his bloody capital gains' to see active service during the war, a fact which did not stop him questioning the patriotism of those who had.[11]

This is not to suggest that Brando's Antony is intended to *be* DeMille, but in an era where politics were intensely personal and driven by domestic and personal matters rather than by the uniforms, rallies and marches which had informed Welles's production, Mankiewicz saw in DeMille a model for Antony, a type who used intimidation and the exploitation of fear and self-interest to carve out not just a personal empire, but a version of the state. If the film's politics have so often been missed the explanation may be not just with the usual arguments about monochrome classicism seeming to move the film outside contemporary events, but with an acknowledgement of an irony at the heart of the Mankiewicz–DeMille battle which finally confuses the film's political position. On 27 October 1950, the victorious Mankiewicz wrote an open letter to the Screen Directors Guild, which concluded with the following remarkable capitulation:

> I ask you, as a voluntary act in affirmation of the confidence in your Guild you so vigorously professed last Sunday night, to set aside whatever reservations you may have concerning any aspect of the oath or its method of adoption, and sign it now. (Geist, 1978: 205)

A principle had been achieved in the battle with DeMille, but Mankiewicz knew which way the wind was blowing. The concession was, he thought, a token, the oath having already been forced through by DeMille back in August, and he seemed to think that playing along with HUAC would buy the guild a little more freedom from scrutiny; but it effectively reversed Mankiewicz's campaign promise to throw out oaths and blacklists with his first real act as president. Ominously, this was to become the first mandatory loyalty oath voluntarily adopted by any of the Hollywood talent guilds, and it set a dangerous precedent. 'If the loyalty oath hadn't gone through the [Directors] guild', said the subsequently blacklisted director Joseph Losey, 'history might have been slightly different, because it started the ball rolling' (Navasky, 1980: 181).

Crowds, mobs and audiences

Mankiewicz was not interested in political parties, and even less in flag-waving demonstrations and marches. It is understandable, then, that his crowds are manipulated by the insinuation of an entertainer, that they are less individuated than in other productions (notably the Meiningen), less self-aware and more pliable, their guard permanently down as they are pushed and pulled by the spectacles offered them. In their dealings with

Flavius and Marullus, the crowd's wit and defiance is pared back, and they quickly fall into step – literally as it turns out – when led by the tribunes. As Flavius moves around the set, the camera tracks him and the crowd obligingly follows, keeping a respectful distance so that the speaker stays visible. This is a crowd which walks, and stands, and looks chastened because it has been told to do so, not because of impulses originating in the crowd itself. Their physical responses are wholly unified, and they generate no whisper of detraction, being wholly malleable, and finally powerless. Their mood changes utterly when Marullus (George Macready, who claimed descent from William) shows them their error, and they shuffle off when Flavius is collared by a watching legionary, but nothing of their new mood survives into the triumphal entry of Caesar which follows. This procession with cheering crowds would have been familiar to theatre audiences fifty years earlier, and if its pageantry, military standards and high camera angles might briefly echo Riefenstahl's 1935 Nazi documentary *The Triumph of the Will*, the brand of Fascism on display is more subtle and domestic, rooted in a crowd which is all too easy to direct.[12]

In the forum scene, the crowd, more individualised than they were, nevertheless remain pliable and largely unthreatening. They aren't a real mob with chaotic energies of their own. They are waiting to be told what to think, what to do. There are a couple of carefully placed women who provide moments of hysterical weeping on command, but the crowd is largely male and, of course, white. There are some moments when they dissent (shouting simply 'no'), but even before and after such moments they are unnaturally quiet, respectful. They seem headless, the 'worse than senseless' 'blocks' of Marullus's lines. The extent to which they turn in Brutus's favour, the completeness of that turn without even muttering amongst themselves – the word which does the trick is 'ambition' – renders them ciphers. This is not a crowd shaped by the mind of a communist sympathiser. It is a crowd of Lepiduses mete to be sent on errands and then turned off like to the empty ass.

There is initially a sense that some of the key men in the crowd – those who shout Shakespeare's responses – don't change their minds: that the most pro-Brutus voice at the end was the man who wanted to hear him speak at the beginning. This suggestion of actual political opinion and constancy, however, is a set-up.

It is the same man who is the first to lean to what Antony says later, the first to turn on the conspirators, calling them 'traitors', and the first to cry out for vengeance after the corpse (another visual reveal) is unveiled. The decision to give all such moments to a single speaker out of so many reinforces a sense of both the crowd's fickleness and its passivity, driven as it is to follow leaders even amongst its own membership. Not surprisingly, the man who applauds Brutus with 'let him be Caesar' generates no irony.

Antony's entrance, cradling as he does the corpse of Caesar, clearly upstages Brutus even before he speaks; it steals focus, and a woman's scream shows that the horror of the spectacle has already begun to trump Brutus's oratory. The camera angles go from Brutus's point of view over the crowd and the crowd's point of view of him, to a shot of Antony with Caesar's body and then Antony's point of view looking down on Brutus *and* the crowd; suggesting that as Brutus supersedes the crowd, Antony supersedes them both. He does so by constructing a visual image, a theatrical (or cinematic) spectacle designed like a DeMille epic, which plays to the eyes and makes fools of the other senses. The crowd – who are spectators now rather than audience – give Antony room in silence, and though they applaud Brutus's final lines, they don't seem to be listening any more.

For Antony the crowd is rowdier and angrier, but in unspecific ways: it's not clear what they are so upset about, and the general shouting and gesturing do not help. Again, there's no one to restrain them, so it's not clear why they are there at all, except that Brutus told them to listen and they – sheep-like – obey. Their anger is not merely void of threat, it's also inexplicable. Their initial wrath at Brutus for the murder made sense, but now that they have been won over by him, it is not clear why they seem so impotently furious.

While Antony has to listen and calculate in order to determine how best to pull them onto his side, there is no sense of danger from them, and he meets their turn to grief for the dead Caesar with something like scorn. By the time he gets to 'O, now you weep', he seems contemptuous, and though he says they begin to feel the 'dint of pity', it feels more like guilt. Antony remains unmoved through the long pan of faces after the corpse is finally revealed, and when he goes back up to read the will, he plays the everyman (no orator like Brutus), less angry because he knows he's won: he just has to stir up a little more fire. The much-debated smile which replaces 'Now let it work', comes less from satisfaction than relief at how easy it was.

If Antony is an entertainer-ideologue, a DeMille pedalling bread and circus in the form of his crowd-pleasing epics and underhand political manipulation, the film can be seen finally as an anxious reflection on the industry itself. Once cinema had been identified as a tool to shape public consciousness, it became an ideological battleground, all too easily used to appeal to the lowest common denominator, the basest and most craven instincts of a populace who were besieged by tales of the enemy within. The liberal, rational and even-handed tactical approach of a Brutus or, for that matter, of a Mankiewicz, are easily swept aside by those prepared to act more cynically. One wonders, then, if it was in part memories of that October night in 1950 that drove a final show of support for Mankiewicz, the Guild's nomination of their former president for Outstanding Directorial Achievement in Motion Pictures for his work on *Caesar*. But when Antony finally looks upon Brutus's body at the end of the film, the location is not on the battlefield where it fell, but already squirrelled away in a tent out of general sight. While Brutus's dead face holds the camera's focus, Antony turns on his heel and marches out the moment his lines (the movie's final lines, delivered cursorily) are done, already moving on, moving past whatever Brutus stood for. The speed with which the film fades to black suggests that his sense of Brutus's irrelevance is probably and troublingly right.

Notes

1. Dowland's version says 'which then offends'.
2. Wonderfully and poignantly, Welles and Barrymore had duelled on national television in December 1940, using none other than the quarrel scene from Julius Caesar, Welles's Brutus triumphing over the older but disregarded Cassius of Barrymore. See Burt, 2001: 204.
3. A version of the gag survives – somewhat anachronistically – in *Dead Poets Society* (1989). The film is supposed to be set in 1959, so the cartoonish version of Brando that Robin Williams performs for his class would have actually been trumped by what Brando actually did in the film. In fact the parody might be said to model still later Brando – from *The Godfather* – anyway.
4. Deborah Kerr plays a spirited Portia in the 1953 film. She knows something is going on, and feels strongly about not being taken into her husband's confidence. She has no voluntary wound (despite the Roman setting), a fact which supports a more domestic reading of

the scene, though her on-her-dignity recounting of her parentage undermines a sense of spousal closeness, as does Brutus's overchaste peck on the cheek, and their tendency to stand facing house front while they talk to each other. She watches the conspirators assembling, fearful, knowing, but powerlessly marginal. She shuts herself away as if horrified, but also deliberate, as if washing her hands of the whole thing. We never see her again, and the strongest sense of a real connection between the couple is the hints – also muted – we see in Brutus after her death.

5   This assessment might be called into question by the final frames of the movie in which the lamp sitting at Brutus's head as Mark Antony ponders his corpse, inexplicably blows out just prior to the final fade to black. The same thing happened to (the same?) lamp on the disappearance of Caesar's ghost, suggesting retrospectively perhaps, that the spectre fulfilled his promise to meet Brutus at Philippi after all.

6   Jean Chothia, for instance, has recently taken Mankiewicz to task for failing to deliver a clearly political film in pointed contrast to Welles's stage production (Chothia, 2003: 115–33).

7   Similar ideas can be found throughout Leger Grindon's *Shadows on the Past*, and Maria Wyke's *Projecting the Past*.

8   The specifics of these events are detailed in Geist's biography of Mankiewicz (1978) and in Navasky's *Naming Names* (1980).

9   Jean Chothia disputes Jack Jorgen's claim that the smile 'says it all', suggesting that the power of his words binds the movie audience to him in ways the smile is powerless to undermine (2003: 121–2). As will be evident by now, I disagree, and think that the power of the visual would trump whatever sense of his motivation which preceded it even without the earlier moment in which he stages being too emotionally overwhelmed to speak. The audience may understand Brando/Antony's charisma and political cleverness, they may even be swayed by it, but they can't miss its deliberation or deception.

10 Geist also claims that for all Mankiewicz's complaining about the lack of funds allocated to the project by MGM, the director was strikingly wasteful in the way he shot in sequence, forcing the constant building and rebuilding of sets. Mankiewicz would later be blamed for some of the now legendary overspending on another Roman epic with loose Shakespearean roots, the sprawling, critical and (at the time) financial disaster, *Cleopatra*.

11 Versions of this complaint were thrown at DeMille at the October 1950 meeting by John Huston who was outraged by DeMille's implications of unAmericanness about men who had fought for their country while DeMille had been 'wrapping himself in the flag' (Geist, 1978: 197).

12 Some critics persist in seeing the film as stressing 'the corruption and tyranny at work in Fascist regimes' (Hatchuel, 2004: xix), though I find such a reading wholly unpersuasive. The echo of Nazi

architecture and eagles is almost unavoidable, since both were derived from Imperial Rome, but this does not make them operative in the film. Welles had already shown how this could be done, and the cinematic medium made a fuller exploration of a Fascist context more than possible, but for whatever reason, Mankiewicz does not make that film.

CHAPTER IV

Wise saws and Modern(ist) instances: Anderson, Barton and Nunn

British *Caesars* saw little in the way of innovation through the 1950s, productions remaining rooted in the pre-war tradition, but in 1962 Minos Volankis staged a production at the Old Vic whose abstract construction set design and equally abstract approach to character and action heralded the play's encounter with new trends in theatre direction and stagecraft. The overall approach was esoteric and conceptual, with a general anti-heroic bent, but critics and audiences were bored and unpersuaded. Character development was reportedly nonexistent, and the ideas in play too remote and arcane to create meaningful resonance (Ripley, 1980: 260–1). In the following year John Blatchley mounted a vaguely First World War production for the RSC which borrowed costumes and – it might be said – ideas from Brook's Brechtian *Lear* from the previous season. The overall mood was cynical and antiheroic, but, like the Old Vic production, it drew little positive attention because it was considered largely an intellectual exercise, one critic remarking that the director's concerns made the theatre feel more suitable to surgical operation than the performance of plays.[1] Such critical responses grew out of the heroic tradition of the previous century but they had been bolstered by the solid virtues of the Mankiewicz film which had become the touchstone of no-nonsense interpretation and skilful execution. In Britain, where the film's latent political content had no clear counterpart, the MGM movie was modern only in its medium. Its values in matters of both content and performance style were seen as stalwartly and praiseworthily traditional, and productions like those of Volankis and Blatchley were seen largely as quirky, attention-grabbing deviants.

Though both were modernist productions, albeit of different kinds, much of what they actually did on stage was fairly

[83]

conventional, and where they were innovative the effect was too easily dismissed because of inadequate execution. They were, however, the beginning of a modernist wave which, in the course of the next decade, demanded greater attention and started to dictate new standards of success. This chapter will consider three productions which model different forms of that modernist impulse: Lindsay Anderson's 1964 production at the Royal Court; John Barton's 1968 production for the RSC; and Trevor Nunn's production, also for the RSC, in 1972. Each staging targeted something it thought inadequate about previous stagings of the play, so that in place of bringing a generalised modernist sensibility to the productions – as had Volankis and Blatchley – they set out to rethink *Caesar* through a new and competing set of stage principles. These were not innovative interpretations of the play, nor did they use the play to grapple with contemporary politics in the way that would dominate the play's subsequent production history. Rather, they came at the play from a new theatrical mindset which brought modern notions of acting, verse speaking, characterisation and stage technology to bear on it. They attempted, with varying degrees of success, not to challenge ideas about the play itself, but about how the play might be realised in the modern age.

In order to foreground the way these productions grew out of, and sometimes in opposition to, the larger theatrical culture, emphasis here will be given to contemporary newspaper reviews. In each case I will focus on an aspect of the staging of *Julius Caesar* as a particular instance of a larger debate surrounding Shakespeare on stage.

Lindsay Anderson and verse-speaking: the Royal Court, 1964

Since *Julius Caesar*'s entrance into school curricula beginning in the eighteenth century, and its becoming the subject of increasingly widespread school study in the nineteenth, the play's long-standing status as a focus for rhetorical and oratorical display had become fused with Shakespeare's literary status. This pedagogical dimension, coupled with (and partly driving) the early twentieth-century move towards 'full text' acting scripts as championed at the Shakespeare Festival in Stratford, generated a sense not just of the sacrosanct nature of *Caesar*'s text, but of how that text should be spoken. While the contentious issues of cutting and delivery have dogged all of Shakespeare's plays, *Caesar* has been a particular lightning rod for such sparring, not least because the question of what the script is and how it is spoken is tied to larger issues about the play's content and meaning.

In 1964, Lindsay Anderson directed *Julius Caesar* at the Royal Court for the English Stage Company. The theatre had opened in 1952, its resident troupe, the English Stage Company, coming into being four years later under the leadership of George Devine, whose mission was driven primarily by writer-centred new work, much of it controversial. The Court staged plays by such leading lights of British nonconformist drama as John Osborne (whose *Look Back in Anger* premiered there in 1956); Arnold Wesker (of such 'kitchen sink' plays as *Roots* and *Their Very Own and Golden City*); Edward Bond (whose *Saved* was staged there in 1965 and ultimately led to the overturning of British censorship laws); and John Arden (whose *Sarjeant Musgrave's Dance* premiered there in 1959). As well as the 'angry young men', the Royal Court was home to unconventional and feminist-leaning dramatist Ann Jellicoe (who achieved notoriety for *The Knack* in 1962) and absurdist N.F. Simpson (whose *A Resounding Tinkle* premiered there in 1957). The company's reputation was thus edgy and subversive, though the form of that subversion was aesthetic as well as political, and the work often challenged notions of dramatic structure and the purpose of theatre, sometimes in ways pushing into the postmodern.

The English Stage Company's decision to stage *Caesar* at all thus generated both excitement and scepticism, though the reviews once the production opened ranged from the bemused to the furious. Looking back from the vantage point of the twenty-first century, that fury – and the word is apt – is itself bemusing, because the production itself seemed fairly tame; but something of the theatre's identity was clearly seen in the production's irreverence, making the show a 'radical assault' on the play, and, by extension, on Shakespeare as an icon of British values.[2]

The production wore its modernism on its sleeve, the reduced cast wearing casual street clothes (sweaters, open-necked shirts, gym shoes) trimmed, in the first half, with toga-inspired sheets and sashes, and a spare, contemporary set in wood (shallow steps, stools and a few other sticks of furniture) dominated by abstract metal sculptures which reminded some reviewers of a human figure (Pompey? Caesar himself?) and others of an oversized Roman eagle. The audience sat close to the action in low light, and key moments were underscored by clashing electronic music and mechanical white noise like planes overhead or motorcycles passing.

The script was cut, but not nearly as extensively as has been suggested by subsequent critics. The opening scene, for instance, often referred to as stripped of its plebeian voices, is merely trimmed, the cobbler's initial sixteen lines being reduced to ten, the carpenter left intact.[3] Frequently deleted lines such as those with which Octavius closes the play, and the Caius Ligarius section of the orchard scene, are left untouched, and the blue pencilling, except in the battle scenes, is light and judicious, mainly used to eliminate what seems digressive or ornamental. A suggestive instance is in Brutus's orchard soliloquy in which Anderson eliminates from 'And since the quarrel / Will bear no color ... ' to 'these extremities', so the speech runs directly from 'Then lest he may, prevent' into 'And therefore think him as a serpent's egg ...' The deleted lines have value, particularly the potentially loaded 'fashion it thus', but depending on the reading of Brutus they may also feel merely vague or padded. The resulting script is leaner and inflected away from the rhetorical, sometimes implying (as does the above example) naturalistic pauses where the meter has been disrupted; but it is neither particularly short nor the hatchet job which has been suggested. Popilius Lena's lines are given to Cicero; Clitus becomes Cinna and Volumnius, Metellus; the second account of Portia's death is cut, and a short bridge passage is added to smooth over some of what has been cut from the Philippi sequence (notably Lucilius's attempt to pass himself off as Brutus and the sense of the battle as two separate encounters); but the final reduction of the text is well under a hundred lines, far less than Welles's, and nothing like the 'Victorian abandon' with which Anderson has been accused (Ripley, 1980: 264).

Though some carped about these editorial alterations, most accepted – albeit grudgingly – that it was done in the name of theatrical contingency and had little effect on the received sense of story and character. Where the cutting was used as a stick to beat the production, it was secondary to issues of verse speaking, which, taken together, were seen to be in violation of the current orthodoxy: Shakespeare should be done uncut and should be delivered in a particular style.

Mankiewicz's 1953 film had countered an English verse-speaking tradition with something more naturalistic, but the

3   The assassination scene in Lindsay Anderson's production (1964), with Ian Bannen as Brutus over the prone Caesar.

difference was one of degree, Brando giving his lines in nothing like the Method mumble for which he was otherwise famed. More to the point, however much the film prepared the way for approaches to Shakespeare which grew out of more Stanislavskian notions of actor-training in America, it had had no such effect in Britain. Gielgud's mellifluous, potent yet nuanced delivery best known from his cinematic Cassius was the supreme instance of this tradition, and its supreme proponent was Peter Hall. Hall had founded the modern Royal Shakespeare Company in 1960 and led it as artistic director for eight years, before taking over as director of the National Theatre from Laurence Olivier in 1973. During his years at the RSC, Hall had honed an approach to verse-speaking which coupled the vocal effects and projection techniques of conventional theatre with a quasi-Elizabethan focus on scansion and poetic texture. For Hall, the sanctity of the line is paramount. It contains, he says, all the necessary clues for pacing and emphasis, and he brought to a sense of the iambic a new and often productive rigour. The *why* of the line – what those of the Method might call motivation – will have to be unearthed or invented by the actor, if necessary, to explain what is apparent to the ear: first comes the form, says Hall, inverting the logic of the Stanislavskian tradition; second comes the feeling.

Hall's convictions shaped the RSC of the 1960s and 1970s, and – since he also directed actors such as Olivier, Gielgud, Peggy Ashcroft and Joan Plowright who dominated other companies – the ripples extended widely. Shakespeare thus became a special case emphasising sound as finessed and undergirded by Hall's directorial processing of what he had learned about text from F.R. Leavis at Cambridge. Though the precise form of his approach has fluctuated a little over the years, Hall's subordination of content to form as dictated by the details of the Shakespearean line characterises his work to this day. These days such an approach is something of an anomaly but in in the 1960s and 1970s it was the voice of authority. Moreover, Hall's rhetorical achievement went beyond what one heard on stage and shaped the discourse which surrounded it, legitimating the mid-century reviewers' gripe that 'no one speaks Shakespeare correctly these days'. In so doing, Hall pushed back at modernism – at least where Shakespeare was concerned – using textual authority to reinforce the notion that acting Shakespeare was predominantly about *speaking* Shakespeare. Of course, not everyone was taken in, but to stand against the new orthodoxy was risky.

Anderson's 1964 production set out to foreground character over rhetoric and did so by utilising ideas about dialogue derived from modernist, naturalist drama akin to the 'kitchen sink' productions for which the Royal Court was known. This did not mean – according to the director – entirely losing a sense of the verse's natural rhythms, but it did subordinate those rhythms to thought, and there is no question that the result moved much of the verse towards prose. At the same time, declamation was outlawed and dialogue became conversation, pitch and volume being dictated entirely through a broadly naturalistic sense of character in Stanislavskian terms, minimising emphasis on the aesthetics of linguistic sound.

In taking this tack, Anderson ran squarely into the accumulated weight and authority of the English verse-speaking tradition; and while reviewers varied in their tastes – most wanting something akin to Hall's approach, some hankering after an older, more musical delivery – the general tenor of their responses was largely the same. W.A. Darlington of the *Daily Telegraph* mused, 'Perhaps the idea was to have a plain, straight-forward, unelaborated production for a change, and let the Bard have a chance to succeed on his own, without gimmicks. If that was it, the whole thing needed to be better spoken, and spoken as verse.' He praised Daniel Massey's Antony for his 'fire', but thought he 'would have done better under a director more insistent on poetic speech', and though he liked Graham Crowden's Casca 'he speaks prose anyway'. J.C. Trewin for the *Birmingham Post* (27 November 1964) targeted the 'deplorable' speaking almost exclusively, denouncing the 'conversational monotone ... the lax speech, and false emphases', and in a longer piece for the *Illustrated London News* he cited a lengthy passage from George Bernard Shaw bemoaning the lack of rhetorical power in Tree's 1898 *Caesar*. He ends scoldingly, 'Insensitive assaults on Shakespeare, in the name of experiment, or the contemporary approach, or whatever the phrase is, have ceased to be amusingly wayward. We cannot be indulgent any more.' *Punch* (2 December) telegraphed the grounds of its objections by announcing at the top of the review that 'the passions of the protagonists must be presented by the actors in clearly spoken language and definite activity'. The modernising of costume and set it dismissed as 'flummeries', grounding the complaint in poor speaking and irritants like the mechanical sound effects. Jack Sutherland, writing for the *Daily Worker* (28 November) clearly wanted to like the modernist approach but couldn't resist bemoaning the 'poor rendering of the verse' which rendered the whole 'distinctly off putting'. Most of these critics seemed unable to consider Anderson's approach as anything but wrong, difference in approach being assessed merely as failure to achieve a Peter Hall/RSC style.

What is clear, however, is that the verse-speaking issues were also a shorthand for a reading of the play which was still largely heroic and yoked to notions of idealism and nobility which were taken as read. Felix Barker for the *Evening News* (27 November) began with a rhetorical question: 'What, I wondered at the Royal Court Theatre last night, would Beerbohm Tree have made of the English Stage Company's pygmy-sized "Julius Caesar"?' Eric Gillett in the *Yorkshire Post* (27 November) denounced the production's 'mediocrity', bracketing its failed verse-speaking with its characters' lack of heroic stature, while Anthony Merryn in the *Liverpool Daily Post* (27 November) similarly lamented that the poor speech meant that the characters didn't feel like 'significant people going through critical times'. An anonymous 'correspondent' in the *Times Educational Supplement* (25 December) allowed Anderson the generalities of his polemic but attacked the dullness of the production in terms of the reduction of the play's heroic scale: 'What he [Anderson] has in fact done is to present the play as if it were a prosaic rather than a poetic dramatic conception, cutting down the characters in the process from something over life-size, which is their true scale, to something under life-size, which is a fundamental falsification.' *The Scotsman* (30 November) flatly called it 'wrongly approached' without poetry and 'lacking nobility', with a 'stark set, annoying music [and] farcical costumes'. *The Evening Standard* (27 November) complained that the production 'has reduced each character to such mundane, naturalistic tones that banality is inevitably the result'. What is lacking is 'nobility' and 'idealism'. 'The flattening out of these personalities, the unrelieved level of conversational communication, makes it very difficult for us to take sides and, therefore, to care.' B.A. Young for the *Financial Times* (27 November) took the principals to task for failing to play the parts as expected. 'Brutus is above all intellectual and aristocratic. This Brutus shows no hint of the cool reasoning he should have brought to his dilemma, and when he speaks the decisive "It must be by his death" he sounds nearer to Machiavelli than to Bertrand Russell.' Bannen was dismissed as a 'rather excitable trade union leader'. Daniel Massey's Antony 'shows virtually no idea at all of how to speak verse, gabbling through it with half the emphases wrong and the climaxes adorned with irrelevant top notes borrowed from the worst features of Sir Laurence Olivier's worst period.' The conversational delivery became an index of a reduced, humanised notion of character which, though precisely what Anderson intended, was considered not just a failing, but a misrepresentation, and a dangerous one at that.

While some of the unease such reviewers manifested may be attributed simply to taste, there were shades of a rearguard panic here which Trewin confesses as 'anger' at what was being done to Shakespeare, particularly at this the quatercentenary of his birth. The speaking of verse as prose was seen as a puncturing of the play's scale, a reduction of the characters and thus of Shakespeare himself, in keeping with the Royal Court's antiestablishment bias. Ronald Bryden for the *New Statesman* (4 December) saw the rhetorical underplaying as 'anti-Bardry', a directorial impulse to cut Shakespeare down to size, to reduce his grandeur through a 'distancing Brechtian naturalism'.

There is surely an unconscious irony in the pairing of Brecht and naturalism in this context. Whatever 'distancing' was happening on stage, it wasn't alienation in a Brechtian sense, since the production's thrust had been to reduce, naturalise and render familiar what was usually grander and more remote. The 'distancing' the critic experienced, then, results from the subversion of his expectations through the creation of characters with whom – contrary to more heroic productions – one might empathise. It is clear from the reviews that assessment of the verse-speaking is code – and pretty transparent code at that – for a notion of what this particular play and Shakespeare in general ought to be, and this was picked up by Anderson himself and challenged in a frank *Times* op-ed rebuff of the Shakespeare establishment.[4] He set out, he says 'with a spirit of discovery … rather than reverence'.

> And having generally been bored by Shakespeare on stage, I want to find out for myself if his writing has really become as unmeaning as if often seems. Does his verse demand a special style of rhetorical delivery? … Cast the play for character and the verse will follow – not rhetorically, but with the music of intelligence and truth.

His intent, or at least the way he chose to frame that intent, was not to throw out the verse, but to subordinate it to character, to support its form and rhythm through thought and feeling rather than accessing the latter through the former, as Hall had tried to do.

The critics were in no way mollified by his approach, and there were numerous indignant letters to the editor published in the course of the next four weeks, many of them attacking Anderson's textual modification but extending to a denunciation of a project they clearly considered to sully the play and its author. Some wheel out the quatercentenary to underscore the horror of 'Shakespeare Improved and Distorted!' while others supply notes on why lines Anderson deleted were actually the core of the entire play (29 December). Robert Speaight, who ravaged the production in his review for *Shakespeare Quarterly*, wrote in to point out that Shakespeare knew things about drama 'far above the heads of our clever young men who so conscientiously contemplate the gutter' (31 December). For his part, Anderson was unbowed and in private correspondence continued for the next thirteen years to rain contempt on a mode of Shakespearean performance geared primarily to the sounding of poetic familiarity:

> The only kind of acting I like starts with absolute naturalness. (I don't exactly mean naturalism). I cannot stand performances that do not have inner reality, which demonstrate instead of experiencing. (In other words the Royal Shakespeare style.) Nor, on the other hand, do I like acting which enjoys too much its inner reality. This reality has to be refined not indulged – and then presented.[5]

> I think you're quite right in opposing my feelings about acting to the tradition at the Royal Shakespeare Company, – in fact to the generally 'established' tradition in Britain at the moment. Or certainly in London. It results, I think, from the victory of the Peter Hall tradition, coming from Cambridge University and therefore very academic or 'conceptual'. Hall, of course, developed the present Royal Shakespeare Company at Stratford, started the Aldwych and now runs the National Theatre. This is theatre without intuition, without emotion – but with a great deal of bourgois pretension and 'intellectual' claims ... I've seen a couple of productions at the National Theatre recently and found them generally dull if not offensive. I saw John Schlesinger's JULIUS CAESAR [in 1977], a dreadful piece of work, with no feeling for either drama or character. The poor actors suffered terribly – including John Gielgud – who really did nothing except speak beautifully.[6]

Anderson's continued frustration with the RSC and the spread of its influence, through Hall, to the National illustrates not only his conviction but his failure to redirect the British acting tradition where Shakespeare was concerned. Though there was to be gradual movement away from the verse-speaking style exemplified by Hall, it was not to manifest itself fully until the end of the century, and parts of it survive intact, particularly in actor training and voice coaching. If Britain in the 1960s and 1970s was to find a modernist frame for this emphatically premodern play, it would have to come to it via some route other than a deconstruction of what Anderson called rhetorical acting.

Those critics who found the approach less offensive to a cherished version of Shakespeare saw something unsettling, but intriguing. Philip Hope-Wallace, writing for *The Guardian*, thought the production a little plain and lacking in richness, rather like a very good college production, but he liked the murmured, conversational tones which he thought were well-suited to the space and made a more immediate connection with its audience (27 November). Moly Hobman in the *Yorkshire Evening Press* (28 November) found fresh contemporary resonance, particularly to the first half, and the *Manchester Evening News* (1 December) found it radical and interesting, calling it 'tautly drawn', full of lurking violence and enigmatic characterisation which makes for 'bold, sweeping brush strokes on a familiar canvas'. Anthony Cooper in the *Financial Times* (4 November) hailed the production as being about soldiers rather than politicians, admiring Ian Bannen's 'bluff Brutus, a man of noble stupidity, hot-tempered, bull-necked and honest'. B.A. Young liked the handling of the mob and the obvious contemporary resonance of their violence against Cinna the Poet, the production's 'best moment'.

The sense of something edgy and engaging in these reviews indicates, perhaps, precisely why some people disliked it so much, suggesting as they do that the play was throwing off its uninspiring schoolroom status. Alex Matheson Cain, writing in *The Tablet* (5.12.64), heralded the production as a new approach which shattered the usual tedious high school frame of reference by seeing the play fresh as the 'picture of a world in sick decline, where the magic power of the *imperium* rests on the shoulders of a nut-like, neurotic old man'. Cain says he saw for the first time Brutus as a sketch for later Shakespearean heroes, 'not the starry idealist of the school tradition, but a remote, passive Hamlet-figure who has no understanding of the necessity of digging into practical politics'. Casca, says Cain, is a 'West-End sort of man', and 'Octavius is a cold little schemer who has neither love like Antony, nor ideals like Brutus, but who is undoubtedly the right person to bear the magic of the sovereignty'. The *Tablet* review makes no claims to academic or theatrical expertise but manifests a clear and surprised enthusiasm for a play the critic has hitherto been baffled by, a play locked in the past and preserved solely in musty textbooks. What is visible here is the hint of a contemporary *Caesar*, a politically relevant *Caesar*, smaller than Welles's certainly, but marked by some of the urgency which would characterise later, more successful productions as it became more acceptable to move away from heroic idealism.

John Barton and character: the RSC, 1968

As the debate about verse-speaking turns out to be a concern for preserving a certain version of *Caesar*'s story, so the question of characterisation similarly turns on issues of heroic idealism and moral clarity. Welles had only partly 'solved' the play's complexities of character and meaning despite a concept production that had gone to significant lengths to clarify the roles, illustrating the difficulty of reconciling subtle textual study with broad-stroke theatricality, even outside the old-fashioned notions of straightforward nobility and honour. England had not yet embraced the Wellesian 'director's theatre' model, and a different variety of modernism was found in the eschewing of unifying concepts in favour of exploring the multiplicity, complexity and, indeed, contradictory nature of characters within the play.

As Lindsay Anderson was mounting his iconoclastic *Caesar*, sights levelled on the Peter Hall verse-speaking method, John Barton was working with Hall (with whom he founded the RSC in 1960) on *The Wars of the Roses*. Four years later, Barton mounted a *Caesar* of his own in Stratford, twelve years since directing an 'Elizabethan pronunciation' production for the Marlowe society at Cambridge University. The 1968 production dispensed with any claim to historicism where pronunciation was concerned, but manifested other aspects of Barton's 'scholar-director' status. Like Hall, Barton came to theatre through literary study and hands-on student work; and though he proved himself adept at textual tinkering in *The Wars of the Roses*, he was able to do so under the guise of someone historically and textually invested in the details of the original. Yet Barton was himself a modernist, albeit of a different stripe than Anderson, and though the core script for his 1968 *Caesar* was very lightly trimmed, he brought a twentieth-century sensibility to the play, not in terms of its politics, but through a commitment to the primacy of character and a refusal to be cowed by the play's heroic legacy. Though the two productions looked and sounded quite different, much of what drove Anderson's sense of the play informed Barton's.

The set was stark, four upstage triumphal arches and three mobile plinths which vanished after the intermission (following the proscription scene). Colours were subdued, the actors wearing leather belts and sling-like sashes. There were no plumed helmets, iron armour, purple robes or other typically Roman visual tropes, and the period was indeterminate. Some critics took it to be vaguely Tudor, but after the assassination, Antony wore a leather jacket, and this – coupled with a style of salute and the programme's reference to the Stauffenberg anti-Hitler plot – was deemed 'half-hearted Nazi' (*Daily Telegraph*, 4 April 1968). Guards, however, marched with staves raised 'ready to whack the Roman crowds as if they were riotous negroes in Detroit' (B.A. Young in the *Financial Times*, 4 April 1968). This mixture of associations with no particular resonance rising to the top led some to conclude that the production was apolitical, particularly since there was no clear message or unity to what unfolded on stage, the play reduced to a 'portrait gallery' (Ripley, 1980: 265–6).

Attitudes to the verse-speaking were mixed, some pleased to find flashes of the old RSC fire *à la* Hall (and particularly delighted by the sheer volume of the tent scene argument),[7] others berating the slowness of delivery, and the pauses which, though they did not disrupt the verse, did render certain portions ponderous. For Barton, the politics of the play were entirely dependent on character, and his sense of character was not completely alien to the kitchen sink drama of the Royal Court. Thus the focus became about what each character perceived and thought, how they adjusted and evolved as individuals; there was no attempt to *solve* the play in terms of its larger political questions. The mapping of character in a strictly modernist sense – with all its self-contradictions, pettiness, ambition and self-deception exposed – was an end in itself. To this end, the text was mined, Barton guiding each actor to build a sense of character if not in isolation, then without concern for overall political or aesthetic cohesion. Because the production was set in a kind of historical no-place, however, there was a lack of material specificity which resulted in a sense of the characters as being separate, almost disembodied, their entire being emerging from language – and thus from Barton's carefully trimmed script – rather than from a world manifested by the play. This was the opposite of those archaeologically informed and supernumerary-saturated Victorian productions, and the result was cerebral and abstract.

Critics found little ground on which to agree, producing reviews almost as unrelated and individual as Barton's characters. They concurred that the storm scene was loud, but not whether the players could be heard over it. Most recognised the centrality of Brewster Mason's Caesar but argued about how he was played; and while some saw no topical resonance at all in his Caesar, others thought they saw echoes of De Gaulle. He first appeared heralded by two columns of marching senators, and he remained potent even at the moment of his death – wrathfully driving Brutus's faltering dagger home himself. He overshadowed the brief second half, his bloody mantle used first as Octavius's standard, then to shroud the fallen Brutus over whose suicide his spectre had presided, the ghost being the last thing visible as the

4   Cassius and Brutus (Ian Richardson and Barrie Ingram) in John Barton's 1968 production.

lights dimmed. But while some, like *The Guardian*, saw him as a dominating presence 'less stricken by princes than stung to death by insects' (Ripley, 1980: 267), others – like the *Financial Times* – called him 'nice, gentle and fatherly'.[8]

Some found Barry Ingham's Brutus weak and muddled, trying to live up to family honour, but not principled enough to make sense next to a strong Cassius (*Ibid.*). Others, perhaps falling back on schoolroom notions of Brutus to make sense of the complexity or contradictions they perceived, took him to be the only principled conspirator.[9] At times Brutus seemed to have vague imperial ambitions (at one point he even sat in Caesar's throne as if trying it out), but such moments were seen as rendering him trivial, even cynical, rather than merely layered or complex. Such a reading was underscored by such moments as his facile use of the second announcement of Portia's death to display his stoicism. Why such a Brutus would be of use to Cassius – played by Ian Richardson as an incisive politician – several critics could not fathom.[10]

Cassius generated the most consistently favourable response, at least in part because he had a fire and determination which reminded several reviewers of Gielgud, though Richardson was more dangerous than noble.[11] As Antony, Charles Thomas showed himself a plausible athlete who felt genuinely for the loss of his friend but became a bully without rhetorical skill in dealing with crowds, B.A. Young calling him 'deceitful, rowdy and ambitious' though 'obstinately likeable throughout'. His final lines over Brutus revealed a glimmer of feeling which had not been suggested by the previous depiction of his brutality and hunger for power. The sense of paradox here was surely Barton's point – that Antony can be a bully and still feel for his departed foe – but that paradox was seen merely as contradiction, and the production's overall lack of clarity, particularly political and moral clarity, was held up as a failing. Some felt that the production finally belonged to Octavius, played by Geoffrey Hutchings (who also played Cicero) as 'an ex public school boy sure of his place in the world which bends to his will' (*Wolverhampton Express*, 3 April 1968).

At three hours, the production was called 'inordinately long in its tediousness',[12] the second half anticlimactic, several critics complaining that it was 'a bore', 'humdrum', and 'lack-lustre'.[13] There are back-handed compliments about the production's lack of 'eccentricities', but critics who carp at conceptual gimmick often finally find themselves bemoaning the absence of a strong directorial interpretation – a vision manifested in bold gestures – and the verdict is ultimately (in the words of the *Financial Times*, 4 April 1968) that the production was 'so straightforward as to seem a little on the dull side'. The *Daily Mail* was blunter (4 April 1968), going with the leader, 'Is this the most boring Roman of them all?' The rhetoric of many reviews lamented a lack of tragic grandeur and heroic status in ways reminiscent of their dismissal of Anderson's production four years earlier. Yet it was also considered emblematic of the RSC of the day, *The Times*'s Michael Billington remarking that it had 'most of the trademarks of the current Stratford style: a spare, economical setting, intelligent verse-speaking, and a critical attitude to standard characterisation' (4 April 1968). Much of that critical attitude was directed at the received impression of monolithic nobility – even the title character's dominance being achieved by force of personality rather than mythic association or political machinery – and on the need to iron out wrinkles and inconsistencies discovered in rehearsal. The production also showed itself uninterested in aristocracy, a fact which – as with Anderson – drew considerable critical ire.

As a version of modernism, Barton's production found greater favour than Anderson because enough of the production was recognisably within the RSC tradition, particularly its focus on verse-speaking. But the repeated complaints about the lack of nobility (both in terms of high-mindedness and elevated class) speak to expectations about this play and Shakespeare in general which were still powerful and resistant to change, while the warts-and-all character focus was (as in Anderson's production) seen as a failure of directorial vision rather than an instance of it. One is forced to wonder if the character-centred work of the production (some of which was reminiscent of what Anderson had done at the considerably smaller Royal Court) was wasted in the 1,500-seat Royal Shakespeare Theatre. Moreover, Barton's collage approach – each character allowed to explore his or her own contradictions regardless of ensemble coherence or even of clear unity within the individual character – was perhaps doomed from the outset, a production (like his 'original pronunciation' student show) destined to be seen as an intellectual experiment. Audiences and critics tend to expect a distinct 'take' on a play, a resolving of its complexities and contradictions, rather than the active unearthing of more. Most contemporary actors assume that rehearsal is the place for such discoveries, but that the movement towards production is when the construction of a clear and univocal arc takes place. The director's refusal to explain the characters to the audience might be seen as pushing the limits of modernism towards the postmodern, or it might be seen simply as a failure to do his job. In 1968, most critics took the latter view.

Trevor Nunn and theatre technology: the RSC, 1972

Caesar's status as classroom text has always tended to reinforce a sense of the play's essential bookishness. Victorian productions had created a strong visual dimension for the play but had done so through antiquarianism and pictorial splendour. Welles had found a new form of spectacle for the play in the Nuremberg lights, but that had come with specific cultural and political baggage. What had not yet been tried was a version of stage spectacle which fully incorporated the technological capabilities of a modern theatrical space to support the strength of the text and its actors through a design component that was impressive but essentially abstract.

In 1962, the Second World War era musical *Blitz!*, by Lionel Bart, opened at London's Adelphi Theatre. Though it was deemed too British for export to New York, it was commercially very successful, running for 568 performances. The production featured massive sets designed by Sean Kenny, featuring Victoria Station, Petticoat Lane and the Bank underground station. It marked a new turn towards the spectacular in musicals, one which made full use of emerging stage technology, and it opened the door to still larger and more lavish stage epics in which the grandeur of the effects was seen to vie with those of the movie industry. The trend for the modern megamusical got up steam with the success of the first Tim Rice/Andrew Lloyd Webber blockbuster, *Jesus Christ Superstar*, which opened on Broadway in 1971 (running for three years despite mixed reviews) and in London the following year. A new weapon had been added to the arsenal of the modern theatre – visual scale, effected through new technology – though it was, in many ways, a throwback to Victorian populist spectacle and at odds with what had defined modernism to date. Such spectacle defined Trevor Nunn's 1972 *Caesar* at the newly redesigned and equipped Royal Shakespeare Theatre in Stratford.

One of the peculiarities of the 1932 Memorial Theatre (or RST) as it was rebuilt after the fire of 1926 was that it sacrificed trap space for what was then considered a state of the art rolling stage, a complex system of lifts and machinery designed to load scenery from below. As well as facilitating swift set changes, this system – modelled on German opera houses – allowed some variance in stage configuration, since the lifts could raise sections of the stage floor by up to ten feet. In practice, however, the machinery proved inefficient, badly installed and – as a result – almost never used. It quickly fell into disrepair. At the end of 1971, Trevor Nunn (who had been the RSC's Artistic Director since 1968), flush with income from the RSC's London theatre, the Aldwych, planned substantial improvements to the RST according to designs by Christopher Morley which would be completed in time for his cycle of the Roman plays: *Coriolanus*, *Julius Caesar*, *Antony and Cleopatra* and *Titus Andronicus*. This news did not sit well with all company members and journalists, some of whom had started to characterise Nunn as a self-promoting empire builder; but the changes proceeded at a cost of some £115,000, the lion's share of which – £90,000 – went on enlarging the auditorium and was quickly recouped in ticket sales (Beauman, 1982: 314).

The remaining £25,000 (roughly equivalent to what was then a four-show budget) were spent on refurbishing the stage machinery in ways mirroring the Barbican. Though considerably less expensive than rumoured at the time (some estimates were off the mark by as much as ten times) the new stage had much the same fate as that it came to replace:

> It proved a technical tour de force, and an actor's nightmare. The company nicknamed it 'the actor trap'; the *Sunday Times* described its cavortings as 'a succession of miniature earthquakes' (315).

It was used in its entirety only once, for the 1972 Roman season, before even Nunn abandoned it and turned his attention primarily back to actors and words; and the refurbishing of the stage machinery might be best considered a design strategy for a single season. The new stage came in for a torrent of criticism (some of it fanned by the rumours of its cost) during the widely panned production of *Coriolanus*, but for *Caesar* – perhaps because the press were more used to it, perhaps because the director's use of it was less giddy – it was widely considered a success and brought to a fairly talky play a degree of spectacle which might have been old-fashioned if it hadn't been so clearly new and, more to the point, modern.

Existing plans of the stage reveal its remarkable complexity and flexibility.[14] The floor alone had seven distinct hydraulically operating units (from down to upstage): a tilting forestage, stage left and right rising bench blocks, and rising centre-stage blocks which could be variously configured (all this downstage of the proscenium). There was then a series of six individually operable steps which could be raised as walls, their tops tiltable to create various effects or match the slope of the floor. There was a downstage elevator, an upstage elevator (both modified from the original stage lifts), and a new set of rear access steps raised by the action of the upstage elevator. The stage could be refashioned in a series of continuous rakes, some of which were extremely steep, or separated into levels. There were also four periaktoi upstage of the proscenium which were built as mobile trucks, and numerous other pieces which could be flown in from above. The opening scene was an extra-textual procession in which Caesar and the senators came down a steep (1 in 8) rake from the highest upstage point to the lowest thrust of the apron over a red carpet which spooled briskly down the slope. The final scene took place on a flat, open stage. In between the two there were twenty cues for adjustment to the stage floor alone and many more to cover flown scenic elements such as banners, and items (such as the statue which dominated Caesar's house) which were brought in on trucks. A version of the full steeply raked stage was used to create the hill from which Titinius spied out the supposed defeat of Brutus, and the central steps were raised to various heights to simulate both the throne of Caesar in the senate and the pulpit from which Mark Antony addressed the crowd. In short, the scenic flexibility and technical complexity of the stage were unlike anything ever seen in Stratford before, and they facilitated a grand visual dimension for the productions, simultaneously supplying a unity to the 'Roman season' which was otherwise lacking.[15]

5   Mark Antony (Richard Johnson) addresses the crowd from the pulpit in Trevor Nunn's 1972 production.

Critical response was largely very positive, particularly after the scathing assaults on the bells-and-whistles approach to an otherwise under-strength *Coriolanus*. Several praised the sumptuous pageantry,[16] and others called for an end to the carping over the new technical innovations,[17] but for many the production's achievement was an appealing balance between character work and the mechanically assisted spectacle. The *Gloucester Citizen* (3 May 1972) called it 'a happy mixture of novel and imaginative staging and solid dramatic performance', observing that the 'highly mobile scenery in white marble was brilliantly designed – now a staircase, now a great white room, a sloping hill, a long road to battle. Its variety was breathtakingly effective and its ingenuity achieved an astonishing illusion of great space on occasions.' The *Birmingham Mail* review (3 May) is similar, foregrounding 'those splendid processions, blood-red carpet and hangings flaring against white setting and costumes. But this time the words, the plot, the personalities grip from the start. The new stage machinery is used sparingly and serves the action well. This is both a stirring and a thoughtful *Caesar*.' Felix Barker in the *Evening News* (3 May) talked about individual performances but was especially struck by the effects of the stage machinery: 'At one moment in *Julius Caesar* last night, four vast statues complete with cornice and plinth came down from the roof to meet three tiers of senatorial seats that rose visibly out of the ground.' John Barber in *The Daily Telegraph* (3 May) saw the spectacle as facilitating a new approach:

> In place of the old austere Stratford way, all now is pomp and ceremony, with thunderous off-stage noises and stage effects that would do credit to a Nuremberg rally ... This clangorous exuberance is a legitimate approach to the extrovert mood of the play, and seems partly inspired by the stage's resources, with its tiltable floor, its revolving periaktoi and rising and falling lifts which speedily rush us from Senate to tent and battlefield, every scene an eye-filler. More interesting than all of this, however, is John Wood's Brutus ...

And there it is. Detectable beneath much of the enthusiasm is an element of guilt, a concern that Shakespeare can't be too much about the visual, and less about the spectacular, and Nunn's achievement lay in offering a complex 'human' dimension to the production that was missing from the *Coriolanus*. So while some critics seasoned their admiration with mandatory grumbling about mechanical tails wagging the Shakespearean dog (Felix Barker in the *Evening News* and B.A. Young in the *Financial Times* (both 3 May), who warned that future directors would find this new 'box of tricks' limiting), they generally seemed to think that the production had enough of conventional merit that the visual could be enjoyed as a bonus rather than belittled as a distraction.

John Mortimer, writing for *The Observer* (8 May) was not alone in finding the fascistic overtones a little heavy handed, but he found more than enough to fascinate him in John Wood's Brutus. 'The much debated question as to whether *Julius Caesar* is, in fact, the tragedy of Brutus', he wrote, 'is answered with a resounding "Yes" by this production and by a performance of quite extraordinary interest, intelligence and technical brilliance from John Wood.' He is logical and shrewd but 'betrayed by his emotional control'. Those emotions appear late, in anger at the camp poet and grief over Portia's death; but while Antony lets his emotions rip and gets a calculated political advantage for doing so, Brutus keeps his head and is destroyed for it. Benedict Nightingale in *The New Statesman* (12 May) saw a different but equally commendable Brutus: an 'insufferable prig' prefiguring 'a familiar type of British liberal more concerned that the purity of his conscience be recognized by society than he should effectively change society for the better'. He seemed to acquire some depth in a fleeting moment in which he made the remark about bearing too great a mind with a touch of irony, but if he had learned anything, it was too little too late, and he was outrageously smug in the tent scene. The middle ground between Mortimer and Nightingale is perhaps implied by Trewin, who praised Wood for a Brutus that was sensitive without being sentimentalised. Such responses suggest a subtlety which – perhaps in contrast to the set – did not over-explain the character, though for some (*The Birmingham Mail* and the *Hereford Evening News*, both 4 May) that subtlety was manifested also by occasional moments of inaudibility, and for Michael Billington, Wood's 'agonized' Brutus severely undermined the production. 'He picks his way laboriously through the text,' said Billington, 'as if it were some dangerous minefield, frantically over-compensating with sudden rushes of verbal energy and making us unwontedly impatient for the character's demise.'

Patrick Stewart's passionate and volatile Cassius also drew a lot of attention, though several thought it unclearly motivated and at odds with the calculation they saw in Shakespeare's text. He was – like Antony – a foil to Wood's Brutus, but the frenzy with which he attacked Caesar was, for some, a little much, and Trewin dismissed what he took to be Stewart's 'florid' interpretation by comparison with 'the sharp sword-thrust of a Gielgud'.

The overall conception was a familiar one and centred on a fascist Rome complete with imperial eagles and blackshirt troops who chanted 'Hail Caesar' during the grand opening procession, after which a haughty and seemingly invulnerable Caesar stared down the audience. Such an approach was, of course, greatly assisted by the sheer architectural virtuosity of the flexible set which stamped each scene with the kind of awe one feels in those outscale 'how do they do that?' moments, where cinematic illusion enters the live and three-dimensional theatre. In short, the theatre's spectacular effects were Caesar's, a mark of his extravagance and power, and as such they went some way towards affirming the title character's centrality to the play, since the potency of the theatricality persisted with his statues long after the character himself was dead. The dictator's long shadow was cast in part not just by the machinery of the state, but by that of the theatre itself.

It was the spectacle which most clearly contributed to the aura of state power, and the reviews contained surprisingly little about those usual flashpoints for totalitarian-leaning productions, the crowd scenes (including the funeral orations), the murder of Cinna the poet, and the proscription scene; and though Caesar himself remained a presence (as evoked by an over-size statue still present in the battles, which did double duty as the ghost), the trappings of Fascism did not clearly survive him. Caesar himself, as played by Mark Dignam, was 'an imperial god-man',[18] 'all powerful – aggression, greed and meglomaniac pride in his eyes',[19] and the *Birmingham Post*'s J. C. Trewin remarked that this was, 'as it should be' in Caesar's play (3 May). His power was symbiotically bound to the wonders of the stage itself, the machinery of which enacted his own gloriously impressive myth.

The stage was not simply modern in its technology, but modernist in its effect. For all the range of different spaces the machinery was able to make, the design remained essentially abstract, a massive white box in which locations were evoked or implied rather than being created naturalistically. In place of the Victorian brand of spectacle (which survived into musicals like *Blitz!*), Nunn's *Caesar* took place in a symbolic landscape which remained largely open and comparatively uncluttered. For all the awe generated by the workings of the machinery, the environments themselves were never intended to overwhelm the human action, even as they manifested the play's larger preoccupation with power.

In spite of the obligatory carping, and the occasional complaints by reviewers that the production was ultimately dull and – at almost three-and-a-half hours – overlong, many clearly found it entertaining. Nunn was clearly doing something right, though Billington's complaints that the energy of the performance itself was low and its rhythm sorely lacking were telling. The new set machinery permitted a fluid variation of 'looks', but Billington largely ignored them and apparently considered them somewhat irrelevant to a production he finally dismissed as 'frankly rather dull'. This may reflect a puritanical or luddite streak, a stoicism not unlike Brutus's on the second announcement of his wife's death, a refusal to be moved by that which moves lesser men; but it may also observe a lack of harmony between the mechanical and human elements of the production. The grand spectacle had, finally, little to say which had not been said before, and after Caesar's death, seemed less clearly motivated by the story than by the company's desire to dazzle. Moreover, it might be argued that the spectacle actually permitted its opposite in the actors, particularly in Brutus, who was small and slow, himself untheatrical specifically because that element – the bold, compelling, impressive element which fires a performance and an audience – was to be carried not by the actors but by the hydraulic lifts, the periaktoi and the rolling stages. What is clear is that the actors disliked the convoluted machinery of the stage, partly because they feared malfunction and instability, and partly because they felt upstaged by it, reduced to puppets by the mechanical virtuosity of the spectacle. When the system did fail after one of the rear hydraulic lifts ruptured a bearing, the production went on quite successfully without it; and when it transferred to the Aldwych in 1973, it did so without any of the rolling stage effects, that theatre being unable to reproduce them. Nunn, who had overused the effects in *Coriolanus*, pulled steadily away from them in *Antony and Cleopatra* and further still for *Titus Andronicus*. The following year he took a well-earned break from directing, and none of the new directors opted to use the rolling stage at all. Indeed, the effects were never used again, and the equipment, like the machinery installed in the original 1932 space, fell into disuse and disrepair, being removed piecemeal over the next two decades to make room for trap space and other stage devices.

It is suggestive that Trewin's critique of Stewart's 1972 Cassius was framed in terms of Gielgud. It had been, of course, more than twenty years since Gielgud had played that role, and though his reprise of it in the MGM film undoubtedly kept his performance alive in the memory, it seems telling that after a series of productions which had tried to move the play politically and aesthetically into the late twentieth century, Gielgud remained the touchstone. No one had stamped the role, or indeed the other roles of the play, quite like he had, and for all the experimentation and discovery of the 1960s and early 1970s, there was no radical rethinking of the play or its characters. The strands of modernism visible in the three productions discussed here are manifested more by shifts in technical approach than by innovative interpretation. For Anderson the shift in approach involved verse-speaking and a general demystification of Shakespearean heroic grandeur; for Barton it involved realising ambiguous complexity in the script; and for Nunn it involved balancing spectacle with actor-centred 'first principles'. Of the three, Nunn's was considered the most successful, and its intertwining of character and visual showmanship was clearly a marriage in which the two partners were seen to legitimise each other, while announcing the RSC's status at the forefront of a new technically sophisticated and rich Shakespeare.

All three of these productions were trying to carve out a way for modern actors and audiences to live under the heroic shadow of the play in the present. Each attempted to navigate a way into the world of the play and its cultural legacy in the light of what the twentieth century had learned theatrically. The result was an alienation from the older form of the play, an alienation which placed the thinking individual against the cultural force of theatrical Shakespeare in general and *Julius Caesar* in particular. None of the three productions, however, seriously tried to approach individual character in the context of post-war politics by engaging the play's political dimension in contemporary terms. Instead they chose to foreground individual character in the context of an abstract modernist aesthetic or with the broad brush intimations of a fascism which had been vanquished almost three decades earlier. Politically they all lacked the kind of specificity which would make them topical, even dangerous. Directors like Anderson were taking aim at a familiar notion of Shakespearean production and, in their own ways, so were Barton and Nunn; but they weren't taking aim at the world outside the theatre. At least in England, it would be some time before the politically immediate aspect of *Caesar* would enter the modernist arsenal.

Notes

1   Peter Roberts, *Plays and Players*, June 1963.
2   The words 'radical assault' are Ripley's (1980: 263), an astounding phrase given the book's publication date of 1980, and one which

clarifies the terms with which he goes on to rubbish the production outright.
3   I am assuming, of course, that the surviving script, kept in the Lindsay Anderson collection at Stirling University, accurately records what was spoken on stage. There is no reason to doubt this, though the script is fairly clean with few emendations and scribbled directions on the facing pages which seem to be directorial rather than made by a stage manager.
4   The piece, which was published on 15 December 1964, is reprinted in Anderson (2006: 297–8), wrongly cited as originating in the *Daily Telegraph*.
5   Letter to Polish-born photographer, Slawek (or Slavik), 25 May 1977. Posted by Slawek himself on his own website www.gotoslawek.org/LA_listy.html, accessed 2 October 2011.
6   Letter to Slawek, 21 September 1977. *Ibid.*
7   Phillip Hope Wallace's *Guardian* review singled out for praise the 'fine high level of decibels' of key moments (4 April 1968).
8   B.A. Young, *Financial Times*, 4 April 1968. Echoing the *Birmingham Post*, John Ripley remarks that 'never in the stage history of the play has Caesar's claim to the title role been so rigorously pressed' (Ripley, 1980: 266).
9   David Nathan in *The Sun*, 4 April 1968.
10 This position was taken by the *Financial Times*, by Peter Lewis in the *Daily Mail* (4 April) and by Ray Seaton in the *Wolverhampton Express* (3 April).
11 Philip Hope Wallace in *The Guardian* is representative (4 April 1968).
12 *Stage and Television Today*, 10 April 1968.
13 The quotes are taken respectively from the *Daily Mail*, *Evening Standard*, and *Daily Telegraph* (all 4 April 1968).
14 I am indebted to Roger Howells, stage manager for the 1972 *Caesar*, for his clarification and annotation of the floor plans, and for several lengthy conversations in the RSC archive in August 2010.
15 It is striking that reviewers made so little of *Caesar* as part of a Roman tetralogy. Despite the recent example of the *Wars of the Roses*, which had been well received for the continuity, foreshadowing and suggestive echoes the cycle created between roles and plays, putting the Roman plays together was seen to generate few new insights or resonances. This was particularly the case for *Caesar*, which had little to build on from the only previous play in the cycle, the largely unsuccessful *Coriolanus*, though *Antony and Cleopatra* benefited from an earlier glimpse of the young Antony. Generally speaking, though the rolling stage and casting between plays created some continuity, the plays were generally treated as quite separate productions, even though they shared Nunn as director.
16 Norrie Drummond in the *South Wales Evening Argus* (8 May), and the *Warwick Advertizer* (5 May).

17 Gordon Parsons in the *Morning Star* (4 May), Michael Owen in the *Evening Standard* and Irving Wardle in *The Times* (3 May).
18 *Hereford Evening News*, 4 May 1972.
19 R.B. Marriott in *Stage and Television Today* (11 May 1972).

CHAPTER V

Glories past: the minor films

Julius Caesar on stage had been defined by the play's classicism, by its oratory, and by a perceived idealist treatment of its characters and subject matter. These factors were gradually stripped away from production in the twentieth century, though it was not yet clear what would take their place. To compound the problem, *Caesar* remained a primary teaching text in a high school curriculum which emphasised the play's literary and historical dimensions to the exclusion of its theatricality. The post-war years had seen significant hardship, particularly in Britain, where the war's costs (literal and figurative) were still being met thirty-five years after VJ day; and in a climate of recession, oil crisis and endemic striking, classical theatre seemed increasingly out of touch with everyday life. In the same period, the gap between high and low culture had widened significantly, and the students who were being taught *Caesar* defined themselves increasingly by their own cultural standards and tastes as represented in particular by various forms of pop music. The counter-cultural impulses in matters of art, social awareness and politics which had begun in the 1960s flowered in the 1970s, so that Shakespeare's primacy (like that of other dead white men) became, for the first time in a couple of centuries, open to question. *Caesar*, one of Shakespeare's most male-dominated plays, its subject matter bound in history and education to official accounts of civilisation and culture, seemed particularly inflexible in the face of shifting tastes and attitudes.

If theatre in general was perceived to have lost track of its roots in popular culture, its position had been usurped by cheaper and more ubiquitous media, notably film and television, both of which were experiencing counter cultural revolutions of their own. The Hollywood studio system was collapsing by the late 1960s as new, avant garde powers were rising, surprising the industry with edgy, stylish and sometimes shocking fare which was meeting with critical and commercial success. By the end of the 1970s the movie industry had been transformed beyond recognition, represented both by a new aesthetic (in the hands of directors such as Bogdonavich, Polanski, Scorsese and Coppola) and by a new mainstream version of storytelling (as offered by George Lucas and Steven Spielberg).

By the end of the 1960s, television had made the shift into colour and had become a genuinely mass medium. In Britain, which would generate the single most important Shakespeare series, the stuffy news and light entertainment programming which the BBC had first offered was undergoing a shift, introducing postmodern comedy like *Monty Python's Flying Circus* (1969–74). Homey crime shows like *Dixon of Dock Green* (1955–76) were gradually overshadowed by tougher material like *Z-Cars* (1962–78) and *Softly, Softly* (1966–76). 1970 saw the beginning of the long-running BBC *Play for Today* drama anthology which was to air some of the most gritty, original and exciting writing for the medium: and by the end of the decade television was an altogether different cultural force.

Popular culture had grown up, become more nuanced and sophisticated, and was questioning of the old verities. Locating Shakespeare in this culture became increasingly difficult, particularly a play like *Caesar* which was seen as among his most bookish, antiquarian and scholarly. For the vast majority of schoolchildren for whom (especially in England) going on to university was not a possibility, particularly in the bleak economic climate, *Caesar* must have seemed more than usually remote, even irrelevant to their lives and world. Much of the classical myth which the play seemed to reify was extensively rethought on television, through the irreverent burlesque of *Up Pompeii* (the original series of which ran from 1969 to 1970), for example, and the politically shrewd, antiheroic *I, Claudius* (1976).

It was in this climate that new versions of the play appeared for film and television in 1970 (dir. Stuart Burge, with Charlton Heston) and 1979 (dir. Herbert Wise, as part of the BBC Shakespeare project). For various reasons neither production was able to capture the zeitgeist of the day, the films tending to enact the cultural gap rather than bridging it. Looking back, we can see that both productions, wary of a modernism they feared would be dismissed as alienating gimmickry, attempted to justify their product's value through a mistaken appeal to older tastes and values. This is a recurring problem for *Caesar*, one that would not be solved until productions began to embrace its political dimension more aggressively, in ways countering the play's investment in the past. These films thus present an image of the play in crisis, anchored not just by a sense of history, but by traditions which prevented the play from keeping pace with changes in the larger culture.

Big screen: Mark Antony rides again: Charlton Heston in 1949 and 1970

Burge's film is not high on many people's lists of favourites, but it merits attention partly *because of* its perceived failures. To understand its goals, however, we must put it in the context of the star who drove it, and that means going back a further twenty years to Chicago. In 1949, David Bradley, formerly a student at Orson Welles's alma mater, the Todd School for Boys, and then completing undergraduate studies at Northwestern University, made a 16mm monochrome film of *Julius Caesar* starring his boyhood friend Charlton Heston, whom he had directed as a seventeen-year-old in a film of *Peer Gynt*. Heston had just started to make a name for himself in theatre and television, though he would not officially debut as a film actor until the following year, and he was the only actor paid for the project. Bradley played Brutus himself and recruited Northwestern acting students to fill out the cast. The result, uneven at best, initially saw only limited release until appearing at the Edinburgh Festival in 1951, after which it enjoyed more extensive attention, even tying for first place at the Locarno International Film Festival in 1953.

From the vantage of the present this last seems unlikely. Much of the movie feels amateurish, and some of the acting is very poor. Nevertheless, it wears its limited resources on its sleeve and, as is often the case with necessity, a certain invention is engendered. In this case, the pay-off is achieved through a visual style and a use of light and shade which press towards the expressionist. The formal outdoor scenes are shot at the feet of the massive columns of several Chicago public buildings: the Elks National Veterans Memorial, various museums, and Soldier Field (later the home of the Chicago Bears). Much is made of the slightly unRoman scale of this architecture, and the toga-clad characters look like ants before it, as if dwarfed by Rome's mythic status or administrative structure. This curious sense of the people's marginal nature is augmented by the film's recourse to exclusionary shots designed to keep the modern city off camera, scenes such as the Lupercal crown-offering squeezing some representative plebs into a tight shot between pillars. The sense of Rome as a place where vast numbers of people actually live, people who have a hand in the political outcome of the play, is absent. The result is a dreamscape in which Rome is both immediate and contemporary, but also a ghost town, a dead window onto a legendary past.

The use of black and white lends the film a starkly contrasted world, but this is not played for moral effect, or at least not in terms of simple binaries. Faces get bright light or are plunged into deep, partial shadow, so that characters like Brutus get a suggestive gravitas and an intimation of complexity which their acting alone could not achieve. Cassius, who is lean to the point of cadaverousness, is a particular beneficiary of this device, emerging as a sinister presence throughout the first half of the action. Camera angles vary sharply, moving from distant shots of actors arranged as on a stage, their faces lost, to extreme, low-angled close-ups where every pore, every facial twitch is laid bare. In its visual dimension the film has a nice sense of detail and perspective; and moments such as Flavius's plucking and scattering the petals of a dry flower on 'these growing feathers plucked from Caesar's wing' get a symbolist treatment which is almost existential. At times, such devices can feel laboured, particularly when they have to bear so much of the film's weight; but they embrace their medium – albeit sometimes preciously – as no other film of this play does, and make this the most clearly modernist of the three productions under consideration in this chapter, despite predating the others by two decades.

Being conscious of itself as film, the movie supplies much which is merely recounted in the play. We see Calpurnia's dream of Caesar's bleeding statue. We see Mark Antony offer the coronet to Caesar during Casca's play-by-play recounting, as we have just seen Cassius's memory of his swimming contest with Caesar. In each case, the visual interpolation risks looking silly (neither swimmer is terribly convincing and the 'angry flood' looks like a mill pond), but the impulse to escape the reliance on words alone is surely to be commended. Cinna the Poet's snobbishly patrician dealings with the cartoon plebs are shown ringed with a fire effect which prefigures how he will die (he's attacked with flaming torches before being stabbed) and what will happen to the city thereafter. The battles, like the crowd scenes, are comically underpopulated, though the camera work manages to convey a sense of event and even something of the grit of combat. The Philippi scenes were shot in the Indiana dunes beside lake Michigan, and much is made of bodies and weapons falling to the sand. The whole is underscored by clamorous brass which overcompensates for the paucity of the soldiers, most of whom are not built for armour and short skirts. Only Heston's Antony looks like a warrior, and in the second phase of the battle he is given some heroic one-against-two fighting to exploit the fact.[1]

Vocal performance is certainly not one of the film's strong suits, a fault resulting from a combination of mannered faux English accents veering towards gangster, poor choice of operative words (there's a particular tendency to play pronouns), and the cost-saving decision to film without a simultaneously recorded sound track, the actors dubbing their voices after filming. Soliloquy is done largely as voice-over, which makes for the camera dwelling for taxing periods on immobile faces; and it is perhaps the attempt to make thought spontaneous that leads to the cutting of the crucial opening line of Brutus's 'It must be by his death', the speech building to a conclusion rather than explicating or rationalising a decision already made.[2] Some of Mark Antony's soliloquy from 'Oh, pardon me thou bleeding piece of earth' is cleverly brought forward and done as voice-over as he shakes the conspirators' hands, taking us into his confidence and onto his side. The device makes Antony, like Cassius, more obviously a Machiavel, deceiving and plotting from the outset.

Heston's Antony is, not surprisingly, the stand-out performance, and he brings a refreshing sense of character to the film in moments such as his flippant damning of his nephew with a drop of wine in the proscription scene. Elsewhere he is a little too reliant on his sonorous vocal style and lantern-jawed good looks, tending to bite off his lines and give steely glares down his aquiline nose. His funeral oration is an expressly rhetorical act, a set piece without spontaneity, and accompanied by grand gesture, impressive rather than indicative of emotional or political motives beneath. Even the understated rumination on the mantle registers a poetic rather then personal dimension and quickly reverts to the same pitch and pace of the rest of the speech. Nevertheless, the funeral oration provides a high point for the film; though it uses none of the visual devices which redeem other scenes, and its brisk, rhythmic energy provides a good contrast to the tent scene – largely uncut – which is merely tiresome, moving from empty bluster to equally empty sentimentality.

What we see in Heston's Antony is an embryonic version of what would become the backbone of Burge's film twenty years later, an Antony who is virile, patrician in his hauteur and sense of rightness, but physical – a bodily presence with an imposing physique which lends itself to rolling around in the sands of combat. He is, moreover, not a scheming politician or manipulator so much as a straight-from-the-shoulder private man driven to oratory by passionate conviction, though his obvious capacity for heroism is tainted by a casual pragmatism in which ends – however bloody and painful – justify means.

Heston wanted a second crack at the part, an impulse in no way dulled by Brando's performance in the Mankiewicz film which had utterly overshadowed Bradley's effort three years later. He made it clear, even after being launched to superstardom (by none other than Cecil B. DeMille) as Moses in *The Ten Commandments* (1956) and winning the Best Actor Oscar for *Ben-Hur* (1958), that he would take a massive pay cut in order to play the role in another feature film. He had, it was clear, a particular set of ideas about who Antony was and his centrality to the story, ideas quite different from Brando's, and the simple fact that any new film would be made in colour seemed to give the project a freshness that would justify its existence as both art and box-office fare.

Tantalisingly, the first person to express interest in taking Heston up on his plans was Orson Welles, who had been working out a deal with CBS to mount the play for television. The deal fell through, but Welles remained interested in the project, as actor or director, and was pencilled into several different roles as planning progressed.

Canadian producer Peter Snell took the reins of the film in 1967, agreed to pay Heston the requested $100,000 plus 15% of world gross, and used his star appeal to raise the rest of the $1.6 million budget (Manvell, 1971: 92). Snell was wary of Welles's legendary excesses as a director, though he continued to consider him for Brutus, Casca and Cassius, though Gielgud – who was already on board to play Caesar – pointed out that Welles was never going to look lean and hungry. Welles was used as another 'name' to draw more talent and money, and throughout preproduction he was touted as being on board; however, 'when shooting began, he was notably absent' (Brode, 2000: 109). Snell had also tried to get Omar Sharif to play Brutus, but when he had proved unavailable, cast – disastrously, as it turned out – Jason Robards, fresh from playing the bandit Cheyenne in *Once Upon a Time in the West* (1968). The rest of the cast was filled out with a good mixture of Shakespeareans and movie stars: Richard Johnson as Cassius, Robert Vaughn as Casca, Richard Chamberlain as Octavius, Diana Rigg as Portia and Christopher Lee as Artemidorus. The director's chair went to Stuart Burge, who had never made a feature film but who was considered a safe option, partly because he had done a TV *Caesar* before (in 1959) which had tried to embrace a sense of visual scale. Money was tight, and for all its Hollywood glitz, this was in real terms an independent film that couldn't afford (or so went the reasoning) to take too many chances.

The film's release date puts it not just on the cusp of a new decade but at a turning point in the film industry, and a glance at the highest grossing films of the previous couple of years highlights the curious spot in which Burge's *Caesar* found itself. The top movies of 1967, discounting the animated *Jungle Book* which made much of its money in subsequent re-release, were *The Graduate*, *Bonny and Clyde* and *Guess Who's Coming to Dinner*, all edgy films in style and content. Of the rest of the top ten, only the Julie Andrews vehicle *Thoroughly Modern Millie* might have been successful ten years earlier, and even the action film *The Dirty Dozen* was marked by darker than usual themes and extreme violence. Other than the Bond film *You Only Live Twice*, the rest (*The Valley of the Dolls*, *To Sir, With Love*, and *In the Heat of the Night*) were all marked by urgent social issues. 1968 brought highly successful sci-fi and horror films to the mix (*2001*, *Planet of the Apes*, *Rosemary's Baby*), musicals (*Oliver!* and *Funny Girl*) and dark suspense (*The Thomas Crown Affair* and *Bullitt*), but added a historical drama (*The Lion in Winter*) and a Shakespeare, Zeffirelli's *Romeo and Juliet*. The top five films of 1969 were dominated by avant garde grit: *Butch Cassidy and the Sundance Kid*, *They Shoot Horse, Don't They?*, *On Her Majesty's Secret Service*,

Midnight Cowboy and *Easy Rider*. Even the Bond film of the group (*On Her Majesty's Secret Service*) pushed the envelope into darker, more tragically unconventional territory. The year *Caesar* came out, the box office was dominated by *Love Story*, *Airport* (the disaster flick which began a decade-long epidemic), *MASH* (dir. Robert Altman), the documentary *Woodstock*, the Second World War epics *Patton* and *Tora! Tora! Tora!*, and antiestablishment pieces such as *Little Big Man* and *Catch 22*.

What is immediately apparent about this admittedly selective list is how little of it would sit comfortably on a movie house marquis with Burge's *Caesar*. Even the *Romeo and Juliet* is markedly different, less a superstar vehicle than Burge's film (its leads, Olivia Hussey and Leonard Whiting, were unknowns), lavishly filmed with a soaring musical score, and stamped with a distinctive directorial look. It was also controversial in its day for its use of nudity, and for energising an old, familiar play with passionate performances from a strikingly young and beautiful cast. Despite its Shakespearean script (radically trimmed for film) and early modern setting, this was an art house film with something of the flair and provocative thrust of its period, and it appealed directly to a younger demographic.

By comparison, Burge's *Caesar* felt out of time, a film which made occasional gestures to the present but which had its feet set firmly a good half-decade or more earlier and woefully out of touch with the cinematic mood of the day, a mood which would produce gritty, character-driven art suspense like *Chinatown* (1974), *The Godfather* (1974), or *Taxi Driver* (1976), or blockbusters such as *Jaws* (1975) and *Star Wars* (1977). Most damaging of all, in embracing the epic form of the late 1950s and very early 1960s, *Caesar* committed to the one approach clearly beyond its financial reach. *Ben-Hur*, the Heston vehicle most obviously recalled by *Caesar*, had been made ten years earlier at a cost (uncorrected for inflation) ten times the budget Burge had at his disposal, and with a cast which included 8,000 extras.

Lynda Boose and Richard Burt call the Burge film 'the last instance in which a definably Hollywood film seriously tried to produce Shakespeare straight' (1997: 13), something they put down to American anxieties about ownership of the Bard, as characterised by the need to surround movie stars with English stage actors, preferably from the RSC. Such a position marks an effective reversal of the triumph seen in the Mankiewicz film, but it needs to be qualified. Burge's film was not, after all, a true Hollywood film, and some of its missteps are about trying to look like one. As its principal box-office draw, the film understandably sought to emulate the epics for which Heston was best known (*The Ten Commandments* (1956), *Ben-Hur* (1959), *El Cid* (1961), even perhaps *The Agony and the Ecstasy* (1965)), but that very approach created unreachable audience expectations. The pastel-coloured togas (surely an attempt to exploit the film's Technicolor advantage over the 1953 film) look cheap, but not as cheap as the armour, most of which is the stuff of community theatre. In the battle sequence Antony is outlandishly attired in moulded cuirass adorned with clumsily sculpted golden lion heads, his helmet bizzarely crested with 'metal' plumes, while the coiffed and boyish Octavius sports a florescent yellow cloak. DeMille's casts of thousands are replaced by scattered and chaotic skirmishing between a few dozen extras, minimal special effects, and glimpses of individual combat which cannot build a narrative of the battle, so that at one moment it's not even clear that Cassius's army is in retreat.

The combat sequences struggle to find any real grit – another legacy of the epic tradition – so the battles feel sanitised and vaguely heroic. Despite the liberal sprinkling of blood around Caesar's corpse after the assassination, the movie's violence shows no trace of the culture which had already seen *Midnight Cowboy*, *Easy Rider* or *Bonnie and Clyde*, and would go on the following year to see *Straw Dogs*, *A Clockwork Orange*, and *The French Connection*. Of course, the play doesn't suit an epic treatment, and however much the orchestral music develops an elegiac note for the final moments, it is far from clear what we are supposed to feel. The story has none of the innate moral clarity and heroic purpose of a *Ben-Hur* or an *El Cid*, and certainly none of the spiritual weight of the *Ten Commandments* or *The Agony and the Ecstasy*. Without a clear sense of tragedy – personal, political, or mythic – the film falls flat, so that Robards' hopelessly stultifying Brutus, intoning lines without suggesting even a clear sense of what they mean, becomes the film's emblem. 'Ye gods!' exclaimed the *New York Times* reviewer, quoting Cassius, 'Must I endure all this?' Despite a 'perfectly viable cast', he continued, the film is 'as flat and juiceless as a dead haddock'.[3]

It begins by promising better, with a voice-over narrative cueing up Caesar's triumphal return to Rome while the camera lingers on the corpse-strewn battlefield of Munda, a landscape of wrecked chariots, shattered weapons and skeletal remains picked over by griffon vultures. The Roman chant of 'Hail Caesar' actually begins in the gaping jaws of a skull in the grass before dissolving into the Lupercal scenes. The image of the circling carrion birds recurs in the Philippi sequence, but little is made of this potentially striking emblem, as if the director is keen to efface his presence once the script itself is engaged. During the credits we see grainy footage of marching crowds, hundreds of celebratory bodies, exotic animals including elephants, and elegant dancing women strewing confetti. The scale of such stuff and its cinematic quality are quickly subordinated to dialogue, however, and the Roman populace ceases to be a force as soon as Flavius and Marullus start to speak. The film does little with the medium's visual dimension, and scenes like the storm are stripped of their supernatural elements and drastically reduced. Even when fairly sizeable crowds can be mustered, as in the funeral oration, the camera relies on close and medium shots so that one never gets a sense of vast numbers of people as one does in in a true epic. Indeed, up to the Battle of Philippi the overall effect is of a small television production trying to relive Hollywood's glory days, surely the consequence of budgetary constraints and Burge's prior directorial experience.

The text is trimmed lightly and largely intelligently, but it loses some of its playable specifics. Portia (a warm and intelligent – if slightly plummy – Diana Rigg) has made proof her constancy, she says, but doesn't say how, and Antony remarks to the servant, apropos of nothing – the reference to his own eyes watering being cut – that passion is catching. Robert Vaughn's pensive, watchful Casca is deprived of his remark about being a man of any occupation who might have cut Caesar's throat, so his initial sympathies are unclear. The second report of Portia's death – always a potentially interesting moment – is cut, so Robards' Brutus loses a complexity he could really use.[4] Richard Johnson's slightly stagey Cassius in his Sheriff of Nottingham beard acquires some tragic pathos before his suicide, but he and Robards are in different films, and no textual manipulation would have been able to establish any chemistry between them. Worse, the film steps back a half century or so (and follows the final version of the Mankiewicz film) in eradicating the murder of Cinna the Poet. This substantially dulls the film's political edge in what must be considered a whitewashing of Antony, the consequences of whose handiwork are reduced to some generic running about, barrel-smashing and torch-wielding. Momentarily we glimpse a body in the street, but who it is and how it came to be there (or even if it is dead) we are left to wonder.

It is as a ghost that Gielgud's Caesar works best, not because there is anything dramatically potent about his appearance in the flame from Brutus's lamp (which he persists in calling a 'taper'), but because he is – like the movie tradition being reanimated by the film – a kind of echo of past classicist productions. No one looms over this play for the three decades or so in the middle of the twentieth century like Gielgud, who played Antony at the Old Vic in 1930, Cassius for the RSC in 1950, and Caesar for the National in 1977, in addition to his film roles for Mankiewicz (1953) and Burge. Here he seems slightly doddering (literally so on his return from the Lupercal festivities), fatherly to Calpurnia, inflexible to the senate, but never obviously dangerous. As always, and as Lindsay Anderson remarked (see Chapter IV), he speaks beautifully, and he implies complexity and thoughtfulness, but this is not his film, and his demise leaves only absence. Even his ghostly reappearance in the lamp flame is a quotation of the same device in Bradley's film.[5] If Mankiewicz implied a shift towards a more Method-driven Shakespeare in the conquest of Brando's Antony, Burge offers nothing but remnants of cinematic forms which are shop-worn and out of fashion.

Predictably, it is Heston's Antony that renders the film worthy of consideration at all. He had grown significantly as an actor since 1949, and though some of his early reliance on physical and vocal swagger survives into the new film, this is a considerably richer and more complex Antony. He is, for one thing, twenty years older, and though still imposing, he has a certain paunchiness which humanises, even undercuts, the loincloth-wrapped Aryan ideal he was for Bradley. Some of what was emerging then has now hardened into trademark – the clipped, tight-lipped speech punctuated with snarls and swelling with indignation, the steely gaze and sardonic private amusement – but he also brings a thinking, reacting presence which stands out in this largely mannered and wooden production. Initially, his age makes him seem miscast at least as an athlete, and his reddish mop of hair sits most unfortunately on his overly pink face; but once Caesar is dead, Antony is able to dictate the part in ways which go some way toward taking focus from what the production has otherwise saddled him with.[6]

In the funeral oration he handles the 'plain speaking' aspect of the part solidly, and though the pitch and sarcasm escalate quickly, he finds real beats within the speech. Throughout he is conscious of the crowd and of the conspirators (some of whom are still pointedly in earshot), even as he winds up the passionate oratory which manipulates them. He's best when he is small and reflective, as when he considers the mantle, using the turn he creates with a sudden tear of the fabric to drive into an impassioned denunciation of the conspirators. The unveiling of the corpse itself is another swift, grand gesture designed to swell the action, and this pattern of calm whipping into storm and back characterises his performance throughout. It is a welcome break from the stiffness of the other principals, and it allows him to make personal connections with the crowd, speaking to them not en masse, as Brutus did, but personally, moving among them, addressing them earnestly to their faces. This Antony sees a crowd as a collection of individuals, or at least sees that as the way to access their communal power. As he returns indoors, he trails the will nonchalantly so that it flaps in the breeze, suggesting a lack of concern for its specifics, that it was a means to an end. But his appeal to the crowd's self-interest does not dull the edge of his passion, and the end in question has more to do with justice than with a bid to power. He manipulates the crowd, but does so impulsively, and without Brando's cunning deliberation.

We surmise that his motives are pure because the film gives us no reason to question his earnestness, his sense of outrage for his dead friend shifting plausibly into delight at his handiwork through a time lapse cut by the film between 'Here was a Caesar! When comes such another?' and 'Now let it work.' He walks up into the Capitol as the crowd stampede, and there is a transitional scene of rioting before he appears in the street among them, by which time his grief and anger have been replaced by knowing delight in ways which do not undermine the sincerity of the previous feelings. He strolls about, indulging in a cup of wine gathered impulsively from a ruptured barrel, then tossed aside; and this slightly reckless lack of concern for his own safety recalls the swaggering airborne cavalry officer played by Robert Duval in *Apocalypse Now* who sips coffee as shells explode around him. Such self-indulgence resurfaces in the proscription scene which takes place in a bathhouse, where he is massaged by a muscular black man (a scene Heston claims credit for devising), and in the moments before the battle when we see him reclining, absently eating and drinking as preparations for war go on around him. This is an Antony who indeed 'revels late o' nights'. It is one of the few touches in the film which seem to catch a true 1970s mood, a luxuriant hedonism which emphasises body over mind, impulse over scheming. At least in the terms of its own period, it makes Antony appealing, particularly against the stiffness of the conspirators or the slightly priggish Octavius.

With Heston looming so large over the production, it is tempting to read it in terms of the actor's own politics, but this is surprisingly tricky. Though known for his outspoken conservative views, his presidency of the National Rifle Association, and his stumping for presidents Reagan and both Bushes, his Republican sympathies developed comparatively late. In the 1960s he campaigned for civil rights (with Marlon Brando), called for support of President Johnson's gun control act of 1968, and protested the Vietnam war. Such were his liberal credentials that in 1969, during the build-up to the release of *Caesar*, he was approached by the Democratic party to run for the Senate on their ticket. He declined after a good deal of soul-searching which had, apparently, more to do with a reluctance to withdraw from acting than doubts about the party he would be joining; and he never clearly articulated what it was in the 1970s that moved him to more conservative views. But whatever liberal positions he espoused on social *issues* in the 1960s, he reveals a political *attitude* in Burge's film which goes some way toward indicating his subsequent shift in political position.

What we see in Heston's Antony is what Brode calls a 'rugged individualism' (2000: 112) which is manifested by his dealing with the crowd in the forum, and by a tendency to view matters of power and social structure in terms of personal morality and the adherence to a private ethical code. Such a view seems to square fairly well with the attitude of the Screen Actor's Guild president succeeded by Heston, Ronald Reagan. Heston's Antony is a kind of superman, a figure out of Ayn Rand, perhaps, who towers imperviously over the lesser mortals rioting in the Roman streets, his elevated rank born of innate talent and a commitment to following his heart which gives him strength and surety of purpose. Around him are slighter, more unmeritable men than

Lepidus, and the film seems to assume the audience will like him regardless of his actions. In the bathhouse proscription scene which Heston says he wanted to feel like a gathering of mafiosos, the orders to damn his sister's son and to restrict the provisions of Caesar's will are rendered as simple pragmatism from a man who sees a larger picture. Ending the scene with Antony's line dismissing Lepidus – 'So is my horse, Octavius' – gives him a wryly knowing and commanding presence rather than the snide or petty man who waxes on for a further twenty lines as in the play.

Brode thinks the film under-rated, but much of what he prefers to Mankiewicz's version is what the script retained that the MGM film cut. He particularly likes the preservation of Shakespeare's paralleling of Brutus and Cassius with Antony and Octavius, particularly in moments like the pre-battle parlay which Mankiewicz eliminated. Brode confesses that much of what the film attempts, however, is badly hampered by Robards' incompetence. Sarah Hatchuel credits Heston for his variety compared to Brando but gives the palm to Mankiewicz for his approach to cinematography (Hatchuel, 2004: 169). Kenneth Rothwell speaks for many critics, however, in concluding his thoughts on the film thus:

> Perhaps it is time to acknowledge that far from being one of Shakespeare's most accessible plays, *Julius Caesar* remains as remote and aloof as the statue of Pompey before which great Caesar fell. Seduced by the ease of costuming an entire cast in togas constructed from bed sheets, countless directors have rushed in who might otherwise have avoided its complexities. (Rothwell and Melzer, 1990: 122)

Rothwell's implication that the play cannot simply be delivered 'straight' recognises that audiences had started to find the play simply dull, overly familiar and disconnected from the interests of their period. Whatever problems Burge's film suffered because of budget issues (including those bed sheet togas), the final problem with the film is that its only compellingly interesting dimension is in Heston's conception of Antony. Beyond that, the film won't take a position, won't explore or innovate, but relies instead on the familiarity of the story, the weight of its language, and the glow of its cast. Such things are not, finally, enough,

Back to school: *Caesar* at the BBC, 1979

If Burge's timing was unfortunate, his *Caesar* clinging to an era which had already passed, the timing of the BBC Shakespeare project was, at least on the surface, uniquely fortuitous, coming as it did in the glory days of British television drama. As Susan Willis suggests, a few years later the project would never have been approved, British television moving steadily towards a more American model which minimised the staging of serious standalone drama (Willis, 2002: 5–8). Even in this moment, however, the project encountered significant opposition, particularly over the cost of mounting all thirty-seven plays over a six-year period. The solution came in the form of substantial funding from overseas, but such funding came with an entirely different kind of price tag, one which would shape the aesthetic and political dimensions of the productions themselves, reinforcing some of the problems Burge had encountered and leading to a production of *Caesar* which was stiffly neutral.

Between 1937 and 1996 the BBC aired an astonishing twelve different versions of *Julius Caesar* on television. Some, such as those from 1937 and 1955, were merely excerpted scenes, and one – the atmospheric 1994 *Animated Tales* version – ran for only twenty minutes; but others were considerably more ambitious and were practically full-scale productions of a largely uncut text.[7] As early as 1938 a 141-minute modern dress adaptation by Dallas Bower was broadcast live, making it one of the largest television projects undertaken to date. Though it was well received at the time, no recording was made. A second full-length production directed by Leonard Brett aired in 1951 and a third in 1959, the latter directed by Stuart Burge. There were four productions in the 1960s, two traditional and two modern dress.[8] The last major production was that mounted in 1979 as part of the BBC Television Shakespeare project and directed by Herbert Wise.

Given the prior success of the play on television, its disappearance after 1979 (save for the *Animated Tales* version and 1996's *Shakespeare Shorts* which consisted only of 3.1) is suggestive, though there was always something about the grand sweep of the Television Shakespeare Project which seemed to intimate definitiveness. The introductory shots of English historical landmarks and the pompous brass fanfare which framed each production were part of a mission often criticised as flat and dull, a monument to Shakespeare which did not clearly live and breathe and which, in its obviously problematic attempt to be somehow 'straight' – without obvious conceptual bent – somehow failed to be much of anything. The rationale behind such an approach grew out of competing notions of what Shakespeare on the theatrical stage had become, coupled with a specifically pedagogical dimension. These productions were to be tooled for classroom use, particularly for American classrooms where, it was argued, seeing competent Shakespeare on stage was simply not possible for many students. This impulse to provide a Shakespeare largely uninflected by 'concept' or innovation became part of the series' brief at the behest of the US fiscal backers. The American underwriters were Morgan Bank, Exxon, the New York City Public Broadcasting Service (PBS) and Time/Life, who were the BBC's distributor in the United States. The terms of the brief specified running times of no more than two-and-a-half hours, Renaissance period settings except where the plays expressly demanded otherwise (as for *Caesar*), and 'maximum acceptability to the widest possible audience' (Willis, 2002: 9–11).

Cedric Messina, the producer of the first twelve plays and the project's initial deviser and champion, agreed to these terms partly because he needed the money if the venture was to proceed, and partly because he did not see them as being at odds with the goals of the project. This was not to be Shakespeare for theatre-goers steeped in the latest or most radical innovations of approach or concept, nor were they for scholars invested in shifting academic trends and perspectives. Indeed, what came up most frequently in the initial debates about the viability and appeal of the series were variations on the idea that the series would bring Shakespeare to people who otherwise might never get to see it acted.[9] The question of what constituted 'maximum acceptability' was considered sufficiently vague to allow directors a certain freedom, but there is no question that the pressure to reach the 'widest possible audience' without giving offence of any kind led to many productions which were extremely tame.

Caesar was one of them. It was the fifth to be taped, but the third to be screened in the UK and the first screened in the United States, a change which attests to its centrality as a high school text.[10] It has all the problems evident elsewhere in the series' low points: flat, rhetorical acting, constrained sound-stage interiors and implausible exteriors, over-tight camera angles making for visually dull 'talking heads' theatre, a failure to embrace a filmic medium in terms of scale and scope, and a refusal to deviate from a 'straight' interpretation which makes for timid direction and the pretence of 'concept free' performance. In this case that means stock Roman sets and costumes. The whole enacts an uncomfortable mid-point between theatre and film: long takes of stagily blocked actors in mid- or close-up shot, the absence of filmic sound and visual effect,[11] and acting which is too big for the medium.

The familiar problem of the performed play's tendency to subordinate character to rhetoric is heightened by the film's baffling attitude to soliloquy and aside which is usually – but not always – done as voice-over. There is no clear logic as to what stays inside the soliloquising characters' heads, so the sudden break from that convention is bizarre, particularly within a line – as when Mark Antony suddenly breaks from his internal monologue to bellow 'butchers' in the 'O pardon me thou bleeding piece of earth' speech – or downright nonsensical, as when Portia uses both spoken and unspoken utterance in her 2.4 asides and then wonders if Lucius heard her. If soliloquy and aside can be delivered internally (in ways upending the early modern stage convention), then why is she speaking aloud at all when she knows she can be overheard? Before going to the Capitol, Metellus's 'so near that your best friends would wish I had been farther' is given as voice-over but Brutus's 'that every like is not the same' is spoken aloud, and there are countless other instances in which the logic of what is speech and what is thought (voice-over) is impenetrable. Apart from these confusing and jarring moments in which the speakers cut back and forth between voice-over, the larger problem is the tediousness of watching long impassioned 'speeches' delivered as actors furiously think, sometimes for minutes at a time, the camera dwelling on every pore of their faces while they try to convey the intensity of their words with steely or conflicted looks and the occasional gesture or movement which can't help but read as illustration. Part of the problem is the series' assumption that television is an essentially realist medium which necessitates a particular brand of intimacy. Willis is enthusiastic about this aspect of *Caesar*, particularly the close-ups and voice-overed soliloquy, because they foreground the psychological drama (2002: 197–8); but she does not address the extent to which such an approach clashes with a theatre script which is driven by a different, less realist notion of character interaction and the representation of thought. In avoiding the script's innate theatricality, Wise's attempt at realism ironically suggests its opposite, the characters coming across as implausibly rhetorical and long-winded.

Despite the proximity of the cameras to the actors, no one is allowed to make contact with the audience by engaging the camera directly (as Derek Jacobi does in Rodney Bennet's *Hamlet* in the same BBC series). No one ever looks into the lens. The audience is close to the performers but not connected with them, not inside the fourth wall except – problematically – when we are hearing their thoughts. The fact that we are hearing thought which is apparently unmediated in the soliloquies simplifies the characters and makes them, paradoxically, less interesting because the potential for their words being prevarication is correspondingly less; for all the closeness and intensity of the audience's gaze, the sense of the characters' humanity is actually diminished. In moments such as these the generic oddity of the film and its neither-fish-nor-fowl format looms particularly large, the whole becoming dreamlike and surreal; one can almost sense the actors' awkward awareness of those too-close cameras following them around the set while they try to perform the play, corralled like cows so they stay within shot.

Daniels calls the production 'well spoken' and it is, to a fault, but this is not to say that the performances are bad. Though most are a bit stiff and overlarge, there is much to commend: Charles Gray's bluff but frail Caesar, for example, whose eyebrows twitch and face sweats when he gets nervous and who has to steel himself to bluster away Calpurnia's fears, showing private relief in the temporary decision to stay at home as she wants him to. He looks devastated by the events of the Lupercal – old and stumbling – and his discussion of Cassius is a furtive whispering to Mark Antony. His only false moments come immediately prior to the assassination, when his gestures get statuesque and overblown, though this makes sense in context and underscores how much of his constancy is actually the myth which grew up around a younger man.

David Collinge as Casca and Richard Pasco as Brutus also turn in credible performances, though they both suffer from the usual problems – a Cassius who gets fey in the tent scene and a Brutus who remains largely opaque and a bit boring, too in love with his own nobility – both tending to orate even in intimate moments. Cassius persistently rolls his 'r's and, like all the actors (save the plebs who have comic dialects) speaks with a high gloss Received Pronunciation which seems to come from a former age of Shakespearean delivery. Portia seems bent on being a BBC newscaster. Casca sounds like he's auditioning for *Private Lives*. It's tempting to read such choices as intended to suggest patrician hauteur and a hint of class politics – and it's true that Antony sounds less like an aristocrat than the conspirators – but they play more like the remains of an elocutionary Shakespeare, enshrined not just in a particular tradition of verse-speaking but in an elevated and elitist notion of both the Bard and the BBC. The core conspirators are not declamatory, but they over-enunciate, revelling in the sound of the lines while simultaneously over-explaining them: Cassius touches his shoulder when recounting how Aeneas bore Anchises, and raises one finger when referring to 'one man', as if we might miss the gist. On stage such things might pass largely unnoticed, but under the persistent mid- to close-range camera lens, they look expository, even condescending.

Pasco's Brutus is more an ideal than a man, and his dealings with his wife move from coldly abrupt to somewhat stiffly apologetic without clear reason. In the tent scene he overturns a table – more choleric than Cassius by far – and seems momentarily to consider using Cassius's dagger on him before returning it. His final scenes show him aged and beaten by the implications of defeat, though the effect is deadening and slow. Sometimes, as in the orchard scene, it feels as though each actor is waiting for their turn to speak – perhaps a consequence of filming logistics – and Brutus suffers particularly in such moments because he has the most to say. The resultant sense of Brutus's separateness from all the conspirators save Cassius, and even from Portia – a separateness that has at least as much to do with the other actors as it does with Pasco – lowers the dramatic stakes considerably.

Keith Mitchell initially seems too old for Mark Antony, but once we are allowed to forget the idea that he participated in a race during the Lupercal, he steals the show. His is an Antony much like Heston's, genuinely stirred by deep emotion over the assassination, and his dealings with the forum crowd are – surprisingly – the production's most plausibly naturalistic moments, though his gleeful laughter at the end is unexpected and hard to explain without throwing out what seemed so real before. Still, when he 'comes down' (from the studio set's 4ft platform) into the crowd to discuss Caesar's mantle and show them the corpse, he connects with people in ways that make the shift in audience sympathy perfectly believable and not obviously manipulative. He is clearly drunk in the proscription scene; and though he is convincing as a soldier, his world-weary amusement makes him increasingly feel like the production's political compass. He's a bit of a cynic, but without the hard, Machiavellian edge of Brando's Antony, say, and his self-deprecation suggests a resigned sense of playing his part till such time as he will be outmanoeuvred by Octavius: something we sense is coming soon. His denunciation of Lepidus lacks its usual spite, emerging – it seems – from previous conversations with Octavius, the young Caesar apparently choosing to ignore what he knows to be true despite the fact that Lepidus is both contemptible and a liability. It's a fine, nuanced moment in a production which tends to prefer broad rhetorical posture.

The crowds – dressed in official pleb outfits whose varied hues fail to suggest either reality or individual identity – generally have that familiar 'pre-blocked' look. That said, they seem to listen and respond as people and are only clearly deficient when used as window dressing (standing around the streets waiting to applaud a procession, for instance). During the funeral orations they react plausibly, the individual lines of the script just audible but subordinate to a general pulsing hubbub that does not attempt to unify response or mood until very late in the proceedings. This lack of unification and the occasional ambiguity is refreshing, as in the first scene when the cobbler and carpenter leave snorting with laughter and pointedly *not* 'tongue tied in their guiltiness'. Yet the biggest missed opportunity of the production is the cursory treatment of Cinna the Poet, whose scene lasts 75 seconds and is (partly as a result) completely devoid of menace or weight, the scene ending abruptly before it is clear what will happen to the hapless poet.

The generic look of the plebeian costumes is in keeping with the obligatory togas of the conspirators and the legionary armour at the end (the quality of which varies widely). It takes a physically imposing actor to carry off those short tunic skirts and arms bare to the shoulder, and neither Brutus nor Cassius measures up, so that from the tent scene onwards they look not just out of their element, but slightly silly (and the unfortunate choice to put Cassius in short white armour trimmed with gold exacerbates the problem). Haircuts are the unavoidable Roman mop tops. The sets are similarly generically Roman, and though passable when they are supposed to be interiors, they are distractingly bad when they include flats of painted columns against a painted sky. The 'battle' scenes are also shot on a studio set and, despite spirited attempts to create rocks and trees that look real, feel cramped and underpopulated. There is no attempt to suggest actual armies, and there is only one moment of combat involving three or four soldiers prior to the death of Cato, so the battle itself feels drawn out and slow, bereft of energy or visual interest and generating a sense of anticlimax that reaches maddening proportions during the interminable scene in which Brutus searches for someone to aid his suicide.

Sometimes there is an odd disconnection between the language and what is actually happening on camera. While some of that is of the familiar but frustrating 'concept failure' type (referring to doublets which are actually togas, for instance), other instances suggest a more pervasive sloppiness, as when Brutus dutifully remarks that Titinius's 'face is upward' when he is actually lying face down on Cassius's body. The soothsayer hesitates when he sees Portia in the street, as if he knows something of her husband's business and wants to avoid her, but he then cheerfully recounts his concerns without regard to her demeanour which should (in its posturing distraction) warn him to silence. Brutus's and Cassius's assessment of Casca as 'blunt' and 'rude' are always tricky, but here they make no sense at all, Casca being both fey and teasingly knowing. Cassius's 'who's there?' in the woefully unimpressive and rainless storm is absurd, since he is standing only three feet from Casca in light only a little lower than the previous scenes. Ligarius shows no sign of sickness despite everyone's talking about it. In all of these moments, one senses a production which has not grown organically out of interaction and discovery but has been driven by technical demands, caught between a realist medium and a non-realist script which it is bound to follow to the letter. Like the voice-over soliloquy problem, the whole feels like a series of fragments rehearsed in isolation, given prefabricated shape, and then bolted together. Such capable actors should not have had to work in these conditions.

However much the sponsors of the series can dismiss the opinions of scholars and frequent theatre-goers as not coming from their target audience, a question arises as to the nature of the Shakespeare being represented by the BBC and the play's pedagogical function. No doubt Wise's *Caesar* brought performed Shakespeare into the classroom, but there is something perverse, something fundamentally untheatrical, about a production whose driving concept is an assumed absence of concept. The result may clarify lines, it may reinforce a sense of characters where the page has only speech headers, but in its artificial insistence on offering the play 'straight', the production at its worst seems little more than book illustration.

There is no question that many productions within the series found ways to be interesting, innovative and even challenging within the project's mission brief. For *Caesar*, however, the accumulated cultural baggage was too great. Anxious not to offend that 'widest possible audience' and limited to a sense of period which made the play's politics remote in the extreme, the production could only enact a kind of monument to the schoolroom version of the play without any of the concessions to contemporary culture which might have made the play more accessible to its audience. Indeed, what this and the Burge film both manifest is *Caesar* at its nadir, lost in a period which had enshrined the play in education but had been unable to keep it from drifting further and further out of touch with popular culture. The BBC's Shakespeare project manifests an awareness of the problem, but the total failure of Wise's *Caesar* to appeal to a younger audience in matters of style, setting or casting in some ways compounded the problem.[12] This *Caesar* may not have offended the 'widest possible audience', but it must have failed to hit the mark with its true target demographic: students. It is hard to imagine the teenagers who were then cheering for iconic punk bands like The Ramones and the Sex Pistols finding much to excite them in such a production, even if they had found other approaches to ancient Rome (such as *I, Claudius*) compelling. Small wonder, then, that after a rash of television productions earlier in the century, Wise's was the last live action *Caesar* filmed for British television (as Burge's was the last 'straight' Shakespeare film with a distinct Hollywood patina). It would take a rediscovery of what these productions seemed most careful to avoid – *Julius Caesar*'s political imminence – to bring an excitement back to the play in performance.

Notes

1. Elsewhere the desire to present the play visually runs into technical problems. The storm scene gives us lightning-illuminated statuary, but nothing clearly supernatural, and references to anything that might be supernatural (other than Cinna's now baffling remark about seeing 'strange sights') are cut. Off the battlefield there is a curious absence of blood (presumably because of the difficulty of cleaning costumes and reshooting on location), something which is noticeable in Portia's curiously invisible voluntary wound, and unavoidable in the assassination itself, with its subsequent hand-washing, shaking and the performative display of 'red' weapons in the streets, in which neither drop nor stain can be seen. This is perfectly excusable, of course, but it does tend to undermine the film's attempt to foreground its visual dimension, putting it in tension with the language.
2. Brutus here is as he is throughout the film, woolly and soft, face and body tending to flab, and unkempt 1950s quiff showing him a man out of time and not sure why he's there.
3. Howard Thompson, 4 February 1971.
4. Burge and Robards had clashed as soon as rehearsals began, and the latter – who was emerging from an acrimonious divorce from Lauren Bacall – stopped attending rehearsals in order to spend more time drinking. He justified such a step by saying that this would make his performance more 'spontaneous' on camera (Brode, 2000: 109). Nothing could have been further from the truth, and the muttering, halting, robotic result contaminates the entire film.
5. The film contains other visual echoes of Bradley which may have come from Heston, such as the image of Caesar's bleeding statue in Calpurnia's dream.
6. Not least of which is his costume in the first half: a vaguely liturgical robe of greenish-gold and a shapeless shift beneath with an oddly frilly neckline
7. Despite its brevity, the stylish *Animated Tales* version is intelligently cut and has strong visuals. Much is made of the supernatural imagery of the play here rendered in psycho-symbolist terms which use the storm in particular to foreshadow both the assassination and the subsequent tragic events. The vocal talents are excellent; and while much of the script is lost (the funeral oration feels particularly abbreviated), what remains is given real weight.
8. The traditional productions took place in 1963 (the middle three episodes of *Spread of the Eagle* which presented all three Roman plays) and in 1969 (in colour, directed by Alan Bridges). The two modern dress productions were in 1960 (dir. Ronald Eyre) and in 1964 (dir. John Vernon).
9. Wise used this very argument to justify the use of a Roman rather than Elizabethan setting, despite his feeling that the play was more

clearly Elizabethan than Roman, saying that 'for an audience, many of whom won't have seen the play before, I believe [an Elizabethan setting] would only be confusing' (Willis, 2002: 93).

10   The first four plays to be taped were *Romeo and Juliet, Richard II, Measure for Measure* and *As You Like It*. In the UK they were screened in that order except that *Caesar* preceded *Measure*, airing on 11 February 1979. It was broadcast three days later in the United States.

11   One rare exception is Caesar's ghost, which appears as a massive head greyly superimposed over Brutus's bed. The effect is clumsy and the two actors are seen to inhabit the same frame without any sense of inhabiting the same space, making it impossible for Pasco's Brutus to interact with the spectre in a specific way.

12   Later productions would use resonant casting choices such as John Cleese as Petruchio or Felicity Kendall as Viola to tap into a TV-savvy audience.

CHAPTER VI

The Romans in Britain: *Caesar* under Thatcher

Peter Holland, in his review of David Thacker's 1993 production of *Julius Caesar* at The Other Place, recalls going in with low expectations because of the 'sad history of the play in recent Stratford productions' (Holland, 1994: 194). Those low expectations were quickly turned on their heads by one of the most exciting productions in recent memory, but they are telling, both because they suggest the disappointment with which prior productions had generally been received and because – perhaps paradoxically – there had been enough productions in recent years to constitute a real history. Between the formation of the RSC's permanent company in 1960 and 1979, there had been only four productions of the play (one about every four-and-a-half years). Between 1983 and 1995, however, there were five (one almost every two years), more than there were of *The Winter's Tale*, *Twelfth Night*, *Othello*, *Hamlet*, *Lear*, or *Macbeth*, more than any other history play (English or Roman), more in fact, than any play except *Romeo and Juliet* which also had five major productions.[1] Such numbers are a little arbitrary, of course, dependent on where the start and end dates are set,[2] but they remain suggestive, particularly when coupled with Holland's sense of the play's 'sad history.' In the mid-1980s and 1990s, *Julius Caesar*, like a bad penny, just kept turning up.

Exploring the paradox of the play as a frequent but largely unexciting offering at the RSC in this period will be the subject of this chapter, and with that paradox comes a problem at the core of this play and its stage history. While *Julius Caesar* is clearly about political theatre and theatrical politics, the two elements which construct those hybrids often sit uneasily together on the modern stage. How does a company stage political ideas without taking sides so completely that all nuance is lost, and how are such ideas made insistent and compelling rather than the stuff of abstract intellectual debate? Clearly the play is political of itself, but the remoteness of its period and the perceived sententiousness of its rhetoric, as we have seen, creates special challenges. Audiences often want a more dangerous Caesar than the one the text presents, or they want echoes of a world with which they are more familiar. Welles gave his audience both, but subsequent directors have generally felt that such a strategy flattens the play, makes its moral concerns too clean and simple. The trick, it seems, is to find ways for the production to speak its full range of meaning if not in a contemporary voice, then at least in a recognisable political register. We do not need to see someone we know in the title role – a Hitler, say – but we do need to connect with the play's political dimension in ways that produce a deep, even visceral response.

The Britain of the 1960s and 1970s lacked the kinds of dominant political figures to make *Caesar* feel topical, but the 1980s and 1990s positively brimmed with analogues to the story of a dictator's demise and its aftermath. The nation in which Ron Daniels' 1983 production opened at the RST was as divided along lines of class, geography and race as it has ever been in the modern era, led as it was by a prime minister who generated deep admiration and violent antipathy in almost equal measures. If the previous decades had struggled to find ways to make Shakespeare's play feel relevant to the lives of its theatre, film or television audience, the 1980s and 1990s had no such problem, even if companies did not always know what to do with the connections open to them.

Margaret Thatcher emerged from her first re-election campaign in the summer of 1983 riding a wave of nationalist fervour generated by war against Argentina over the Falkland Islands the previous year. She wielded a contempt for communism abroad and socialism at home, and through investment in monetarism promised triumph and affluence in the face of deep economic slump. She sought to dismantle the 'culture of dependency' she viewed as inherent to the welfare state, and preached the doctrine of the Keynesian free market hand-in-hand with a return to Victorian imperial values. Yet in spite of her three terms as prime minister, Thatcher's approval rating was, on average, only

40%, the second lowest of any twentieth-century British prime minister, rising only to 55% after the Falklands war. She was personally combative, sure of her own convictions and willing to override dissent from all quarters in pursuit of policies often presented in terms of crusade. It is not overstating the case to say that she was and remains the most divisive figure in modern British history. Historian Andrew Marr neatly sums up the divide:

> On the one side were those who felt they had at last a warrior queen for hard times, a fighter whose convictions were clear and who would never quit, someone who had cut through the endless dispiriting fudging of earlier decades. On the other were those who saw her as a dangerous and bloodthirsty figure, driven by an inhumanly stark view of the world. To the cartoonists of the *Sun*, *Daily Mail* and other right-wing papers she was a Joan of Arc, a glorious Boudicca, surrounded by cringeing wets, apelike trade unionists and spitting Irish terrorists. To the cartoonists of the *Guardian*, *Daily Mirror* and *Spitting Image* she was simply mad, with sharply carved vulture's beak nose, staring eyes and rivets in her hair. (2007: 405)

She was the Iron Lady – as the Soviets had christened her – or Attila the Hen, both nicknames nervously teasing out the familiar remark made both pro and con, that she was the 'best man in the conservative party', whose stalwart determination could get positively Caesarian. In the face of large-scale demands for U-turns in her economic policy, she delivered a withering speech to the Conservative Party which famously concluded with the line 'turn if you want to. The lady's not for turning.' She was constant as the northern star, and until late in her unprecedented third term when massively unpopular tax policies finally gave real force to dissent within her own party, she seemed completely unassailable from within and without.

On 12 October 1984, four months after Ron Daniels' production had returned to Stratford from the Barbican, Margaret Thatcher was the target of an IRA assassination attempt which left five people dead and many more seriously injured in the bombed ruins of a Brighton hotel. While the casualties included senior ministers and members of their families, the prime minister herself was unharmed and continued doggedly with her work until she was brought down six years later. Since assassination had not figured in twentieth-century British politics as it had in the United States (one obvious exception being the murder of Louis Mountbatten, also by an IRA bomb, in 1979), one might expect this detail to throw the other points of resemblance between Caesar and Thatcher into such sharp relief that she was clearly present in all productions from the period.

And, in a sense, she was. The programmes from those productions are shot through with topical political reference, and there is no doubt that the debates raging just beyond the theatre door seemed to bleed into the concerns on stage. Nevertheless, Thatcher herself remains a curiously palpable absence on stage despite both her dominance of British politics until 1990 and the way her final years shaped the government which followed. However much she saturated the cultural and financial climate of the theatrical world, however much she so resembled the title character with her war victories and her steadfast and autocratic government, her insistence on fierce personal loyalty, and her bifurcating of the nation, no major production of the period ever managed to do more than evoke her in the most abstract and indirect fashion.

One reason for this, I suspect, is simply a matter of gender. *Caesar* is one of Shakespeare's most single-mindedly masculine plays. Despite the obvious parallels with Thatcher in the play, it requires a particular leap of the imagination for an audience to see a specific female leader in the physical presence of a male actor. No company attempted a cross-gendered Caesar until 1993 at the tiny Barons Court theatre, and to have done so earlier would have made the kind of unavoidably insistent association which reduced the play to mere political illustration. The play resisted literal association with the British prime minister, and had that connection been insisted upon it would have overwhelmed the play in problematic ways. It is difficult to imagine, for instance, a major British production flirting overtly with ideas of assassinating a Thatcher figure – however unpopular she was in some quarters – after the 1984 bombing. The RSC couldn't literally stage Thatcher in *Caesar*, but the immediacy of the play's political concerns was undeniable, and each production had moments when the audience could glimpse the Iron Lady brooding over the theatre.

Ron Daniels' 1983 production went through a radical revision during its Stratford run before transferring to the Barbican. In its first incarnation, key first-half moments centring on Caesar's public appearances and the funeral orations were recorded by cameras in the house and projected live onto a large upstage screen. The effect, as most reviewers agreed, was the sense of an insistently modern and televisual politics, adding a slick and spectacular dimension to the play's rhetorical set pieces.[3] The projection aimed to solve the perennial problem of the crowd scenes by turning the on-stage audience into a mere sample of those to whom the images were being broadcast, and gave a new emphasis to the idea of audience/populace/*voter* manipulation through the dominant media of the late twentieth century. This was particularly topical because the British political world was experiencing a collision between an old school, straight-from-the shoulder Labour opposition which disdained media gloss and the prime minister who – notoriously – had recently hired media consultants and public relations firms in order to fashion a more endearing popular image. In contrast to Michael Foot, the famously shabby Labour leader of the day, Margaret Thatcher had emerged coiffed and deliberate in front of the camera, a benign, Victorian aunt smiling on children, the hectoring and condescending tone which had characterised her early career and which Clive James had compared to 'a cat sliding down a blackboard' now carefully polished away (James, 1981: 119–20).

The projection device magnified the performers but also, of course, dwarfed them; and while there was something provocative in the resultant gap between the scale of Caesar's public persona and that of the actual man, for instance, the director came to view the projection as intrusive and distracting, and therefore cut it entirely before the end of the Stratford run. The result was that audiences saw two quite different productions. The later version was not substantially rethought or reblocked when the video was removed; and though some may have found the projection superfluous, there is no doubt that without it, the production got smaller without becoming more intimate. It also lost a technological contemporeity which the programme gestured to through quotations from current political figures, but which felt at odds with a production eschewing the modern in its vaguely nineteenth-century Prussian uniforms, generically old-fashioned poor people, and broad-shouldered ceremonial robes which suggested samurai restraint.

Political immediacy was also muted by an emphasis on the pictorial, at least in terms of costume and blocking. For the first

6 Caesar (Joseph O'Conor) and his senate with rear projection, Brutus (Peter McEnery) bearded on the right, in Ron Daniels's 1983 production.

half, the stage floor was marked with lines suggesting steps. Actors tended to keep their distance from each other, speaking from stillness. Even the crowd scenes felt muted and arranged, everyone carefully spaced, and the battles were marked by parades of colourful flags before dissolving into anticlimactic and abbreviated scrapping. Caesar's public scenes, particularly his processional entrance into the senate, were a dazzle of gold capes which moved the Rome in question squarely into the Vatican, the liturgical effect heightened by a crashing pipe organ which began as part of the spectacle but slid during the assassination into theatrical underscoring.

Out of this emerged a play which was concerned less with Caesar (played by a stentorian Joseph O'Conor), than with curiously fragile Mark Antony and with the collapsing friendship of Brutus and Cassius. Emrys James' Cassius was from the outset the most mobile performer in this otherwise fairly static production, a flamboyant, even playful character who toyed gleefully with being a Machiavel in his first soliloquy but later treated Brutus like a schoolboy conceding his place on the team to a more able athlete. It was Cassius who ensured that Caesar was dead, Cassius who menaced Mark Antony with a knife when he failed to endorse the assassination in the right terms; but his status rode with the fortunes of the conspiracy. He shrank almost physically in the course of the production, and his whining performance in the tent scene desperately tried to coax Brutus back to him. In this, most strikingly of all the production's choices, he failed completely. As Cassius became weak, miserable and desperate for attention, Peter McEnery's Brutus grew hard and isolated, filled with anger and self-loathing. A part of him blamed Cassius for their predicament; but even more, he despised himself for ever having been taken in by so slight a man. By the end of the scene he did not even raise his eyes from the maps and battle plans, as Cassius begged for a more genuine reconciliation than was evident in Brutus's dismissive pronouncements that all was well between them. In the first half, Brutus had been stoic, pensive and marked by an edge of almost priest-like authority,[4] though his nobility had been edged with anger over what Caesar might become. Now, he foreshadowed Macbeth in his isolation, his callousness and his resignation to see things through to their inevitably bitter end. The production thus became, oddly, the tragedy of Cassius, his arc marking the realisation of his own empty bluster, his lack of standing with the soldiers (he was completely ignored during the strategising with Titinius and Mesala), and the loss of his friend. Finally he resolved to meet Brutus's dismissal with a flippancy which he took with him to his death; but this empty posture revealed how little there was left of him.

David Schofield's Mark Antony was boyish and dreamy, grief-stricken after the assassination but rarely showing the kind of calculation often associated with the part in modern performance. He spoke 'O pardon me thou bleeding piece of earth' in an almost romantic tone, and addressed 'lend me your hand' not to Octavius's servant (who had already exited) but to the corpse of Caesar itself. During his funeral oration he remained largely composed, his voice soft, rhythmic and ethereal in ways making it difficult to assess his feelings, and he seemed steered by the turn of the crowd. After showing the mantle, he moved downstage of the carefully arranged horseshoe of people around the body to talk directly to the house – here the close-up projection of him on the wall behind must have been particularly potent – and showed what seemed to be genuine amazement at the generosity manifested by Caesar's will. The reflective pause in his final couplet when told of the conspirators' flight ('Belike they have had some notice of the people / [beat] How I have moved them') was chilling, but not because it revealed any Machiavellian glee. Rather, it seemed to have just dawned on him what he had done, and his response was one of trance-like curiosity. Something of this persisted throughout the production; and though he was clearly in control of proceedings during the proscription scene, he tended to speak straight to the house in a manner which suggested an instability of which Octavius was wary. Octavius's remark about some who smile containing in their hearts millions of mischiefs was clearly a reference to Antony who, recognising it as such, slapped him hard across the face. This eccentricity persisted into the scene before the battle, Antony moving from dreamy composure to volatile outbursts; and when he gave his final lines over Brutus's corpse, he collapsed sobbing, something pointedly at odds with the triumphal music which ended the production.

In effacing current political resonance – particularly after the excision of the upstage projection – Daniels' production sought strength in the personal, but the effect was of characters lost in a stark, cold world, unable to connect to each other or turn their political ideas into anything more than abstract solipsism. The bareness of the set, the formality of the clothes, the inability of the actors to close the substantial physical space between them, all created an almost existential isolation, so that even scenes of potential intimacy like that between Brutus and Portia were driven by frustration, suggesting people who couldn't quite reach across the divide this world inevitably created.[5] The motif of all this distancing was darkness – a recurrent feature of RSC productions from this period – which Irving Wardle, reviewing for *The Times*, saw as an invitation to view the world of the play 'as a fatal machine grinding along its predestined course irrespective of human will'. Key moments throughout – particularly the storm scene and subsequent meeting at Brutus's house – were so minimally lit that it was often hard to see who was on stage or what they doing. Though such lightning might have made for fine dramatic emphasis if used more sparingly, it only served to further alienate the characters and the audience. For Wardle this all conveyed a certain 'belittling' destiny, but it may not have had so clear a sense of purpose. Brutus's angry ruminations under the shadowy outline of tree boughs in the darkness of his orchard echoed a moment from Beckett, and the production as a whole spoke less of fate than of fatalism, the growing awareness of what we should have always known, that altruism, principle, human connection, love – in all their disparate forms – are either illusory or unsustainable.

Terry Hands' 1987 production had much in common with Daniels', partly because they shared a designer in Farrah who favoured a sparse, open look which tended to reduce the scale of the players on the RST's broad proscenium stage. This production was, like its predecessor, often extremely dark, though more was made of lighting effects – particularly cross-hatched spotlights, follow spots, and up-lights akin to Welles's famous Nuremberg effect. The tent scene was, again, the highlight of the production, though here Roger Allam's Brutus and Sean Baker's Cassius were more in amity by the end, and the trajectory of the scene included a more emotionally rooted treatment of Portia's death which clearly informed Allam's solemn and ruminative delivery of his 'There is a tide in the affairs of men' speech. When Cassius tried to force Brutus to kill him, there was none of Emrys James's showy brattishness, and the moment was both urgent and desperately sad for both men. While Daniels had driven them apart, Hands united them in their sense of on-rushing tragedy; and with the air thus cleared, they were able to move through the final scenes with brisk dignity.

As is often the case when the tent scene steals the show, however, the production was politically less compelling than it might have been, despite a more obviously autocratic Caesar (played first by David Waller and then by Daniels' Joseph O'Conor).[6] There was much kowtowing to this Caesar, a habitual reverence such as one might bestow upon a medieval king – not presenting him with your back, for instance, and being very quick to kneel or flat-out grovel if he seemed displeased – but he was so comfortable in his authority that he showed little that might arouse fear in the audience. Indeed, some of the moments which might have hinted at menace, such as his remark to Ligarius about being less an enemy to him than his ague, were deliberately undercut; mock seriousness that played on dread turning into laughter and a tickling hug. His 'good morrow' was bellowed into the ear of a clearly hung-over Antony. While Michael Billington saw this Caesar as 'nakedly Fascist' in ways which limited the play's finer moral points, it was a boys-club style Fascism – Caesar as captain of the rugby club – a man of real power tainted by caprice, but also companionable and indulgent. In short, what made him dangerous was less obvious in his personality and actions than in the deference and focus which others gave him. On that great open stage he was a magnet among iron filings, and they reflected his every word and step with movements of their own. In his final moments Caesar came closest to showing why he might be a tyrant, spurning Cimber with his foot and declaring himself constant as the northern star, not as one speechifying for an imagined audience, but revealing a genuine – and alarming – sense of self. It was the closest the production came to a genuinely Thatcherite moment.

Such an approach puts a great deal on what is not seen. We were invited to imagine Caesar the bully in Decius's cringing; and that might have worked well enough, had not the production asked too much of its audience's imaginations elsewhere. The darkness in this production was not simply the low and vaguely natural light of night of Daniels' production. Here it was stylised and used to give focus to the empty platform with its brick backdrop, a choice which tended to isolate the speakers even more than Daniels' twilight had done. To make matters worse, though the underclass appeared at the top of the show to be cajoled by Flavius and Marullus, and later as a gaggle of cheerful hoodlums who first raised Cinna the Poet on their shoulders as a hero then hurried him off to execution on the discovery of his name and profession, they vanished entirely for the forum scene. As a result, first Brutus and then Mark Antony delivered their spot-lit speeches out front to no one but the house. To compound the problem, Mark Antony's speech was underscored by piped generic crowd noise: sounds of a football stadium fading in and out over a transistor radio, periodically turning into implausible unison responses that sounded less like serious theatre than panto ('You will compel me then to read the will?' 'Yes!' [He's *behind* you!]). What was surely supposed to draw the audience into the moment did the opposite, stripping the moment of any immediacy and spontaneity, reducing the dynamic to that of an oration more at home in a production from 150 years previously. Writing for *Shakespeare Survey*, Stanley Wells observed that it was like watching 'actors demonstrating their skills at an audition' (1994: 174).

There was no intermission, and the centrality of Caesar to the latter part of the play was reinforced by the presence of a large statue at the beginning whose shadow persisted through the production. Caesar's ghost was seen stalking the battlefield at the end, though the production had little supernatural dimension, and Caesar's influence might best be seen as symbolic. Brutus killed him reluctantly but decisively, delivering the killing stroke himself, and the sombre mood which descended upon the conspirators thereafter suggested a feeling that they had done something morally right, but hard. Artemidorus was recast as Lepidus, which went some way toward explaining his position in the triumvirate, though the true power was shared between a mutually distrustful but finally unemotional Antony and Octavius.

For all its potential resonance, the production's consideration of political murder remained largely abstract, its white-robed perpetrators remote, dignified and – the tent scene notwithstanding – wrestling with things which stayed in their own heads rather than penetrating ours. The violence was as stylised and muted as the lighting, the play's core ideas playing cerebrally, even aesthetically, but without visceral imminence or a clear sense of cultural context. In this the piped noise of the invisible forum crowd became both cause and effect, an alienating device which, like the orchard scene whose darkness made it work almost entirely as sound, reduced the play's theatrically interactive dimension to a collection of well-known speeches. The curtain call recognised that it was Brutus and Cassius's show, but audience response was itself dignified, even polite.

Steven Pimlott's 1991 RST production had many elements in common with Hands' and Daniels', showing almost baffling continuity in terms of elements which had not been particularly successful in those earlier productions. Light was low to the point of blackness, on-stage audiences were small, assisted by piped sound, and scant attention was given to the final battles, here cut to almost nothing. The programme was similarly packed with text and images invoking contemporary political parallels (including one picture of a scary, barking Thatcher), but the production itself offered little to make such parallels explicit or even relevant. Few of the performances seemed to access much in the way of character, and audience response was correspondingly muted. What separated this production from the others was its Caesar who, in Robert Stephens, was clearly a man not of the same mould as those around him, a man of such commanding authority that it was immediately clear why everyone was afraid of him; thus his assassination effectively killed the production. If anyone evoked the spirit of British politics in the period, it was Stephens' haughty and autocratic Caesar, a man whose presence instilled awe and fear and whose absence would leave a vacuum in the political world that none of those involved in his murder could possibly fill.

Although Thatcher's leadership had been challenged in 1989 by Sir Anthony Meyer, she had weathered the storm without significant distress; but the poll tax, her hostility to recent economic policies in mainland Europe, her support of the first Gulf War and her continual defiance of both public opinion and voices from within her own party culminated in the resignation of Geoffrey Howe (her deputy) and Nigel Lawson (Chancellor of the Exchequer). Finally Tory golden boy Michael Heseltine challenged her leadership directly. Thatcher fought the challenge but, on 22 November 1990, when it had became clear that she could not win, stepped down speaking darkly of betrayal.

In this context, it is not surprising that the highlight of Pimlott's production, the point at which it seemed to really breathe with life and relevance, was the assassination itself. Robert Stephens was a commanding actor with a powerful and plummy voice which he could modulate rhythmically to create a clear sense of thought. He had a knack for finding surprising operative words so that what might have turned into bluster and posturing played as deliberation, even calculation; and he was able to deliver all his lines prior to the assassination ('northern star' and all) with absolute command while *sitting*. He always seemed to be the cleverest man on stage and, coupled with his imposing physical presence (this in spite of being played as both frail and deaf) and his certainty of his own rightness, he was indeed a colossus bestriding the narrow world where men like Brutus and Cassius

7 Robert Stephens as an Imperial Caesar in Steven Pimlott's 1991 production.

crept about below. Stephens needed no Nuremburg lights or brownshirts to play the fascist, but neither was he clearly undesirable as a leader. In dealing with the soothsayer, he showed kindly understanding of what he took to be the man's infirmity, and he seemed to warn Brutus against conversing with Cassius who, in this production, was hard, brittle and petty. The audience grasped Cassius's anxiety about Caesar, might even have sympathised with the need to get rid of him, but the murder itself would be difficult, and replacing him, impossible.

In the end, the conspirators surrounded him like hyenas trying to bring down a lion. Caesar fought back, brandishing Casca's dagger against them, forcing them to stifle him with his mantle, the assassination then dissolving into a breathless, graceless mugging in which it took a full two minutes for them to bring him down and another minute for him to die. In that agonisingly long sequence there were moments when it looked possible that Caesar would outlast them all, that he might not actually be mortal, and that their terror of him was clearly justified. He managed the defiance to spit in Brutus's face on 'Et tu Brute', something he had done earlier to show his contempt for the augurers who said that Caesar should not go forth. Until the very end it was not clear that he would not vanquish them, and the conspirators were left panting, exhausted and shaken by the experience. Nervous tears gave way to still more nervous laughter, but even as they washed their hands in his blood they seemed wary, as if he might get back up and knock their heads together. Stephens glowed with the Iron Lady's certainty, her influence and the dread she inspired in those who had finally mustered the courage to bring her down. Perhaps most topical of all was the absence which followed Caesar's death as the conspirators, crowd and theatre audience considered who could possibly step into the resultant void.

Given the topicality of the moment, it is difficult not to see a missed opportunity in the production's failure to find weight and energy in the crowd scenes. The murder of Cinna the Poet was graphic and bloody, and the mob mentality glimpsed then and in the earlier encounter with Flavius and Marullus was transferred to the truncated battles whose armies recalled rampaging football hooligans (another condition of Thatcher's Britain). But the production's attitude to the Roman populace – the forum scene – was deeply unsatisfying. Peter Holland depicted the funeral orations as 'operatic' in both the separateness of their staging (the speaker stage right and facing out front, the on-stage crowd in a huddle stage left, also facing out) and the frankly bizarre manner of rendering the crowd's scattered reactions as a choric, unison response which – as in previous productions – stripped the crowd of any individuality or capacity for thought (Holland, 1992). The mindlessness of the mob may have been what Pimlott was going for, but the effect (even in the opening scene) was condescending intellectually and wooden theatrically. If the funeral orations are to have power, their speakers must be more than puppeteers. Holland also complained about the inordinately lengthy intermission which did not come until after the proscription scene, and which, at thirty-five minutes, ran almost as long as the second half.[7]

The battles with their red/blue-clad soldiers (fresh from a Manchester United v. Chelsea clash perhaps) felt like an afterthought, without much in the way of actual combat, the scenes pared down to the suicides and run confusingly together. Mark Antony's apparently genuine emotion on finding Brutus's body seemed to make clear to him how poorly Antony was cut out for this world so he abandoned it, dropping his sword and storming off, leaving Octavius seated regally down front alone. But if Pimlott was trying to show layers to Antony, the gesture came too late: he too fell victim to the stiffness of the forum scenes and the formality and restraint which dominated the production from Caesar's death. Even the proscription scene was dark and flat, the characters seemingly going through the motions so that they seemed to feel nothing at all. In the tent scene, Brutus and Cassius resorted to shouting at each other, but there was no sense of urgency or emotional weight, even the report of Portia's death shuttled off in the darkness like a news bulletin. Their farewell speeches before the battle were static, distant and robotic, and the scene ended without so much as a handshake. The darkness, the lack of visual interest, and the stiffness of the performances made the audience miss Caesar all the more; but then perhaps that was the idea. Peter Holland saw in the red and blue of the armies a direct echo of the contemporary political parties '(Octavius as Neil Kinnock?)', but any such associations came less from connection to who was still on stage than from the absent Caesar. However clear it was that this hard-nosed Octavius would take over from the (apparently) overwrought Antony, this was a production about the creation of a political vacuum and the inadequacy of those who remained to fill it.

Of course, the lack of political stridency in these productions was not simply a matter of its being too difficult to stage a Caesar in the Thatcher mould, or even the persistent anxiety about staging domestic assassination in the wake of the Brighton hotel bombing. Another key issue was that which always wanders the battlefield of theatre like Caesar's ghost: money. Leftist activist theatre had come under attack early in Thatcher's regime, most dramatically and publicly over two Howard Brenton plays, both staged in 1980, which caused a firestorm of protest and recrimination, much of it with significant financial implications.[8] The first of these, *A Short Sharp Shock*, was a bare-faced assault on the logic of monetarism presented in caricatures of the current administration. It broke Royal Court box office records despite being absurdist and clumsily structured, and prompted parliamentary calls to cut off the company's public funding, but it was seen by comparatively few people who did not seek it out expressly for its political content. The Royal Court was not a tourist destination, and had been long known for its leftist leanings. Brenton's next play, however, opened at the National Theatre, then under the leadership of Peter Hall, and it produced not just a fierce debate about public funding, but also legal action against the director, Michael Bogdanov, for public indecency. The play was *The Romans in Britain*.

Most of the fuss about *Romans* fastened on a scene in which a Roman soldier attempted to rape a male Celt, because those who wanted to close the show down thought that an indecency case might be winnable based on existing laws, so long as the gap between the real and the fictive could be collapsed. What the play was actually about, however, was the reconsideration of national myths and colonial imperialism with specific reference to the relationship between Britain and Ireland. This had been a largely taboo subject for English theatre, and though the legal battle over indecency took the spotlight (fought in increasingly ridiculous terms over the minutiae of what actually took place on stage) the play foregrounded the paradoxical barbarism performed by people who considered themselves the civilised amongst the savages. The Anglo/Irish implications were quite clear, even if they got lost in the moral outrage of Mary Whitehouse who had spearheaded the legal challenge. In addition to the calls for Hall's resignation and threats of discontinued funding for the National Theatre, Bogdanov was personally and privately prosecuted under the 1956 Sexual Offences Act (the police having refused to prosecute under the 1968 Theatres Act). After several days of evidence, Whitehouse's lawyer convinced her to retract the charge (incurring costs of £20,000), so no verdict was given. In order to finance their defence, the National had established a special emergency fund which had put such a strain on resources that they refused to withdraw from the fight when Whitehouse offered to drop the charge if both parties paid their costs. Despite the National's eventual victory, the process sent a message to the theatrical community, warning them of their precarious financial situation.

The finance issue involved more than the possibility of prosecution. As had become clear in the early rounds of the battle over *Romans*, a company's financial state was very much about public support, particularly that received from the Arts Council. The 1980s were an uneasy time for theatre artists in England, as public funding was brought into line with monetarist policies which demanded a measurable financial return on any public investment. Companies began borrowing Tory rhetoric to demonstrate precisely how their productions promoted auxiliary spending, while the Arts Council chimed in that theatre promoted 'the "can do" attitude essential in developing the "enterprise culture" this government hopes to bring to deprived areas' (Peacock, 1999: 54). This fascinating revisiting of the entrepreneurial logic historians see as underlying theatre in Shakespeare's own day demanded that theatre justify itself in order to merit support. In 1985 Peter Hall remarked that such justification should not be necessary for the same reasons that education needed no justification, and that the soul of the country lay in its arts, whose contributions to the nation could not be measured simply in the terms prescribed by the market economy. The problem was not that the money was not available. Indeed, many companies were able to stay afloat or even expand during the period in question; but companies certainly felt that to get the money, they had to prove their worthiness, and this undoubtedly affected the content of their productions.

Leftist companies such as Roland Muldoon's CAST had their funding cut outright, but the RSC was able to weather the storm. In 1985 they negotiated a three-year sponsorship with the Royal Insurance Company worth about £1 million, though there was some anxiety about reliance on a corporate support which was considered fleeting. In 1986 the RSC lost about £1 million in American tourist revenue due to fear – said Terry Hands – of terrorism, and a similar amount in 1988 due to the exchange rate.[9] In 1990 they were forced to close the Barbican over the winter due to a £4 million deficit, only to have the Arts Council forgive the debt and increase their funding by 8%. In 1986, the government-commissioned Cork report ('Theatre IS for All') proposed increased funding, but this could not fully eradicate what Peter Hall called the 'loss of nerve' among companies who felt the lack of moral support even more than the lack of financial support (Hall, 1985: 7). In the final analysis, most theatre was considered not dangerous enough to merit putative measures, even where funding was concerned, and – as D. Keith Peacock points out – was subject to the same kinds of cost-cutting as were education, health care and local government (Peacock, 1999: 60). Whether or not the chicken of timidity preceded the egg of funding support, there was a symbiosis, even if it was manifested solely as a persistent anxiety about what would happen if Madame Thatcher decided she did not like what you put up on stage.

Whether this situation led to politically timid productions across the board at the RSC is too broad for my study, but it seems unavoidable that – at least in terms of the politically charged *Julius Caesar*, a play with obvious parallels to issues of contemporary politics and governance – the company opted to mute the *Romans in Britain* challenge in return for ongoing subsidy. Daniels and Hands chose to stage the play in ways which replaced obvious political associations with the concerns of private men, of individuals wrestling with conscience and relationships. Pimlott's staging was the most clearly resonant in topical terms; but taking place in the safer space of the post-Thatcherite years, it achieved that resonance almost exclusively on the shoulders of Robert Stephens, whose potency and danger evoked that which had already past.

After the historically unspecific Britishness of previous RSC productions, David Thacker's 1993 staging at The Other Place embraced a more global perspective, but in doing so it managed to find a curiously local topicality which its immediate forebears had missed or shied away from. The programme foregrounded political crisis and war in China, the Philippines, Afghanistan, Iraq, Nigeria and what had been until recently the countries of the Eastern Bloc. His cast was more racially diverse, his Caesar evoked a Ceausescu or a Yeltsin, and his battle scenes – by far the best I have seen – felt like newsreel from Bosnia; but ironically the effect had a curiously British resonance which former productions had lacked. In this it was helped by dialect, the cast using a variety of regional accents not generally heard on the RSC stage except for comic effect, so that the whole felt grounded and familiar while the previous three RSC productions had been constrained by that linguistic no-man's-land which is RP. While the crowd which tore Cinna the Poet contained women in vaguely Muslim headscarves, their British regional accents made them chillingly familiar. The other thing which Thacker used to brilliant effect in creating a sense of community with the audience was the space itself.

The Other Place was an intimate studio theatre seating about 140. In its first incarnation it had played host to one of the landmark productions of *Macbeth* (starring Ian McKellen and Judi Dench); and it was the special energy of actors on a small stage in close proximity to the audience which set the tone for its success. As such, of course, the venue was not an obvious choice for *Caesar*, which tends to be large on stage, and not only in the notoriously difficult crowd scenes. For all its domesticity and occasionally talkiness, *Caesar* is an expansive play conceptually, more a *Lear* than a *Hamlet*, and one might wonder how such a cockpit might hold the vasty fields of Philippi. The solution came in part from staging the production in promenade, the action moving around a stage on which the audience were standing or sitting, a device I have never seen used to better effect. It facilitated a smaller, more naturalised and more obviously contemporary acting style which was perfectly at home in the production's suits and ties, its modern battle dress, and its swaggering politicians with their audience-steering security detail. It also lent a ready solution to the vexed crowd scenes. It is not uncommon to seed the house with plants who call out 'we will be satisfied' on cue, but such responses usually feel like a clumsy theatrical ruse. They almost never prompt audience engagement and when they do, it tends to be jokey and distracting. Here, the very fluidity of the crowd, its need to adapt to where the main action was taking place, made the plants tougher to spot, and they seemed so close and so comparatively numerous in so small and tight a house that they really seemed to speak for the audience. The engagement of a promenade audience is, of course, of a different kind than the engagement of an audience watching from behind the fourth wall, and the act of such engagement can be heady in ways which, paradoxically, take one out of the fiction even as one joins in its construction; but the majority of the audience seemed genuinely connected, thrilled even, by what was happening around them. The production built a community of players and theatre-goers of a different and more collaborative order than that

8   The conspirators stand over the dead Caesar, as the audience look on in David Thacker's 1993 production.

which is usually produced in theatre; and however much one might want to dismiss the promenade device as a gimmick or its effect as a kind of hysteria, the audience's obvious enthusiasm for what they had experienced was impossible to deny. *Julius Caesar* is rarely so exciting on stage.

Nor did Thacker's production lose dimension or subtlety in being so theatrically compelling. Indeed, the intimacy of the space and the proximity of the audience fuelled a knowing familiarity among the conspirators; and after the exuberant chaos of the opening crowd scene and the photo-op passage of Caesar en route to the games (guided through a throng of cameramen by discreet secret service operatives), Brutus and Cassius were small and conversational. The crowd sitting and squatting at their feet limited their ability to move around, so their exchange focused on vocal emphasis and pace, each line coming out of thought. Cassius was no showy manipulator, but an old comrade who knew Brutus well and who was working out his feelings about their predicament aloud. Casca had to check his diary before determining whether he was free for dinner, and Cassius's soliloquy on how he would woo Brutus with anonymous letters was thoughtfully improvisational. The contrast with Caesar's slick and swaggering mingling with the crowd was palpable: we were shown the gap between the media-driven gloss of public politics and the private, human scale of the drama beneath, both rendered startlingly contemporary and plausible.

The battle scenes played on such audience uneasiness, creating a running chaos of gunfire, explosions, even helicopters and mortars, through the cramped, dark and smoke-wreathed space. There was no light but that which came from heavy ordinance, and the two armies were – in their modern battle dress and balaclava helmets – indistinguishable, an image of civil war in which friends and families take up arms against each other. Prisoners were marched across the stage in ways evoking the atrocities of Bosnia, the audience parted by soldiers in gas masks with submachine guns.[10] Everyone ducked as shells were heard to whistle overhead, and the fighting and killing were brutal, real and constant. It was like falling into the *News at Ten*. But if the battles were an ordeal even for the audience, it was the kind of ordeal which bonds a community: the curtain call which ended the show was consistently received with the rapture of people who have witnessed not so much a production as an event whose intimacy and cultural immediacy made them feel like integral participants.

The political dimension of the play was gendered male even more expressly than usual in that there was a sense of the boardroom, the boys' club, in the way the conspirators interacted. In the tent scene it became clear that Cassius desperately needed the camaraderie with Brutus which the conspiracy had afforded him. For Brutus's part, the revelation of Portia's death came hard and led to a cautious but heartfelt reunion with Cassius, two soldiers or business partners confessing the bond between them in ways that would not violate the terms of their masculine culture. Public notions of self interfered with private impulses, friendships and weaknesses, so that the play as a whole seemed to be exploring a divide most clearly figured in its title character. That divide is a common feature of productions – the mythic Caesar jockeying for space with the deaf Caesar – but here the politics of such a division were made clear. Prior to the assassination itself Caesar arrived ready to give a speech at a lectern with a microphone, and was irritated to be drawn from what was scripted into a debate about what was amiss that he and his senate (the latter a polite afterthought) needed to address. The petitions of the senators were interruptions, and his response – 'constant as the northern star' – began small but built as he pounded the lectern like Khrushchev. The public event slid into a private one and back, ending with a murder which was both a political event and the outpouring of a deep personal resentment, particularly on the part of Cassius.

Such a dynamic set the stage nicely for Mark Antony – played by Barry Lynch at his most insinuating – whose speech over Caesar's corpse ('Oh pardon me thou bleeding piece of earth') began in intimate quiet and swelled to a deafening roar which was without precedent in the production, unnerving the audience with the force with which private grief drove into public vengeance. This dynamic continued in the funeral oration when Antony actually put on the 'mantle' (a military jacket) and found out Caesar's wounds on his own body, mapping the public outrage in personal terms.

The production was at its best when it combined intimacy and modernity, as when Cassius tore up a propaganda poster while musing on his fears about Caesar's rise in the storm scene, in the female aide's feeding of documents into a shredder during the proscription scene, or in the little discoveries made by actors forced to simply talk to each other. Casca's remark that Caesar would be crowned 'tomorrow' was given great weight and received as news by Cassius in ways forcing a new urgency on proceedings. Likewise, Brutus and Portia found a strong intimacy long before her catalogue of male relatives and her voluntary wound. Brutus's soliloquy, however, revealed a paradox at the heart of the production. Being forced to give the speech to the audience clustered about him transformed what might have been mere thought into rhetoric, so that Brutus's true feelings receded behind the words. This happened elsewhere in the production too, so that when characters spoke to other characters, their conversation tended to feel spontaneous and honest; but when they spoke in soliloquy, it was hard to discern a difference from the orations and confident politicking of the public scenes. The characters, in other words, seemed at their most genuine in intimate groups; but when alone, they seemed to close off their secret inwardness, becoming unreadable so that there was far less distance between the swaggering Caesar, who always had one eye open for the cameras, and the private, contemplative Brutus. This was a version of politics in which everyone was always 'on' because the insistent presence of the audience demanded it; and the sense that in the world of 24-hour cable news, there could be no real privacy for public figures lent a further modernity to the production. By extension, the public politics were an outgrowth of private relationships, so that Peter Holland was able to write that 'the drama of Thacker's production was not one of the politics of ideology but of the humanity and hence corrupted nature of commitment, a commitment generated by individual psychology rather than political analysis' (1994: 195). This he saw as the positive side of those troubling evocations of recent dictators whose demise the audience had – rightfully – cheered. The play is 'far more uneasy about the manipulation of the mass of the people than I would like to be about the fall of Ceaucescu or the events of Tiananmen Square … Still, the sight of David Sumner's splendid Caesar playing to the television cameras with the assurance of Yeltsin or Clinton on walkabout, beaming but surrounded by bodyguards, was too good to miss' (194).

The success of such a production might be set against what was generally perceived as the unmitigated disaster of Peter Hall's production two years later which took place at the RST and seemed to return to everything Thacker had beaten back. There was a massive sculpture of Caesar's head along with some generic Roman icons. The programme was packed with frescoes, mosaics and extracts from Plutarch; and while it included some stage history, there was no politics to speak of. The production delivered on what the programme promised. The general lack of specificity became almost archetypal, with the set, costume and acting style invoking a mythic environment populated by types and a notion of the Roman populace that was virtually choric. Where Thacker's crowds had felt engaged, contemporary and real, Hall's were separate, abstract and vaguely – but unproductively – Brechtian, speaking in robotic unison and in profile while Brutus and Antony addressed the house out front. The crowds stood in dutiful silence until scripted to declaim with one voice, and remarks such as Antony's 'Oh, now you weep' were wholly without justification. The resultant sense of alienation was fuelled by what is sometimes called 'iambic fundamentalism', an unflinching adherence to the rhythm of the line as the sole carrier of meaning, the words rattled out at a pace seemingly designed to prevent audience comprehension, let alone connection. The production might have been trying to force some distance between the audience and the story, to prevent them from being sucked into its personalities so they could assess its action more objectively. It might have been trying to focus on the forces of history rather than its players, might have even been trying to make a point about the delusory nature of audience engagement in politics, showing how crowds are hysterical and easily manipulated. But if Hall was attempting to do these things, he was unsuccessful, and the result was generally seen as a failure of naturalism, not a conscious attempt to be something else entirely, and the political world of the play evaporated as the production devolved into something between Greek tragedy at its most staid and a community theatre production of *Les Mis*.

Such observations raise a question which haunts this chapter and, perhaps, this entire book. Given the play's educational and theatrical history as a study in oratory and classicism, how does a production make its political core feel urgent and relevant without the kind of overt cultural echoes which flatten the play's nuance (*à la* Welles), feel gimmicky, or evoke the kinds of parallels Holland worries either don't quite work or leave the audience unsettled? Perhaps there is always *some* value in unsettling audiences a little; and though I understand the anxieties about creating literal political allegory, I don't think Thacker's production finally did that. Rather, it made glancing reference to current or recent events sufficiently deftly, to generate only a general sense of currency rather than the echo of a particular political location. Despite Thacker's visual allusions to eastern Europe, his use of an intimate promenade device, British regional dialects and more general contemporeity of suits and uniforms created a far more local resonance than had the previous RSC productions which had sought association through abstraction. The gestures may have been to situations and figureheads known best from the news media, but the community – actors and audience – were British. If such intimacy caused audience hysteria, the thrill of being close to the actors as they created characters who seemed so familiar even with Shakespeare's words in their mouths, then it was in accord with a play in which one of the key political lessons is that passion is catching. Hall's retro corrective (it is difficult not to see it in these terms when placed alongside Thacker's production) seems to have wilfully missed the point, falling back as it did on a ritual model of theatre which effectively denied community and privileged the text. Ironically, even this homage to the words was in pursuit of a notion of metrical correctness that denies language its basically communicative dimension. Few audiences could have followed Hall's story if they had not previously studied it, so relentless was the pace; indeed, one might even see an enactment of the play's class politics in the production's refusal to actually engage its audience.

To be fair to Hall, part of his attachment to speaking the text, the whole text and nothing but the text springs from a desire to (in John Barton's phrase) 'embrace the ambiguity', to allow the play's full complexity to work on an audience without significant inflection which might simplify or – in modern political terms – 'spin' the moral or political content. Though I am sceptical of the efficacy of such an approach, it seems to have an ethical core, though this too is a kind of director's theatre. What it risks, of course, is dullness, while its opposite – productions which are heavily cut or overtly shaped to generate particular political effects – risk absurdity and/or shallowness. I alluded earlier to a 1993 Barons Court production which made self-evident what had been only obliquely and indistinctly present at the RSC over the previous fifteen years; it cast a female Caesar to draw an explicit connection between Shakespeare's assassination and the Iron Lady's recent ejection. This strategy was about as far from Hall's as could be imagined, and it failed for different reasons.

The Barons Court theatre is a small, 50-seat house in a pub basement: although the production ran for four weeks, its total audience was still a fraction of that which would see an RSC production.[11] The show got no major critical coverage and has no scholarly record. Even the theatre's own archive has been lost, much of it accidentally thrown out, so my sense of it is built largely out of a brief correspondence with the director, Ron Phillips. His approach to the production was straightforward:

> In this case, Mrs. Thatcher had been defenestrated a few years earlier and the circumstances of her overthrow were remarkably similar to what befell Caesar. A trusted band of fellow Senators/Ministers had conspired to bring about the fall of their leader. Both tragic acts were huge mistakes, resulting in ultimate disaster for their respective countries ... the adaptation just wrote itself.[12]

The script was largely uncut. The conspirators were cast with an eye to their physical resemblance to Thatcher's former allies, Howe, Heseltine *et al.*, though Carole Street, the militant actress playing Thatcher herself, did so with no attempt to mimic the former prime minister, resisting her all-too-immicable voice and mannerisms. That she *was* Thatcher, however, was undeniable, and in her vocal and physical presence she suggested what the director termed 'the lady's qualities'. Phillips's programme note began with vague gestures towards Shakespeare's enduring value, the madness of reducing his presence in schools, and the need to keep the plays in production fresh and relevant. This last thought provided a segue into the lines which cue the audience into what they are about to see. Shakespeare on stage does not need to refer back to Hitler or Stalin for topicality:

> No, there is a potential theme closer to home ... just a mile or two from the site of the Globe Tavern. Picture the Bard, therefore, as he places a fresh piece of parchment in his typewriter and begins to write anew the story of the timorous mice and their problem over who will bell the cat ...

For all the playfulness of such an image, however, the production was intended to be a serious replaying of Shakespeare's tragedy, its earnestness undiminished by its contemporeity. Audiences, however, came expecting – and determined to find – a comedy. As Phillips says:

> The assassination of Mrs. Thatcher was a scene of great anguish (the stabbings were performed with rather too much relish) and I personally found it almost impossible to watch. All of our audiences, however, laughed their collective heads off; the reviewers were little better, dwelling on non-existent comic moments. It is scarcely surprising, therefore, that the play fell between two stools, disappointing those who came to see one of the great tragedies of the ages and those who demanded a belly laugh.

It is impossible, at this distance from the production, to fully explain the audience response. Theatre is fragile and any number of factors can upset what a production is trying to do; but it seems likely, given the cultural climate of the day – the glee with which the country watched the drama of Thatcher's 'defenestration' – that audience politics overwrote the efforts on stage. Phillips's own agenda was clear. The production was, he says, 'intended as a tribute to one of our finest leaders who had taken the country from the economic abyss into which it had fallen under incompetent Socialist rule to the prosperous, world leader status which she bequeathed to us'. The cast, however, were to a man, left-leaning politically, though they concealed this fact during casting; and though Street confessed to having developed a grudging respect for Thatcher as a leader through playing Caesar, she 'detested' her. Whether any of this political antipathy came through in the actual performance is hard to say, though that reference to the stabbings taking place 'with rather too much relish' seems suggestive. Phillips himself explains the audience's determination to find humour in Thatcher's demise as the result of media 'brainwashing', particularly through the vitriolic lampooning of television satire, but I began this chapter by discussing Thatcher as a divisive presence, one who triggered deep and powerful feelings because of what she represented to different constituencies. In the 1980s and 1990s it was impossible to be ambivalent about her. She had always triggered a visceral response which grew in part out of geography and class, but after almost two decades in the public eye her very presence – the particular theatricality of her personality – produced an almost Pavlovian response. It is unsurprising that a small theatrical production was unable to alter the assumptions of its audience, and that – in those days of poll tax riots – many who came to see her assassinated in effigy as Caesar, were there like the cobbler of the opening scene: not as blocks or stones but as feeling citizens who came to triumph over her political blood.

Whether *Julius Caesar* is suited to be a paean to whatever political figure might be glimpsed in the title role is, of course, debatable, and another explanation for the Barons Court production's lack of success may be that, though the play struggles to justify the assassination, it also fails to provide a simple panegyric for Caesar's greatness. If Welles's take on the play flattened its complexity in the production's assault on Fascism, Phillips's intention to celebrate Thatcher must have run into similar over-simplification. Building a successful production of the play is not simply a matter of finding the right amount of topicality (too much for Phillips, too little for Ron Daniels), but it is clearly important if the modern audience is to grasp the play's politics in their own idiom while not being overwhelmed by an ideological agenda. If the production offers a simple polemic, audience response will be determined simply by the extent to which they share the company's politics. One need not want to hear the play delivered in a wholly neutral voice to find such an approach reductive.

Notes

1. Technically there were six RSC productions of *The Taming of the Shrew* between 1983 and 1995, but one (Barry Kyle's) actually opened in 1982, one (Di Trevis's of 1985) was a small-scale tour, and a third, Bill Alexander's 1992 production, was a remounting of his small-scale staging from 1990. Similarly there were also five productions *of A Midsummer Night's Dream*, but one, Bill Buffer's 1988 production, was a small-scale tour.
2. To cover simply the period of Thatcher's regime reduces the list to three (Barry Kyle in 1979, Ron Daniels 1983–84, Terry Hands 1987–88) though we should surely include Steven Pimlott's 1991 production which was in the works when Thatcher resigned in November 1990.
3. John Barber, writing for the *Daily Telegraph* (31 March 1983) likened it to 'a huge anti-theft monitor in a supermarket'.
4. John Barber, writing for the *Daily Telegraph* (31 March 1983), went so far as to see in McEnery's bearded Brutus a Christ-like figure.
5. Even during Gemma Jones's supplication to Brutus they stood apart, and when he raised her from her knees he seemed irritated that she knew so much of the conspiracy. Though some form of intimacy was found by the end of their exchange, he hurried her off on Ligarius' arrival, and when we next saw her in the prelude to the assassination she seemed merely frantic.
6. Tom Matheson in Horst Zander's *New Critical Essays* says that Waller replaced O'Conor, while it was actually the other way around (Zander, 2004: 311).
7. The length of the intermission was dictated, apparently, by the complexity of removing first half set units, particularly a massive doorway in the upstage centre wall.
8. For details of these plays and the surrounding fiscal climate, see D. Keith Peacock's excellent *Thatcher's Theatre: British Theatre and Drama in the Eighties* (1999), pp. 85–100.
9. *PM*, Radio 4, 13 January 1988.
10. One of the guards leading the line of prisoners was played by the actor who had been Caesar.
11. The production dealt with the impossibility of crowd scenes in so small a house by recasting Mark Antony's funeral oration as a television broadcast.

12 All quotations from Phillips are from his private correspondence with me in autumn 2009. I am extremely grateful for his assistance in sketching out this largely unknown production.

CHAPTER VII

Accents yet unknown: global *Caesars*

Despite *Julius Caesar*'s popularity as a text for study all over the world and its prominence on the nineteenth-century stage, many nations which have a long and varied history of staged Shakespeare have shown little interest in *Caesar* during the twentieth and twenty-first centuries. In the Soviet Union the play seems to have been considered too republican for its dictators, but not clear-sighted enough about that republic to be a useful tool for those opposed to communism. In Japan, *Caesar* flourished during the Meiji Restoration but subsequently played only the most marginal of parts in that country's history of staged Shakespeare. This chapter will consider those places where *Julius Caesar* has been a significant force on stage, first in those countries most clearly marked by European Fascism and then in the postcolonial cultures of India and South Africa.

Given the many variables which govern a play's performance history in places with widely differing cultures and histories, it seems unreasonable to expect consistent patterns to emerge; but in the case of *Caesar*, some tentative observations might be made. First, the play's political valences, though they have come increasingly to define the play in the Anglophone world, are by no means givens, particularly in cultures in which Shakespeare's play has 'classic' status and in which a general sense of value – often defined in literary terms – can blunt any dangerous or subversive edge. Second, *Caesar*'s historical content, coupled with its classic status, makes the play ripe for the kind of reimaginings which radically rethink not just that content, but its legacy as an artistic and cultural product. Third, such reimaginings, particularly in post-colonial nations, often take shape in indigenous forms, so the play becomes not just the contested site of cultural value which we might expect, but also a means of legitimising and spreading those indigenous forms. In the process, the specifics of *Caesar*'s politics are applied to topical issues and figures in ways bolder and more direct than is common in England and the United States, the foreignness of *Caesar* often broken down as the play is reduced to its mythic or other essential components. What seems consistent is that the act of staging *Caesar* outside England and the United States is always an engagement with the past and with the cultural geography with which that past is entwined; in some sense, therefore, staging *Caesar* is always political, however much the performers might think of the play in other terms.

Wrestling with the past: *Julius Caesar* in Germany, Austria and Italy

Since Welles, the political topicality of *Julius Caesar* has had expressly totalitarian overtones, and one might expect the history of the play in the Axis countries of the Second World War and the Soviet empire which emerged from it to be especially telling. But despite a long-standing fascination with Shakespeare, *Julius Caesar* has only the most minimal performance history in Japan, Russia and East Germany, while in Italy, Austria and Germany productions – though seeming to walk dangerous political lines – have eschewed direct political association with past or present regimes. It is tempting to assume that the play would be considered too politically subversive or unstable to be stageable under a dictatorship, but there is evidence – admittedly inconclusive but fascinating all the same – to suggest that this is not the case. That evidence comes from Germany.

The major production of the inter-war period was directed by Max Reinhardt in May of 1920 at the Grosses Schauspielhaus, Berlin. Reinhardt was something of a throwback who admired the massive productions of the nineteenth century, but was invested in 'character, spirited invention and scenic innovation', favouring 'wit, imagination, rhythm, harmony' over politics and ideological concepts (Hortmann, 1998: 41). Though a little old-fashioned, Reinhardt's traditionalism lay not in his failure to embrace the play's political dimension so much as in his resistance to the then fashionable interest in abstract expressionism, an approach which dominated what surely should have been the most politically charged production in the play's history, that directed by Jürgen Fehling at the Staatstheater, Berlin, in 1941.

The Nazi attitude to Shakespeare was complex and bizarre. As Wilhelm Hortmann points out, Shakespeare was staged with astonishing regularity in early twentieth-century Germany, performed largely in translations by August Wilhelm Schlegel working with Ludwig and Dorothea Tieck, translations which had been well-known for a century. Before the Third Reich, Shakespeare was the most performed dramatist on the German stage. For many twentieth-century Germans, Shakespeare was an essential element of German culture, more so – some argued – than he was in Britain. During the First World War, fears of holding on to so English an icon had been frequently and loudly dismissed as coming from English critics who were blinded by a kind of historical accident. Spiritually, psychologically, culturally Shakespeare was German, and his ubiquity on the German stage and in the German language proved as much (Hortmann, 1998: 2–4). The Nazis promoted the German playwright, Friedrich Schiller, but Shakespeare continued to be staged at an astonishing rate throughout the years of the Third Reich, the two authors alternating for the title of most produced dramatist in Germany.[1] It might be said that Nazi theatre shows less evidence of prescription than might be expected, though that fact has more to do with complacency than tolerance.[2]

The Nazis certainly shut down productions and censored scripts, but their ire tended to fall on producers who were known enemies (London, 2000: 33). Where Shakespeare was concerned there seemed to be little to prompt official anxiety, and censorship tended to be literal and inflamed by issues of who was doing the production. So, for example, all the Bohemian lines about cross-breeding plants were cut from *The Winter's Tale* when it was performed in 1939 at a Jewish theatre (Rovit, 2000: 202–3). In general, however, Shakespeare was perceived to be in accord with the Nazi preoccupation with heroic protagonists and the depiction of major events, and in general Shakespeare continued to be regarded as a German dramatist, an exception to bans on foreign or potentially subversive material, even in Jewish theatres (Gadberry, 2000: 103). At the outbreak of war in 1939, all production runs of English dramatists were terminated, exceptions being made for only two; Shaw (another bastion of German intellectual culture who was conveniently classed as Irish) and

Shakespeare (London, 2000: 236). By March 1941, however, Propaganda Ministry permission was needed for productions of Shaw (who had by then become more vocal in his support of England) and Shakespeare. Some 3% of all Third Reich productions were of Shakespeare plays, second only to Schiller, and in 1939–40 there were eighty-five Shakespeare productions and only eighty-two Schiller (239). Though some Nazi zealots wanted Shakespeare banished as unGerman, these were very much in the minority, and the official line persisted even in the mouths of the most ardent Nazi sympathisers: Shakespeare showed a spiritual affinity with Germany which came, in part, from writing in a country which had been free of Jews, from his reliance on German sources, and other 'pseudo-historical and bogus anthropological arguments' (241). The canonical translations of Schlegel and Tieck triumphed over more modern versions by Hans Rothe, who was pilloried by the staunchest Nazis not so much for his use of contemporary German and his tendency to editorialise and interpolate, as for his deviation from the familiar text, which betrayed a lack of nationalist sentiment comparable to deviating from Luther's Bible (242). In May 1936, Goebbels gave a speech on how classic literature must be 'rescued from 'literary experiments' which endangered the 'eternal value of their works', and there was virtually no performance of Rothe's versions afterwards (243). Modern dress productions or those which alluded to recent culture were similarly denounced as blasphemies. Shakespeare was a known quantity, wedded almost mystically to ideas of German identity and socio-cultural value.

Even so, there is something remarkable about the way in which Shakespeare plays were valued on the stage. *Hamlet*, unsurprisingly, given its grand romantic background dating back to the time of Schlegel's translations, was extremely popular; but it was only the third most frequently produced Shakespeare (staged 94 times) in the years of the Reich, after *Twelfth Night* (135 times) and *The Taming of the Shrew* (101 times) (London, 2000: 244). The next most popular were all comedies: *A Midsummer Night's Dream, Much Ado About Nothing, The Comedy of Errors* and *As You Like It*. There were a lot of *Merchant*s coupled with Marlowe's *Jew of Malta* (86 in 1933 alone) since they were perceived to reinforce anti-Semitic ideology, but (other than *Hamlet*) the tragedies and histories were less frequently produced. This might be considered evidence for the Nazi avoidance of a more overtly political

Shakespeare, but there were still prominent *Lear*s and *Macbeth*s which clearly dodged the charge of subversion.[3] John London concludes that though some productions were overtly pro-Nazi and a few had anti-Nazi leanings, there were many more which treated the plays without political implications of any kind, being either generally supportive of a larger German world-view in abstract terms or, more commonly, simple entertainment (250).

In March 1937 Jürgen Fehling directed *Richard III* at the Staatstheater in what many perceived to be anti-Nazi trappings: updated costumes looking like German military uniforms,[4] a colossal set rendering the people ant-like and a limping title character many assumed to be Goebbels. Some critics responded enthusiastically and in terms which rendered the critique of tyranny astonishingly contemporary; indeed, Fehling had to be protected from Göring by famed actor-director Gustaf Gründgens. The fact that the production happened at all attests to the resilience of the myopically pro-German way in which the Nazis persisted in evaluating staged Shakespeare, and it goes some way toward explaining why Fehling was able to stage *Julius Caesar* in the same theatre three years later.

Fehling was violently anti-Nazi, but he was also manic depressive, artistically eccentric to the point of egomania, and fascinated by powerful men who altered history. Whether intentionally or not, these factors conspired to make his *Caesar* a paean to the title character and a study in the misguided and destructive conservatism of the conspirators. It could be pointed out, of course, that such a reading sits better with the script than does one which sees in it an invocation to the overthrow of a dictator, a fact which – for some – hobbled even Welles's production. There was nothing in Fehling's production, however, which suggested overt connections to his country's present. Costumes were stock Roman togas, tunics, and gowns with classical lines. The set was monolithic: steps and podiums and oversized columns for the formal scenes, less literal spaces for other parts of the play, still over-sized but pushing into the abstract with walls at curious angles and – in the case of the proscription scene – a sloping, triangular ceiling with a circular hole cut out of it. It was expressionistic; but although it was a form of expressionism shaped by the director's own passionate idiosyncrasies, it was not a mode suited to political critique.

For all his anti-Nazi feeling, Fehling was largely uninterested in political critique in specific, literal terms; and, of course, he had to be careful. People knew that classical plays could be topically resonant, and even plays by Schiller – the Nazis' darling – contained incendiary lines about tyranny and freedom of thought which led to censorship and outright proscription.[5] But while it is tempting to agree with Bernhard Minetti that 'in the Third Reich, pieces like *Julius Caesar* – when played straight – became political plays', all the reviews suggest that Fehling did 'everything in his power to enhance the role of Caesar and mark him out as the man of the future. His fall, therefore, must appear as a historical catastrophe, and his murder a crime of mythic proportion' (Hortmann, 1998: 143–4). Some even saw the production as celebrating the kind of dictatorial leadership they knew all too well, seeing echoes of the dead Weimar republic in Brutus's tepid liberalism. Subsequent critics went so far as to label the production – inaccurately, in my view – Fascist.[6] One oft-cited detail is that Werner Krauss, who played the title role, had embraced Nazism and had starred in some of the period's most anti-Semitic films, notably *Jud Süß* (the play in which Welles had first made a name for himself in Dublin), though this association is surely semiotically unstable. The casting of Krauss might be said to underscore the link between Caesar and the Fuhrer in that it evoked Nazi policy by association, though this renders the production no less ambivalent.

Fehling's brand of expressionism slid away from both realism and political polemic. 'Theatre as a didactic strategy, as part of a programme of ideological manipulation or in the service of specific causes or general enlightenment was alien to Fehling's nature' (Hortmann, 1998: 145). He dismissed Brecht's nonillusionistic, epic theatre in favour of a theatre of 'deliberate pathos' (146), in which he would stir the hearts of his audience, shaking them to their very core in pursuit of a specifically theatrical catharsis. What this meant in effect, however, was that he embraced passionate affect in his actors; and for *Julius Caesar*, that meant he was less interested in Brutus than in Antony. Gustav Knuth was 'directed to eliminate all traces of conscious planning and scheming from the role. He was to appear as the warm, open-hearted friend, unsuspecting and generous, dragged into politics almost against his will but, once involved, an unstoppable force' (146). He was a passionate presence driven by feeling and vision, creating almost by accident a sense of 'history in the making, being pushed toward anarchy or order by headstrong agents' (146).

But if this is what Fehling meant by 'deliberate pathos', it necessarily limited the production's political potency and even – for some – suggested a position quite opposite to his own. Caesar's status as a history-maker, even in death, appealed to Fehling, who considered the title character 'more revolutionary than his opponents who kill him in the name of freedom ... They act ... from blind idealism but they look backward and do not understand Caesar's visionary projection into the future' (145). A key moment in the production which attracted a good deal of close scrutiny was the murder itself, in which the conspirators were immediately struck with horror at the enormity of what they had done. They couldn't speak. They could barely stand. For a long moment the stage held the unavoidable dread of something now beyond their control, something irrevocable and earth-shattering. Far from inspiring any real conspirators in the audience to tyrannicide, the production must inevitably have given them pause.

Fehling was trying 'to preserve and repossess the classical heritage ... not to surmount or overcome it' (147). Theatre had to remain 'below the level of rational discourse and ... the horizon of intellectual insight', and his production was thus visceral and monumental, aimed at stirring hearts more than minds, in keeping with a version of art that spoke to 'emotional and spiritual rather than rational values' (147). Finally it must be said that though Claus Von Stauffenberg, who directed the 1944 bomb plot against Hitler, was arrested with a copy of *Julius Caesar* in his possession in which Brutus's speeches had been underlined, he would not have been inspired to assassination by Fehling's production (143). Indeed, though tyrannicide was in the air throughout the war years, Rudolf Hess, though remarking that *Caesar* could be a dangerous play in the wrong hands, applauded the production, apparently confident that what he had seen had suited Nazi ideology.[7] It is telling that the only clear instance of *Julius Caesar* being used as a prompt to tyrannicide in Nazi Germany was one of private reading, in which a would-be assassin could focus solely on the parts which best suited his interests and intent, and ignore others. Had von Stauffenberg sought the same clear and single-minded inspiration from a stage production, he might have had to leave half-way through.

This is not to say that the play cannot be subversive. Dennis Kennedy makes a compelling case for Leon Schiller's 1924 production in Warsaw – designed by the Pronaszko brothers – as targeting the 'veiled dictatorship' of former First World War hero Josef Pilsudski, though even this was not the kind of production in which each element of the story correlated directly with something in reality (Kennedy, 2002: 106–7). Rather, it used an approach to the crowds which made them unified and stylised in motion (rejecting the individualisation of the Meiningen tradition) so that they seemed both elemental and manipulated by the powerful for their own ends.[8] But even here, political critique was veiled and oblique, lying primarily in the minds of the spectators who were willing to see through kaleidoscopic and Cubist modernism to issues of their own day.

Schiller's production would have worked less well and less overtly in Nazi Germany, where notions of modernism were more circumscribed, where the totalitarianism of the regime was a good deal more overt and draconian, and where Shakespeare was both more mythic and more embedded in a species of nationalism. After the war years, those mythic ideas were complicated in German-speaking countries by the populace's desire to leave their Nazi past behind; as a result, there has still been no major production of *Julius Caesar* in Germany or Austria which has made direct connection to the regimes which drove the Second World War.

Post-war German people sometimes *thought* they were going to get something more directly retrospective, as did those who queued for tickets to Fritz Kortner's 1955 production at the Residenztheater in Munich, curious to see an 'Adolf-Caesar' (Hortmann, 1998: 207). What they got instead was emblematic of the new German theatre's iconoclastic move towards naturalism which set the tone for much of what has come since, and which sought to correct the lack of realism in expressionism and the lingering tendency to stylise, particularly in the depiction of supposedly noble characters. Like Brecht, Kortner despised '*Überrumpelungstheater*' such as Fehling had used in which audiences were emotionally overwhelmed (207), and did not want the audience to 'luxuriate in the dumb delights of unconditional identification' rather than recognizing the contradictions in all the characters: 'Ambivalent responses were best' (207). Despite strong feelings about Germany's culpability in the rise of Nazism and the roots of the war, Kortner's 'inclination lay neither in the direction of Brecht's political didacticism nor in Piscator's documentary theatre of exposure and accusation' (204–5). Seeing in the theatre's reverence for the idea of the hero something of the problem which had permitted Hitler's rise to power, he embraced a notion of the heroic which had more to do with the maimed, rebellious and morally outraged survivors of the war. Kortner despised the absolution of theatrical villains through pathos and wanted to depict real people. For classical plays, this meant trying to make everyone psychologically credible, in this case 'a Caesar without genius, a worthy, somewhat philistine paternal tyrant, and an undemonic Antony', the latter being termed by critics a 'small time clerk' turned tactician and demagogue (206).

Kortner's was a sceptical reading of the whole text, not just its heroic valences; so instead of having the intermission at what was then the traditional point – after Mark Antony's funeral oration – he put it after the death of Cinna the Poet, so that the audience saw the effect of the oration before applauding it. The assassination itself was messy, anticlimactic and indecorous, without the clear high purpose or sense of elemental tragedy common to past productions, including Fehling's. Battle scenes were ambiguous 'sinister exercises in slaughter taking place on a set strewn with corpses and cadavers of horses' (207). If critics saw anything of recent history in the production, it was an echo of the unsuccessful conspiracy against Hitler in 1944, not so much in its principles as in the butchery and failure which pursued it. Critical response was mixed. Though Gerd Brudern's Brutus was well received, many saw casting problems – particularly in Caesar (Paul Verhoeven) and Mark Antony (Ernst Ginsberg) – as the reason for a loss of the play's traditional grandeur. Kortner's iconoclastic realism thus foundered on the rocks of a familiar monumentalism, the lack of mythic power being seen as failure of vision rather than deliberate intent.

In recent years, Caesar has returned to Austria; but, as in Germany, local politics have not figured overtly in performance. In 1992 Peter Stein directed the play for the Salzburg summer festival at the Felsenreitschule. The venue, a reconstruction of a seventeenth-century riding school, is huge and demands large-scale choreography if the actors are not going to become minute and insignificant. Stein's set was a wide bank of gently rising white steps, and they were used pictorially to suggest who was rising and who was falling politically, so that the story was conveyed as much through 'symbolic blocking' as through language (456). Though some thought it a slightly ridiculous throw-back to the days of Reinhardt or Lang, Stein reverted to crowds with over a hundred extras. The toga-draped cast was made up of top name actors, all quite distinctive, so that unity could be achieved only with the broadest of strokes, movement and gesture being both stylised and old-fashioned, a vestige of the heroism Kortner had so decried.[9] The conspirators were all older men, suggesting a rearguard action defending something that was already lost. The stand-out performance above the more generalised ensemble was Gert Voss, who played Antony as a tactician from the start, but one who was also prone to odd eruptions of passion and contortions of body, making him 'unpredictable and inscrutable' (456). Audiences loved the production, but most reviewers were cool, finding little that was original or striking beyond the effective use of the space itself and the theatrical energy of the crowd scenes.

What is striking about all these German-language productions is that they eschewed the specific political valences so central to productions of the play in England and the United States, and the case of productions staged under the Nazis in particular suggests a number of things. First, it reinforces the literalness of censorship – the idea that subversion can exist only in specifically subversive acts, obvious visual echoes, or incendiary utterances. Second, it shows how much subversion is contained not so much by the theatrical space – subversion dissipating at the final curtain – but by assumptions the audience bring to the production. In the war years, the centrality of Shakespeare not just to German culture but to a (bizarrely propagandist) notion of what German culture was permitted the perception of heroic ideals to strip the play of its potentially topical referentiality. With hindsight it is hard to understand why *Julius Caesar* was not a political powder-keg, and to an extent – as the case of von Stauffenberg suggests – it was; but for many its explosive nature was clearly contained, or at least theatrically containable, by its mythic status. The German productions discussed here, particularly post-war, also attest to the problem of the play's political ambivalence. For all its appeal as a play about standing up to tyranny, *Julius Caesar* refuses to unequivocally take sides, and such equivocation facilitates both extremes of the twentieth-century German performance tradition: grand and mythic on the one hand; small and character-driven on the other. Hitler himself was never clearly personified in Caesar, but one wonders both what kind of production could have gotten away with doing so in his own lifetime, and – given the second half of the play – what more recent production could have done so without seeming nostalgic for what he represented. Far from avoiding their political history, then, German and Austrian productions have adopted what may be the only honest and ethical position available to them in their particular cultural and political context.

One solution to the problem was proffered by Falk Richter's 2007 Burgtheater production in Vienna, which approached the play without the topical referentiality of recognisable figures from life, but addressed larger issues of the place of the media in contemporary political discourse. The initial translation was made by the well-known German novelist and playwright Helmut Krausser, a specialist in Roman history, from which Richter constructed his own 'version' (his words in German are 'Bearbeitung' or 'Fassung') of the play.[10] The actors wore contemporary dress on a wide, shiny stage featuring a broad and steep ramp with occasional steps, all black, and screens on which were projected images of a statue-like Caesar.[11] The production was stylish and crisply acted with a wonderful naturalism owing something, perhaps, to Kortner, great efforts being made to convey the ambivalent humanity of the characters. Caesar was an imposing presence in slightly shabby business attire – more a union leader or shop steward than a CEO or president – and the conspirators wore clothing in a limited range of blacks, browns and whites all tending to grey, while Calpurnia wore an ivory nightdress and Portia wore red.[12] Antony, a young businessman, showed real passion when confronted by the bloody corpse of his friend, and this drove him through the funeral oration. But the production was about more than the individualised characters. It took particular aim at what the director calls 'neo-liberalism' and the media that supports it, particularly in matters of globalisation and war. The only toga in the production was worn by the projected news announcer who reported Caesar's death and the people's desire for vengeance.

9   The public, represented by the video images, tear apart Cinna, the poet, played by video artist Björn Melhus who collaborated with Falk Richter on the production (2007).

Richter says that the idea for the project originated partly in Robert Greenwald's 2004 documentary *Outfoxed*, a study of Rupert Murdoch's media imperium and Fox News's part in manipulating the election of George W. Bush, through asserting his victory long before the matter had adequately been resolved. This calculated intervention in the electoral process, and the way other networks followed suit, demonstrated, says Richter, the power of the media to affect the political process for their own economic reasons. Richter saw in Fox's coverage something closer to an advertising campaign whose aesthetics recalled Goebbel's work as Reich Minister of Propaganda, particularly in its anti-Kerry bias. Connecting Fox and the US company Halliburton, controversially linked to the 2003 Iraq war, gave Richter the impetus to shape his *Caesar* production so that its use of media and its militaristic drive drew on the memory of Nazism to point an expressly European finger at the Bush administration and also, to an extent, at Berlusconi's Italy. As Richter says,

> The US is a world power. But maybe it is in the same state that Rome was before its decay. Hard to say. But in the Bush Era when we were producing our *Caesar* it looked that way. It looked like the US was turning into a soft fascist state,

exhausting itself by too many wars and conflicts, the government getting lost among competing economical interests. And Fox was the medium ... the power behind the false elections, the war on terror, the strong anti Kerry campaign, the strong anti-UN, anti-Europe and anti-international law drift in the US ... So we used *Caesar* to fictionally raise the question: Will there be resistance? And to draw a theatrical parallel between the super power USA and the super power Rome.[13]

The playing space was designed to suggest that it was under the control of a media empire with large screens on which ran Fox-style news trailers, and whose front man became Antony. Brutus, weak and misguided, assumed that the assassination would return the nation to a democracy which had been effectively suspended by Caesar's constant 'state of emergency'. But Caesar's apparatus of power was 'post-democratic' and inhered in a supportive media which knew on which side its bread was buttered. The system, with Antony at its helm, easily survived the loss of Caesar himself, because the system – like Fox – preys on the irrational fears and resentments of the populace instead of advancing the kinds of logical argument which are central to Brutus's position. The production was about 'democracy today', says Richter, so it must have been interesting to see former speaker of the first chamber of the Austrian parliament, Andreas Kohl, and former Chancellor, Franz Vranitsky, applauding the first night's performance loudly.[14] Fascism, the production seemed to say, is elsewhere; and it is disguised, as it often was, as populist news.

Shakespeare's presence in Italian culture is not nearly as strong as it is in Germany or in countries with strong colonial ties to Britain. Unsurprisingly, major Italian productions of *Julius Caesar* are comparatively rare and – lacking the monolithic equivalent of Schlegel's translations – are more freely adapted in the production of what is, after all, a story from local history. It was performed in 1979 at the Teatro Olimpico in Vincenza by the Teatro Populare di Roma company, under the direction of Maurizio Scaparro; and John Francis Lane, reviewing cursorily for *Shakespeare Quarterly*, praised its lack of gimmick or modern dress and referents, saying the director allowed the words to 'speak for themselves'.[15] All crowds were cut, rendering Antony's funeral oration a kind of aria, reinforcing the general impression of a play as driven by a handful of powerful manipulators to whom the people were no more than a power source. Lane saw this as topically echoing contemporary Italian politics in the light of recent political assassinations, particularly in Turin and Milan, but this association, Lane asserted, was wholly in the minds of an audience steeped in knowledge of the political climate. The production itself did nothing to make such connection explicit, and the whole sounds curiously operatic in its disconnection from the world.

One of the most controversial productions of the play in any country was Romeo Castellucci's 1997 *Giulio Cesare*, which toured world theatre festivals for five years. The production was based on Shakespeare's play and material from the Latin histories, and was staged by the Cesena-based company founded by the director and his sister, Societas Raffaello Sanzio. Castellucci's approach was radically destabilising. As he says in an interview:

> Work with the classics demands that we confront the traditional, but that is precisely why the work can surpass the traditional, but never in a literary way. Therefore one mustn't tackle these classical texts as a superstitious person who believes the classics to be safe; quite the opposite. One must make an effort to put them to the test of fire, in order to better determine their supportive structure, which leads exactly to the revelation that they speak to everyone, to the frail and private nature of every individual. And the book, as object, is no more. (Castellucci, 2004: 16)

Though the production's postmodernism got the most attention, the director's aim was not primarily cerebral. According to Castellucci,

> [I]f there's no emotion, for me that's it, it's over, it's only a sterile idea ... I always demand that an artist move me. I even ask that of a visual artist. For me the emotional wave is the ineffable nucleus of a work, its breath of life ... Irony is interesting when it's fierce, when it rips your mind apart. That doesn't always happen. The artists have to be damn good. (18)

Dennis Kennedy studied the production enthusiastically and in detail as the final example of his *Looking at Shakespeare*, and remarked that 'it was the best version of *Julius Caesar* I've ever seen, but there wasn't much *Julius Caesar* in it' (2002: 355). The paradox stemmed from Castellucci's radical revisioning of the play as a study in celebrated rhetoric which he then subverted and reinvented in surprising ways: one character gave Flavius's opening speech with a laryngoscope down his throat so that the miked sound could also be 'seen' in the movements of his larynx on a screen, Brutus inhaled helium to distort his voice, and Mark Antony – played by an actor who had no vocal chords – used a voice synthesiser. The director explained that last choice thus:

> Mark Antony is the one who wins the oratorical competition, so working with someone who has no larynx meant having a new voice that came from the viscera, from deep down inside. Mark Antony's speech is completely focused on Caesar's wounds, it recalls the number of stab wounds, the blood that came out of them, the fact that the wounds are "silent mouths" which have no other voice at that moment but his, Mark Antony's. Well, this character in the shape of this actor actually talks from a wound, to make the speech truthful, outrageous, and moving. The most amazing thing of all is that this type of emotion is really stimulated by a consciously rhetorical use of the body and voice. (21)

Cicero – viewed by the director as integral to the conspiracy (an idea derived more from history than Shakespeare) was represented by a massively obese, naked man who sat on one side of the stage and never spoke. The juxtaposition of sight and sound also used incongruous physical images – a live horse, a set which began as a kind of random museum of Roman statuary but became a post-apocalyptic wasteland, and – most controversially – two severely anorexic women who, together, played Cassius in ways visually echoing the Nazi concentration camps. As Kennedy puts it,

> in Castellucci's *Caesar* the past was unapproachable, a series of ironic quotations jumbled together, yet impossible to leave behind. A play about the power of rhetoric was rendered in visual terms by visual artists. The final step had been taken, a border crossed: voice became visual, language physical, and scenography became performance. (355)

Kennedy saw the production as indicative of a kind of postmodern evolution towards the visual, and I have some sympathy for his enthusiasm, particularly immersed as I am in innumerable reviews which seem to hold speech – the lines and their 'effective' delivery – as the *sine qua non* of Shakespeare in performance. Yet championing the visual over the verbal in performed Shakespeare still feels like a critical cul-de-sac. Some critics found it pretentious and self-indulgent, even offensive; and as Kennedy himself suggested, the play as play was almost incidental, becoming a vehicle for performative commentary rather than what we normally expect from modernist and pre-modernist theatre: story, character, a particular kind of dramatic coherence, and so forth. But it did grow out of the play, and perhaps even more so from those 'Latin histories' which Castellucci cited as crucial to the production, particularly their accounts of the devastation of Philippi, here rendered in quasi-nuclear terms, so that Kennedy finally called the production not so much postmodern as 'neo-expressionist, iconoclastic, and aberrant', 'a subjective rendering of [the play's] recessive themes' (355). Such a production could only be interested in its country's Fascist period in the most generalised way, seeing it as a stage in that 'unapproachable' past which has led to the present.

Post-colonial *Caesars*: India and South Africa

Shakespeare has been a part of Indian culture since the eighteenth century and was frequently performed in English by schoolchildren and by amateurs and professionals of all levels, driven – often directly – by enthusiastic Brits, and by a reverence for the supreme dramatist of a language which had become the conduit of education and high culture. After India achieved independence from Britain in 1947, productions of Shakespeare in indigenous languages became more common, the translations tapping into those elements of the stories that made them feel familiar to audiences used to their own brand of folk drama. Utpal Dutt, who directed *Caesar* once in English and later in Bengali, remarked that his village audiences were receptive to Shakespeare because the Jatra plays to which they were accustomed were similarly 'full of blood and thunder and high-flown prose' (Trivedi, 2005: 179). Interestingly, both of Dutt's Calcutta productions (first in English for the Amateur Shakespeareans, 1949, then in Bengali for the same company, now named The Little Theatre Group, in

1964) used modern dress and had Fascist overtones which some saw as derived from Welles' 1937 production. The earlier of the two used modern battle-dress, gunfire and Cubist stained glass, Caesar himself vaguely Hitler-esque in hat and coat, with the conspirators as leftist partisans (228–9). The production was praised for its intelligence and clarity, although, predictably, reviewers found fault with the reductive politics which did not clearly enact Shakespeare's republicanism. However derivative and Eurocentric the approach might have been, it was striking because the concept immediately placed the production on the cutting edge of the post-war period, since – Welles notwithstanding – few major theatres elsewhere were exploring so topical an embrace of the play's political dimension in 1949, and none in England. The professional production of 1964 at the Minerva Theatre used a nineteenth-century Bengali translation by Jyotirindranath Tagore but retained the Fascist look, and though the production had a 'thematic resonance' for the area which had a significant socialist history, 'there was no consistent attempt to localize the mise-en scène' (229). Despite its Bengali script and its resonance with both the political and dramatic traditions of the region, the production was not clearly *about* India; rather, it enacted a partial appropriation of the European in which its own innate foreignness was foregrounded. Of course, any reflection on European Fascism was certainly relevant to India, since the Second World War had played a significant part in the country's recent history and independence.

Alyque Padamsee (the so-called 'Bhagwan of Indian English theatre')[16] organised a small production of the play in Mumbai in 1977 with a female Caesar, using the script as a vehicle to respond to the recent Emergency in which, from June 1975 to March 1977, Prime Minister Indira Gandhi suspended elections and civil liberties, bestowing upon herself the right to rule by decree. Though he modified relevant pronouns from male to female to suit Usha Katrak's Caesar, he left the text otherwise unaltered and in English, renaming it simply *Caesar*. In doing so he sought to make the kinds of comparisons he later made during his popular production of *Evita*, in which he projected phrases from the prime minister's 1975 Declaration of Emergency to make explicit the link between Eva Peron and Indira Gandhi. Padamsee (who is prominent in both theatre and advertising) is wedded to an English script and to traditional ideas of articulation and diction, which goes some way to explaining his 2007 decision to promote a three-CD audio set of *Julius Caesar* by veteran actor Pratap Sharma who read all the parts: a device to excite students about Shakespeare (though one which works by sound alone). For Padamsee, Shakespeare remains something best performed in English and without alteration, though this does not prevent a play like *Julius Caesar* from echoing a specifically Indian political present.[17] While Padamsee felt fewer constraints (cultural, fiscal or political) than did the RSC under Thatcher, partly because his was a considerably smaller production, his *Caesar* did what the RSC productions were unable to; it made a direct association with the current regime in spite of the dictator-figure's gender.

More recently, Ebrahim Alkazi directed Arvind Kumar's Hindi translation of the play for Delhi's National School of Drama in 1992, emphasising the friendship between Brutus and Cassius and having Shrivallabh Vyas, who played Caesar, reappear to aid Brutus's suicide as Strato (Desai, 2001: xxxvi). That same year, what Desai calls the 'most controversial' Indian production was performed for the Motley company at the Tata Theatre in Mumbai, directed by Naseeruddin Shah and Vikram Kapadia. This was a substantial production with a large number of actors[18] working on a set of multiple levels, and it sought to assert a bleakly cynical political vision: 'Politicians come and go and nothing really changes.'[19] The production was considered unsuccessful – even by the company which staged it – partly because its scale was unmanageable and partly because it was not patronised by regional schools, even though the play was a part of their curriculum. The company was also charged with being 'way too intellectual and elitist'[20] particularly because of their focus on English writers; and though the company changed, the 1990s were a period of great upheaval in the local theatre scene. There seems to have been a rift between practitioners staging classic English plays which some considered elitist, and those staging Hindi and Urdu drama, which others dismissed as amateurish and lacking in literary or theatrical craft. The Tata Theatre's directors saw *Caesar* as rich enough that it did not need an Indian context for relevance,[21] and they accused the local practitioners of indigenous drama of hiding behind exoticism to disguise as 'true theatre' what was actually just poor product.[22] Ironically, in the light of the elitist charge, Desai complains about the production's use of textual interpolation and cutting, suggesting that the production was not sufficiently pure for Shakespeare devotees and not sufficiently populist for theatre-goers. Whether the school groups stayed away because the production contained too much Shakespeare or not enough is unclear. Heeba Shah, Naseeruddin's daughter who continued to work with the company for many years thereafter, remembered the closing of the production as the directors' decision:

> I played a messenger in Motley's *Julius Caesar*. My father was Brutus and Benjamin Gilani was Cassius. Akash Khurana was Caesar and Kitu Gidwani was Portia. We had about 25 shows, then father closed it because he said it had become 'too commercial'. It was the most expensive Motley production with period costumes and a cast of 80–85 ... Since then we have stuck to a cast of 15 and minimal props and costumes.[23]

What 'commercial' means in this context is unclear – other evidence suggests it does not mean 'profitable' – but it seems that the company had hoped to draw crowds with a spectacular version of the play retooled for popular tastes, though not, apparently, enough.

The Tata production is illustrative of the double bind in which recent Indian staged Shakespeare seems to fall as the culture struggles with the place such material should inhabit in the post-colonial world. *Caesar* continues to be a familiar touchstone of dramatic – or at least *literary* – greatness, but its life on the stage in traditional form seems endangered. Since the mid-1990s, there have been kathakali dance productions of the play, some of which have used the pakarnnattam technique in which a single dancer plays all the parts. One such performance took place in 2005 by Suresh of the Margi Kathakali School in Thiruvananthapuram. The performance lasted an hour and 'depicted some of the dramatic moments in Shakespeare's play culminating in the assassination of the Roman dictator and his horrid realisation that those who conspired against him included his friend Brutus'.[24] Accounts of these productions have little to say about the dance as interpretive or even constructive of the play; they say more about how to teach the types and gestures of the kathakali form. Indeed, instead of embodying the natural interplay of two living performance traditions, the practitioners involved seem to have chosen *Caesar* as a familiar story in order

– ironically – to broaden the appeal of kathakali. Shakespeare's play was suitable because of its iconic appeal, the sweep of its story, and the scale of its characters. Sadanam K. Haikumaran, founder of the Sadanam Kathakali Academy, who mounted the play (renamed *Charadutha*) in 2010, puts it in these terms,

> As a Kathkali artiste I am very keen on observing the depth of the characters in various mythological plays. Here we are trying to emphasise on the original form of Kathkali while it's [sic] sanctity is not being contaminated.[25]

The 'form' can be uncontaminated in spite of the production's curious cultural hybridity because kathakali is a performative medium rather than a body of plays. Curiously, however, the result enacts two different forms of nostalgia, one for the indigenous art form, the other for Shakespeare's story. The teaching of the former, as part of a process of cultural reclamation after India's lengthy subjugation to Britain, ironically makes use of, even appropriates as reverse-colonialism, the familiarity of the non-Indian story (*Caesar*) which was an instance of that very cultural subjugation. The kathakali performances escape the charge of elitism levelled at some 'straight' productions, partly because their medium is less verbally driven, though one wonders if it is also because 'elitism' might also be code for 'British'. To what extent the two elements which come together in such hybridised creativity will survive, separately or together, remains to be seen.

India has a thriving and prolific film industry but to date has not produced a screen *Julius Caesar*. A 'Bollywood' film – originally scheduled for 2006 with producer Bobbi Bedi – was in the pipeline from celebrity musician/director Vishal Bhardwaj, but seems to have been suspended. Suggestively, Shakespeare figured again in a debate over the quality of indigenous forms, this time screen plays. Bhardwaj said that his interest in a filmed *Caesar* sprung from 'the lack of story writing talent in Bollywood', but his decision to abandon the project came from a desire to do 'something original and exciting'.[26]

Though complicated by its colonial associations, *Julius Caesar* has played a prominent role on stage in various African nations, while also remaining a staple of the educational curriculum even during the darkest days of South African apartheid, where the play was studied by all students regardless of race and ethnicity (Quince, 2000: 59–78). Though Shakespeare's centrality to African culture was always contested and has become more so with the resuscitation of previously marginalised or suppressed languages and cultures, the residual sense of cultural esteem coupled with a democratising rhetoric of universality has maintained his visibility in classrooms and theatres. That very universalism has also lent the politics of *Julius Caesar* a certain African topicality, though using productions for the communication of a clear political agenda has been typically vexed.

In countries recently ruled by the British, such as Sierra Leone, the status of Shakespeare as national poet – and therefore emblem of the coloniser – has been significant, though it is striking that (as in Nazi Germany and postcolonial India) the dominant impulse of the former colony has been to appropriate that emblem through translation rather than to repudiate it outright. Thomas Decker's 1964 *Juliohs Siza*, a translation into Krio written only three years after the end of British rule, enacts a political and cultural conquest in which the title character embodies the arrogance and hubris of the imperial British but also enacts (in its later scenes) the collapse of the idealised democratic republic into the single-party regime which ruled Sierra Leone until 1991. Julius Neyerere, the first president of Tanzania, published a blank verse translation of the play in Swahili titled *Julius Kaisari*.

Nelson Mandela's biographer, Anthony Sampson, looking back from 2001 during a heated debate about the elimination of Shakespeare from the school curriculum, observed that

> *Julius Caesar* had more impact than any other play. Africans saw it as a kind of textbook for revolution. [But] in South Africa the play had a deeper resonance, for it vividly described how an oppressed people can realise their potential against tyranny, and escape from their sense of inferiority.[27]

In 1944, when Nelson Mandela and his colleagues formed the Youth League of the ANC to create a more militant pressure group, they adopted as their motto Cassius's 'The fault, dear Brutus, is not in our stars / But in ourselves that we are underlings.' Sampson also observes that in steeling himself for what might come, Mandela underlined and signed the following passage in 1977 during his Robben Island imprisonment:

> Cowards die many times before their deaths
> The valiant never taste of death but once.
> Of all the wonders that I have heard,
> It seems to me most strange that men should fear;
> Seeing that death, a necessary end,
> Will come when it will come.

Strikingly, of course, the speech is one of Caesar's rather than one of the conspirators', suggesting again that the play's political use-value lay more in its individual utterance than in its dramatic whole. Like the Krio and Swahili translations, these were literary rather than theatrical endeavours, and – as for von Stauffenberg – the play as anti-tyrannical polemic was a productively fragmentable reading text. Indeed, Shakespeare as an African *theatrical* phenomenon has had nothing like the status or visible frequency that he has enjoyed in Germany or in other former European colonies such as India or North America. Laurence Wright, speaking as a 'sober Africanist', discusses staged Shakespeare in South Africa as 'a side-show to a side-show, just one significant strand in the marginal story of colonial drama and its heritage', dwarfed by the performative dance, drama and ritual practices of the indigenous peoples (Wright, 2004: 63). That said, Shakespeare – and *Julius Caesar* in particular – has had a highly politicised stage life in South Africa, albeit one which has not been able to hold onto political singularity of purpose except in highly adaptive forms.

Prior to the Second World War, productions of Shakespeare in South Africa were exclusively the realm of English-speaking whites, but in the post-war years other racial groups (Afrikaners, coloureds, and blacks) began to use the plays as a means of asserting their own position and value. In 1958, a largely 'colored' (mixed-race) organisation – the Drama Centre – staged the play in Woodstock, directed by Carter Ebrahim, who would later become P.W. Botha's Minister of Coloured Education and Culture. For Ebrahim, the play's emphasis on tyranny was politically apposite in reference to the British, to whom Commonwealth South Africa belonged until it became a republic in 1961, though, as Quince shrewdly observes, the director downplayed the play's potential applicability to local oppression and the disenfranchisement of the majority black and mixed-race population (62). 'Finally,' said Ebrahim, 'it was great fun, and that was the important thing. Everybody had a lot of fun' (63).

In 1960, after a marked upswing in racial unrest, prime minister and grand embodiment of apartheid Hendrik Verwoerd survived an assassination attempt. A few weeks later the Drama Centre staged its second production of *Julius Caesar*, this time at the City Hall in Capetown. The cast were all classed as 'coloured' but the director was an Afrikaner, Robert Mohr, and the production was staged in modern dress with a particular emphasis on the crowd, which contained about eighty people. In light of the recent assassination attempt – something the director wanted to explore overtly – the production might have been intended as clearly revolutionary, but the effect was muted by issues of acting style. According to Quince, George Veldman, who played Brutus, was an old-fashioned, declamatory actor, while Cosmo Pieterse, who played Antony, was more modern and naturalistic, and won the audience's sympathy, thereby muting the production's revolutionary edge. That said, the sheer fact of a 'coloured' cast performing this particular play in the context of increasing racial constraint and unrest must surely have created more complex ripples in its audience. In 1966, a second assassination attempt on Hendrik Verwoerd succeeded, the prime minister dying of stab wounds inflicted by a messenger in the House of Assembly. This event loomed large over all productions of *Julius Caesar* until the 1980s, as did the large gatherings at the funerals of activists slain by the police after the Soweto uprising of 1976 and throughout the following decade (Quince, 2000: 60–1).

In 1984 and 1985, *Caesar* was once more set as a school matriculation exam text, and this fuelled several productions, including two by the Federal Union of Black Artists which toured the black townships around Johannesburg. These were small, low-budget productions done 'straight' with little (conscious) directorial bias, their emphasis being the aiding of children to pass exams; but some resonance with the current political situation was unavoidable, though – again – genuinely revolutionary impulses were muted. On the one hand, the vacillation of the crowd seemed unfortunately topical; and on the other, Shakespeare himself was still largely associated with the dominant culture; furthermore, the students (like many in other cultures) seemed dubious of seeking for ideas about their own identity and predicament in the play. Another much larger production occurred in 1985, directed by the politically radical Malcom Purkey for the University of Witwatersrand; this one made more deliberate use of contemporary African cultural referents, particularly in the colours of flags and sarongs. South African army khakis were dyed and modified so as to avoid one-to-one correlation with the current regime, and the combination of modern fabrics with more traditional tribal dress perhaps rendered the costumes too abstract for direct political allusion. Again, acting styles were crucial in determining audience sympathy, and once more naturalism and charisma won the day for Antony and Octavius over the stiffness and petulance of the conspirators. But Cinna the Poet was black and was torn apart by a white mob: both a reflection of apartheid horrors and an inversion of the familiar and hysterical white South African nightmare. Overall, the production's political import was seen as uncertain, even confused, though some saw in it a study of what might happen should the current regime be toppled. Unquestionably, however, the play engaged with the nation's political zeitgeist, even without a simple 'message'.

In September 1993, a few months before South Africa's first democratic, multi-racial elections, the play was staged by the African Shakespeare Company in Johannesburg, under the direction of Karoly Pinter. The production was shot through with topical contemporary reference, although it slid free of any clearly partisan position. The cast was racially diverse, but while the Caesar was white and the crowds black, other roles bore less obvious racial symbolism. Mark Antony and Cassius were white, Brutus and Casca were coloured, and Octavius was black. This might resemble some version of colour-blind casting – should such a thing ever be possible, particularly in so racially defined an environment – but Quince saw the production as dramatising a popular (black) revolution urged on by white agitators, a revolution briefly co-opted by another white demagogue (Antony) but, beyond the limits of the production, destined to fall into the hands of a black military dictator (Octavius) (Quince, 2000: 75–7). This admittedly bleak reading was reinforced by a scattering of elements from South African culture, which included the tendency of white orators to use African words and phrases to imply they were 'of the people', symbolically resonant handshakes, the security trappings of white rule, and even a popular South African soap opera which Octavius watched as Antony killed Casca (who had apparently changed sides after the assassination and subsequent political debacle). Such witty parallels were peppered with more unsettling images of the contemporary South African scene, however, such as when Cinna the Poet's murder was depicted as a 'necklacing'. The final battles were contemporary with mortars and the sounds of helicopters roaring overhead, but the combat-fatigued troops were all black, and the production's ominous projection was all too clear: whatever its evils, the demise of the present regime would result in a blood bath, and most of the casualties would be black.

Shakespeare has been contested ground in these African productions, a locus of power and status to be claimed, with *Julius Caesar* a kind of jaundiced mirror reflecting not just the present but intimating a terrible, looming future. The colonial and domestic perspectives were not successfully married in a single production until the one that garnered the greatest critical attention from outside Africa: Yael Farber's 2001 *SeZaR*, produced for the Grahamstown National Festival of the Arts and restaged at several regional theatres in the UK the following year. Breaking from South African performance tradition, Farber's script was a linguistic amalgam only about half of which was made up of Shakespeare's unaltered Elizabethan English. The rest came

10 From left to right: Porshia (Mmabatho Mogomotsi), Mark Anthony (Tony Kgoroge) SeZar (Hope Sprinter Sekgobela), Sinna (Siyabonga Twala), Kalphurnia (Keketso Semoko), in Yael Farber's *SeZar* (2001–2).

largely from Sol Plaatje's Tswana translation with additional lines in a contemporary idiom, some English, others Tswana, Pedi and Zulu, reflecting the diversity of the cast.

For all the interest the script created – and it was the focus of much celebration in the South African press[28] – this was a visual, even visceral (sometimes literally) production, whose ownership of the play was manifested less by its linguistic re-colonisation than by its reliance on indigenous performative forms and pointedly African settings. Rome was replaced by 'Azania', an unspecific but distinctly African place which could be, as Laurence Wright observes,

> anything from AZAPO's visionary pan-African idyll, to some generic post-independence black state, to the scurrilous Azania of Waugh's *Black Mischief* (1932). What it is not is a neocolonial appropriation of Shakespeare, making vague obeisance to metropolitan heritage by whimpering 'me too!'. (102)

The stage was open and flexible with two mobile steel-girdered towers and an apron downstage of the proscenium. The cast consisted of only eight actors, all black. Costume was generalised African with touches of ancient Egypt, Arab North Africa, and ancient Rome. The production was interspersed with traditional African dance, with drumming, and with ritual stick-fighting for the battles. The actors themselves were well-known at home, several of them from popular television shows. The play's supernatural elements got a distinctly African flavour implying communion with ancestors and the gory rituals of animal sacrifice and augury, the soothsayer becoming omnipresent by virtue of her other job as a uniformed street sweeper. Even Caesar's epilepsy got an African touch suggesting spiritual gifts, though most topical and appalling was the piling of brown limbs up and down-stage of the main playing space, an image conjuring the atrocities of Rwanda. Radio broadcasts announced rioting, reported on the ravages of AIDS, and prophesied erupting violence. The assassination followed *SeZaR*'s refusal to heed Brutus's plea to act in response to a killer virus and menacing foreign neighbours. 'This is a classic invaded on every level by a new reality,' said the director, 'our reality.'[29] Recent African history was constantly in play throughout the production, though this was achieved through eerie echo and half-allusion, so that observers saw – or thought they saw – reminders of any number of African politicos and their acts:

> For South Africans, the assassination of Chris Hani[30] may hover at the verges of consciousness ... And then perhaps the (utterly unsubstantiated) accusation ... that President Mbeki had something to do with this earlier traumatic event may spring to mind. Or was it, ought it to have been, Mbeki himself (who, like SeZaR, has been accused of being too involved with foreign affairs, too concerned with his own image, of not relating effectively to internal affairs of state) who most fittingly stands in the shoes of SeZaR? .... Audiences from further north might have felt impelled to think of the late Laurent Kabila and his son Joseph in the DRC, or the struggle for democratic succession in Zambia, or Robert Mugabe's desperate hanging on to power at any cost in Zimbabwe. Moise Tshombe, Patrice Lumumba, Idi Amin, Jerry Rawlings, Sierra Leone last year, Ruanda before that, Nigeria for the last twenty years, the list goes on. (Wright, 2004: 18)

In resisting direct association, the production became applicable to a broad and tragic range of people and events from recent African history.

The production was raw in effect, but not in execution, the overwhelming response being that this was a depiction of what *was* rather than an explanation for it, a snapshot of Africa playing the same political and military games familiar to all emerging modern nations. Mark Antony was a doomed spin-doctor, trying to make PR out of a hopeless situation. Writing in the *Oxford Daily Information*, Sharea Deckard remarked, 'I have never seen a *Julius Cesar* so raw, so seething with the dynamics of power and betrayal.'[31]

Acclaim was not universal, however, and some English reviewers found themselves feeling queasy about the tension between the revered play and its African incarnation, not because the text was being corrupted or diluted by the nontraditional production, but because the text itself felt unnecessary. Worse, it seemed like a different brand of colonialism. Karen Fricker, writing for *The Guardian*, praised the vitality of sound and movement which characterised the production's self-consciously African dimension and even found the switching of languages 'thrilling' and defamiliarising, but ultimately thought that the Shakespearean verse was a chain around the production's neck:

> Shakespeare holds this production down. The energy dissipates when the text is performed in the original; the English verse simply isn't as powerful, spoken by these actors, as the African language. Why did we need the pentameter at all?[32]

The image of the chain around the neck of an African theatrical event is important, because for Fricker the issue here is an unease with which the production attempted to reclaim its grip on the culture of its former European oppressors. She acknowledges that Shakespeare's play was politically charged for Mandela and that *SeZaR* staged in South Africa would thus play differently – i.e. more radically – in terms of its politics:

> But performing this production in Shakespeare's homeland shifts the context considerably; what might have felt like a liberating mix of classic and native here brings with it a troubling whiff of neo-colonialism. A non-British culture uses a 'classic' British text to contextualise its own relevant and timely tale of greed, intrigue, and betrayal – and then exports it back to Britain, reassuring us, perhaps, that we westerners still have the answers, and the power.

I confess myself baffled by the logical sweep of the argument here, and wonder if in fact the politically correct anxiety about neo-colonialism is actually the projection of a different (and less politically correct) unease about African Shakespeare generally. Why does staging the production in Britain invert its politics, and for whom? Naturally, audience context changes the semantics of a production, and it could be that in the minds of the audience the adaptability of the play to an African context asserts a kind of Western cultural supremacy, but this surely demands a particular and inflexible mindset no production could alter. Fricker's solution, apparently, is that the play should not have been done at all, since her complaints are about the fact of the production, not its execution; and the defamiliarising she so praises would seem to increase as the play – the recognisable Shakespearean text – moves towards its own event horizon. Presumably, she would have been happier, then, less uncomfortable at least, had it kept going until it vanished entirely.

This is the dilemma of postcolonial Shakespeare in production, particularly, perhaps, for a play as politically loaded and yet finally ambiguous as *Caesar*. For some, any production of the play which maintains a connection to the Shakespearean original must always finally be conservative, its subversive energies contained by the status of the original and its place in colonial history, regardless of the ownership or idiom claimed by the performers. This seems reductive, ultimately an enactment of the same cultural condescension the argument ostensibly strives to oppose, since it affirms the logic of its reading (that Westerners should be 'reassured' by the perceived affirmation of their persistent power) over that of what has driven the production and – at least to judge by reviews – the response of its original African audience. The text's associations (British and colonialist) are clearly relevant to the production, but to insist on what such associations mean in spite of the motives of its performers and assumptions brought to it by audiences is to re-enact a colonialist hierarchy of knowledge and perspective. Such a move also refuses that basic principle of theatre, that performance is transformative, that a play – rather than intrinsically signifying any one thing – is remade in production, claiming its own inner logic and values. While I recognise that no play can entirely overturn the assumptions of its audience about what the play, or its author, or its place in history, meant to them when they entered the auditorium, Farber's *SeZaR* seems to have come as close as possible to insisting upon its own meaning and redefining the play in African terms.

Confronted by a language which was not that of their audience, *SeZaR*, the Indian kathakali dance productions, Castellucci's postmodern adaptation, and Richter's media-focused production were forced to engage more directly with theatre's transformative and adaptive strategies. In so doing they remade the play in their own image, or a version of it which interested them, which suited their cultural landscape and political interests. This is a difference in degree from more traditional Anglophone productions, rather than kind, however much we rehearse the old evasion of whether or not a play is done 'straight'. While such adaptive strategies do not automatically make for interesting or well-executed productions, they do at least shake off some of the play's long-standing baggage, finding freshness and immediacy which more conventional productions in Britain and America often struggle to elicit.

Notes

1. Overall under the Nazis, Schiller won out, though the positions were reversed again between 1955 and 1975 (London, 2000: 38).
2. In 1934–35, 52% of all productions in Berlin were by non-German authors (London, 2000: 223).
3. *Lear* received only 4 performances in the year the Nazis came to power (1932–33) but 98 in 1934–35 (London, 2000: 244). *Macbeth* was – astonishingly – staged throughout the Third Reich in a total of 29 different productions, sometimes treated as an anti-British play or a quasi-Nordic 'ballad of fate' (245).
4. This despite a 1935 ban on the use of such uniforms on stage.
5. Schiller's *Don Carlos* contained such lines and his *Wilhelm Tell* was banned in 1942 because of the hero's decision to kill the tyrant (Hortmann, 1998: 143).
6. Horst Zander, *Julius Caesar: New Critical Essays* (2004: 301).
7. London (2000: 249–50). From 10 May 1941, Hess was in British custody but it still seems to have been Fehling's production that he saw. As to tyrannicide being in the air, it might be argued that the Stauffenberg plot's timing was crucial – in that it came after the D-Day landings when many despaired of Germany winning the war, and that Fehling's production belonged to an earlier, more positive ethos. But there were at least eight separate attempts on Hitler's life between 1938 and the (unrelated) Stauffenberg bomb, and that last instance was the conspiracy's third attempt in as many months. As to the widespread nature of dissent against Hitler it might be worth noting that the Stauffenberg plot led to the arrest of over 5,000 German officers who had connections to the conspiracy (Beevor, 2009: 330–9).
8. Images from the battle of Philippi are especially striking, the stage a mass of clashing, modernist lines in the long spears and geometric shields used by the ensemble.
9. The cast included Martin Benrath (Caesar), Thomas Holtzmann (Brutus), Hans Michael Rehberg (Cassius), Branko Samarowski (Casca), Walter Schidinger (Soothsayer) and Rosel Zech (Calpurnia).
10. The director's views which follow are taken from my private correspondence with him.
11. Excerpted moments from the production are available for view on YouTube.
12. The disemboweling of a sheep took place upstage as Caesar's debated his visit to the capital with his wife.
13. Private correspondence with author.

14 According to *News from Austria* 6 (2007) an official Austrian state affairs newsletter available online: http://bkacms.bka.gv.at/Docs/2007/3/22/info6_en.pdf, accessed 25 February 2011.
15 Translation by Angelo Dallagiacoma, Set by Roberto Francia, costume by Vittorio Rossi, music by Giancarlo Chiaramello, *Shakespeare Quarterly* 30: 2 (1979), 308.
16 Chaman Ahuja, India's *Sunday Tribune*, 18 March 2007.
17 *The Hindu*, 1 August 2006.
18 Accounts of the cast size vary tremendously, ranging from forty-five to eighty-five. The *Mumbai Theatre Guide* says seventy: www.mumbaitheatreguide.com/dramas/Articles/09/sep/01-motley-theatre-festival-september-2009-at-ncpa.asp, accessed 7 March 2011.
19 Dolly Thakore, *The Daily*, 11 March 1992.
20 www.screenindia.com/news/30-&-throbbing/490288/, accessed 14 March 2011.
21 So said Shah in interview, www.mumbaitheatreguide.com/dramas/speaks/naseeruddin.asp, accessed 14 March 2011.
22 So said Kapadia in interview, www.mumbaitheatreguide.com/dramas/speaks/vikram_kapadia1.asp, accessed 14 March 2011.
23 www.telegraphindia.com/1080521/jsp/entertainment/story_9297183.jsp, accessed 14 March 2011.
24 http://shakespearemag.blogspot.com/2005/01/kathakali-version-of-julius-caesar.html, accessed 14 March 2011.
25 www.indianexpress.com/news/a-classical-change/568483/, accessed 14 March 2011.
26 www.webindia123.com/movie/interview/april2007/in040407.htm, and www.mumbaimirror.com/printarticle.aspx?page=comments&action=add&sectid=30&contentid=200612140217219378c18973&subsite=, accessed 14 March 2011.
27 *The Observer*, Sunday 22 April 2001.
28 The production was the focus of two different attacks, one from those who thought Shakespeare should be unadulterated and performed wholly in English, and one from those who thought there was no place for the work of a non-African playwright. The two positions are, of course, related. See, for instance, Edward Tsumele's review in *The Sowetan*, 24 January 2002.
29 'Swinging Shakespeare', Edward Tsumele, *Sowetan Time Out*, 8 February 2002.
30 Hani was the commander of Umkhonto we Sizwe, the military wing of the African National Congress, who was gunned down before he could establish himself in the post-apartheid polity.
31 25 September 2001.
32 *The Guardian*, 30 October 2002.

CHAPTER VIII

'Growing on the South': Georgia Shakespeare 2001 and 2009

Consideration of non-Anglophone productions in Chapter VII reveals the fundamentally local nature of theatrical production, something obscured by consideration of film or of companies like the RSC whose profile raises their productions to the level of national or international event. This chapter takes a closer look at *Caesar* in regional theatre, presenting not an overview of the countless productions staged off the radar of the national press, but a detailed study of two productions by a single company, Georgia Shakespeare. I do so for three reasons: first, because both productions are interesting and in some ways unique; second, because I was involved with both productions and thus have an insider's perspective; and third, because they enact that larger truth mentioned above: that most theatre emerges from and for a specific and local community which has its own taste, its own history, its own artistic and political culture.

Georgia Shakespeare (originally titled The Georgia Shakespeare festival), is one of approximately 233 active Shakespeare-driven theatre companies in the United States (Hartley, 2011). It was founded in 1985 by Kirby McLain (Lane) Anderson, Robert Watson Georgia and Richard Garner, the last of whom remains its Producing Artistic Director. It is an entirely professionally staffed company with a core group of forty-three Associate Artists, and other staff, designers, actors and directors hired on a seasonal basis. For the first eleven years of the company's existence they played in a tent on the Oglethorpe University campus in Atlanta, but moved into the purpose-built Conant Performing Arts Centre on that same campus in 1997. The theatre is a 509-seat modified thrust proscenium and is shared with the university, which controls the main stage for six months of the year. Oglethorpe is a predominantly white liberal arts college in a similarly white area of predominately black Atlanta. Georgia Shakespeare's average audience is approximately 90% white, 5% black, 5% other ethnicities. When the company stages its spring 'Shake at the Lake' production – free admission to the general public – in the more ethnically diverse portion of Atlanta's Midtown surrounding Piedmont Park, the audience demographics become more diverse by only three or four percentage points. When they stage productions featuring largely African American casts at their Oglethorpe home, however, as in their 2005 *Romeo and Juliet*, audience diversity shifts closer to 20%. Given the racial make-up of Atlanta, this number is still comparatively small, but it changes dramatically for the company's education programs and school matinées, for which the audience may be 75% black. Both of the *Caesar* productions discussed in this chapter touch on racial issues.

The company performs three shows in a summer repertory season, a stand-alone production in the autumn, a Christmas show, and a spring re-mount in Piedmont Park, with other more minor productions, events, and education programmes running throughout the year. Its annual budget is approximately $2 million, half of which comes from ticket sales, the other half from private and corporate donation. Georgia Shakespeare remains one of only two League of Resident Theather (LORT) theatres in the area,[1] and – with the possible exception of The Alabama Shakespeare Festival – is the largest and most respected Shakespeare-dedicated theatre in the south-eastern states.

Georgia Shakespeare's early years featured several playful, mainstream adaptations of Shakespeare including a (recently revived) musical *Shrew* and a Mafia-themed *Hamlet*. In more recent years, and particularly since leaving the tent, their approach has been more consistently 'serious', less adaptive. Budgets have escalated and production values have increased proportionally, allowing the company to hone their profile and stylistic approach. In recent years they seem to have retired their slogan 'We take classics to the edge', but they have retained an unabashedly conceptual approach to production which tends to be more politically and aesthetically innovative than those of most regional Shakespeare companies. Though some directors are in-house, others are brought in on a per show basis, allowing for considerable variety in the style of approach, but operating within a general ethos which seeks to make the plays contemporary and exciting. This is especially important in a city whose larger artistic life tends to be driven by the inventive urban energies of the New South.

In autumn 2001, the year they got their LORT status, the Georgia Shakespeare Festival staged *Julius Caesar* set in 1930s Louisiana. The show was directed by John Dillon. As dramaturg, I spent weeks in rehearsal, also attending design and production meetings, working on the script with the director, writing programme notes, giving pre-show lectures and participating in post-show discussions.[2] The production's title character was loosely modelled on the governor and senator, Huey Long, who was assassinated in 1935, shot on the steps of the Capitol building he had built in Baton Rouge. It wasn't just the coincidence of where he died that made Long – known as the Kingfish – a suitable analogue for Caesar. Long was a radical populist who sought to overturn the old Louisiana aristocracy, but he was also a demagogue, an orator whose down-home wisdom masked the vaguely Fascist leanings which were evident in the architecture of the Capitol where he was killed. As governor, he was renowned for his public works programmes, particularly his construction of roads and bridges, and parlayed this image of the people's civil servant into real political power, dealing viciously with his rivals, particularly after the failed impeachment bid of 1929. He supported his opponents' rivals in elections and had their family members fired from state positions. As he infamously remarked, 'I used to try to get things done by saying 'please'. Now ... I dynamite 'em out of my path' (Parrish, 1994: 164). He worked to shut down newspapers which opposed him while expanding his own propagandist *Louisiana Progress*. In spite of his public works, he was denounced by many – particularly the old moneyed families of Baton Rouge – as a dictator who had systemically gathered all the power of the state into his own hands. As a senator, Long was unpopular among his colleagues who thought him fiery, overly radical and self-interested, particularly in his opposition to Roosevelt's New Deal, which Long thought insufficient as a redistributor of wealth during the Great Depression. Though his actual intentions are disputed by biographers, Long professed that he would run for the presidency in 1936, and even wrote a book on how he would spend his first year in office (*My First*

Days in the White House). In January of 1935 a paramilitary organisation calling themselves the Square Deal Association used 200 armed men to take over a Baton Rouge court house. Long responded by declaring martial law, banning publications criticising state officials and making it illegal for people to congregate in groups of more than two. Two months before he was killed, Long unearthed evidence of what he believed was a plot to assassinate him which included former governors and members of congress. The circumstances of his death have always been uncertain, the supposed killer, doctor Karl Austin Weiss who was killed by Long's bodyguards at the scene, having very confused motives and no history of political activism or violence.[3] Some 100,000 people filed past Long's open casket prior to his burial.

The points of overlap between the careers of Huey Long and Julius Caesar are obvious, even if there are significant differences (Long had no military background to bolster his political gains), and the production sought to make direct connections. The set was flexible but modelled on the Baton Rouge state Capitol, costume and dialect were region and period specific, and the crowds who celebrated Caesar's initial triumph did so with all the trappings of Mardi Gras: a jazzy, brass procession around the auditorium, carnival costumes including a stilt walker, and beads that were thrown to the audience. The crowd's banners were adorned with the motto 'Omnes Reges Sunt', a rough echo of Long's famous campaign slogan 'Every Man a King'. When the crowd were asked, 'Is this a holiday?' they gave a raucous, affirmative cheer. Of course, the version of Mardi Gras offered was more New Orleans than Baton Rouge, and there were other minor discrepancies that rendered the production more a populist evocation of Long's environs than a historicist recreation. This was also true of one of the production's most memorable scenes, in which Cinna the Poet, played by a young African American actor (Anthony Irons), was lynched on stage. Historically, Long's political constituency involved large numbers of black people for whom he was an advocate; but though race was certainly an issue in Louisiana, the lynching scene evoked something more generically southern, something unsettling that was not contained by the setting of the production. It was a potent piece of theatre which challenged its Georgian audience directly, though it did not grow precisely out of the circumstances of Long's life and death.

Such points of slippage between the theatrical event and the period it purported to represent are telling because they illustrate how the specifics of research – of which much was made in rehearsal – gave way to a production which was not ultimately *about* Huey Long at all. Dillon took certain liberties with the text, heavily truncating the second half, for instance, and eliminating what he called 'Shakespeare's least interesting ghost', but the story he set out to tell was still the story laid down by the play, not that dictated by Louisiana history. Where the two were in conflict, the play won out. On some level, of course, it could hardly be otherwise. The production was not intended to be a history lesson (Louisianan or Roman), so slavish adherence to either period would be nonsensical even if it was feasible. The directorial strategy, however – sharing images and music from 1930s Louisiana, screening the Ken Burns documentary *Huey Long* in rehearsal and making biographies of Long available to the cast – was to create a feeling of specificity among the people who made the production. If the details were lost on the audience, if that audience emerged without ever thinking of Huey Long (who had, after all, been dead long enough to be unknown to many who saw the show), that didn't matter. The aim was to make the story of Caesar feel real, familiar, a mythic story – but from the recent south, not from an ancient and distant past. An academic colleague who saw the production remarked that Caesar's lines on danger knowing full well that Caesar was more dangerous than he, had never made more sense than when they were growled 'by a red neck politician to his wife across the breakfast table'.[4]

The immersion of the rehearsal process in the life of Long – something I had not seen practiced by this company before – created intriguing points of contact which went beyond one-to-one parallels between Long and Caesar. Long's brand of politics, as already mentioned, was roundly rhetorical, and while the footage of his speeches which we watched certainly informed Bruce Evers's bluff and certain dictator, they also informed a broader sense of the play's political oratory.

Lots of localising detail emerged from the production's historical context. The dark suits and fedoras gave the conspirators an air of southern aristocratic point device, quite at odds with the plebeian crowd or the begging, voodoo-Rasta soothsayer. Much was made of handkerchiefs, used for instance to meticulously wipe the ubiquitous hip-flasks or to spread fastidiously

11 Bruce Evers as Caesar (left) hectors Decius (Brik Berkes) and Calphurnia (Teresa DeBerry) over breakfast in John Dillon's Georgia Shakespeare production (2001).

on the stone steps before Casca would deign to sit. All the actors spoke with a hint of southern dialect (not something they usually employ), most with the understated and softly musical drawl of the gentry. Evers's voice for Caesar was quite different; brazen, luxuriant and confrontational, a particular kind of swaggering braggadocio nicely parodied by Chris Kayser's slick and dapper Cassius as he recounted the swimming contest and Caesar's sickness. Class loomed large, Caesar a dangerous upstart usurping the natural dominance of the conspirators, country gentlemen whose every syllable bespoke their genteel southern *sprezzatura*. Surprisingly, the speech rhythms of the dialect served the iambic verse remarkably well, particularly in the mouth of Evers, in whom the marriage of Shakespeare and 1930s southern bluster emerged clear, pointed and natural.

Other details similarly established a specific world for the production. Caesar's guards wore the Fascist-leaning brown shirts of the period's Louisiana troops, and there was no doubt that they were constantly on the alert and ready to report whatever they saw or heard back to the King Fish. Brutus considered the murder from a white whicker chair on what looked like a plantation house porch, and Caesar's breakfast was furnished in covered dishes by servants (some of them black) in white mess jackets. Mark Antony began the play as a rake in shades and two-tone shoes. Caesar's funeral involved a large and ornate casket covered with floral tributes and was brought on with a military honour guard to a plaintive jazz trumpet dirge. Cinna the poet was found out with hand-held flash lights. In the second half of the play, while Octavius and his men were uniformed soldiers in jackboots, the conspirators and their forces in their oilskin jackets and sunhats looked like aristocrats on a hunting party, a nice image of how out of their political depth they were.

The meticulous work to evoke the period seemed to load the dice, and my concern at the time was that it might deprive the audience of anything other than a window into that period; but this was not the case, partly because the production turned out to be more flexible in its intent, especially in the second half, and partly because theatrical meaning gets shaped by things other than what the production team controls. In this case, it was an accident of history.

Two weeks before the production opened, the terrorist attacks now known simply as 9/11 took place. More pointedly, there were, in the immediate aftermath, a handful of reprisal attacks on Arab or Muslim Americans which made the headlines. Still, the company was surprised to find that audience members saw allusions to such attacks in the lynching of Cinna the poet. That theatrical moment had been designed to evoke southern, racial memories which, given the continually loaded racial politics of Atlanta (a blue city in a red state primarily because of its Democrat-leaning black majority), seemed particularly unavoidable. As cited above, Georgia Shakespeare's audience is primarily white, though the balance shifts when African American actors are figured prominently, and the company had been braced for various kinds of response to this representation of Georgia's all too recent past. But talk-back audiences and eavesdropped lobby conversations drove the 9/11 point home. Moreover, the site of the disaster (what became known as Ground Zero) was inadvertently echoed in the post-apocalyptic second half set, in which the Baton Rouge Capitol building's façade was replaced by a bombed-out ruin: I suppose that for some, the whole play might have become a study in cultural trauma and the desperation which rises when monoliths – emblematic buildings or monumental leaders – are destroyed. Here the sense of collapse and chaos was augmented by the corpses of others killed in Octavius's and Antony's purges which hung against the cyclorama. At times, and in spite of all the production had attempted to make explicit, there was an atmosphere of shock, of deep communal grief, which had little to do with Louisiana and everything to do with New York.

As large-scale cultural concerns shaped the meaning of what was built on stage, so did small-scale backstage concerns. The comparatively large cast of the production was drawn from both its core repertory players and from another company in the city, the Atlanta Shakespeare theatre, also known as the Shakespeare Tavern. The Tavern is a smaller, less financially well-endowed operation which claims an Original Practices (OP) approach to staging Shakespeare, which they do in a small, dedicated downtown space.[5] The two companies have markedly different approaches and resources, and seem to play largely to quite different audiences, each tending to use the logic of their respective methods to claim – usually tacitly – a brand of superiority. Though relations are generally amicable there is a simmering rivalry between them which flares periodically, particularly over funding, slights in the press, or perceived personal affronts. They don't often share actors, and Dillon's *Caesar* was unusual in the number of Tavern actors it involved. They tended to be cast in smaller roles, something which I heard commented upon several times in rehearsal in half-joking terms: 'at the Tavern I'd be Brutus: here I'm Strato …' From time to time there was a palpable tension between members of the cast, some of which was demarcated along company lines, and which spilled over into the last scenes of the play, where the taunting rivalry between the two military camps was clearly fuelled by something real. Saxon Palmer, who played Mark Antony and who was then considered Georgia Shakespeare's golden boy (he subsequently became a regular on and off Broadway) and could be quite acerbic in rehearsal, was a particular lightning rod for some of the percolating resentments, and it was he who became the focus of the production's boldest – and final – choice.

As Antony knelt down-stage to deliver his final lines over Brutus's corpse, Octavius came to stand immediately up-stage of him. Octavius suddenly drew his pistol and put it behind Antony's head. Antony looked up, not turning, but knowing, and as the stage blacked out, there was the deafening report of the gunshot.

12   The closing image of Dillon's 2001 production. Antony (Saxon Palmer) stoops to Brutus' body as Octavius (Gregory Thomas Isaac) levels his pistol.

Audience response was, predictably, mixed. There were dry remarks about there being a very disappointed Cleopatra somewhere, but some liked the way the gunshot capped off the play's preoccupation with intrigue, double-dealing and the ruthless trumping of personal relationships and loyalties by the lure of political power. I was conflicted by the choice, recognising its dramatic power and the way it gave a 'twist' to the end of the story which was genuinely surprising, but also worrying that we had deviated too far from the original. Of course, the manner of that deviation was insulated against the usual complaints: it added no lines, rewrote nothing, wilfully misread nothing, merely adding a kind of final stage direction (which productions always treat as their prerogative). Some audience members who didn't know or remember the play well didn't even realise that they had seen anything unusual.

The director would not be drawn into extensive debate on the matter. He liked the final coup, thought it gave the production a nice sense of closure and made the case (fairly, I think) that no discussion of *Antony and Cleopatra* – or even of *Julius Caesar* as a known and studied text – was relevant to how this production should end. The moment was provocative; and that, he thought, was a good thing, even if it led to people dismissing the production as *wrong*. At one point I pressed for cutting the at-black sound of the gun, arguing that the final outcome of the visual tableau should be left ambiguous, Octavius drawn and poised to kill Antony, enjoying his moment of secret power, but without conclusion. In time, however, I got used to the scene as executed, and came to quite like it, finding it too late in the show to be disruptive, and seeing it as growing naturally out of tensions and interests that were very much of a piece with both the play and the production. The moment was *Caesar* escaping its historical confines just as the production had escaped the literal truth of Huey Long, the story following its own logic without the circumscription provided by either Plutarch or the Shakespearean script. That final shot was also seeded in all the Antony/Octavius scenes, in which a bitter resentment of each other grew, particularly on lines such as 'I have seen more days than you' and 'why do you cross me in this exigent?' These were men thrown together by political fate but temperamentally unsuited to be partners and increasingly divided over their final purpose. Yet that final gunshot was also a product of in-fighting within the cast; and when the director discussed the choice with the cast prior to committing to it, those who spoke up most in favour of the gunshot's inclusion tended to be the Tavern actors, several of whom (including Gregory Thomas Isaac who played Octavius) were happy to see Palmer's Antony finally outmanouevred and defeated.

Character dynamics elsewhere inevitably took a back seat to the larger concept, but Chris Kayser's Machiavellian Cassius deserves mention, particularly for his first half manouevring and manipulation. When he embraced Casca on 'there's a bargain made' he smiled wolfishly, as if he had caught him in a trap. Bruce Evers perfectly caught the balance between swaggering good old boy and menacing dictator in his Caesar. When he demanded if Caesar should send a lie to the senate, he slammed the breakfast table with his fist, and his rage against Decius was sudden and terrible, but quickly undercut with laughter and hearty shoulder-slapping. There was more delighted laughter from Caesar at Decius's remark that they should break up the senate till Caesar's wife have better dreams, but a chill silence when Decius went too far by speculating that some would say Caesar was afraid. Palmer's Antony was mercurial and conversational but adept at carefully modulated moments of rhetoric which powerfully evoked the image of his dead friend. When he built in volume – even punctuating his feelings with Caesar-like slams of his hand on the coffin ('But were I Brutus [Bang] and Brutus Antony [Bang], there was a Brutus …') – the effect managed to be both dramatic and plausible. Charles Horton's Brutus was less well received, most critics and audience members finding him too cerebral and understated, too lacking in passion, though I think his performance made sense within the southern aristocratic milieu of the production, and such complaints about Brutus on stage are common. He wore a grey suit in the first half, while all the other conspirators wore black, and was always a pawn disguised as a leader: pleasant, well-meaning and thoughtful, but ultimately naive and completely incapable of either expediency or military organisation. His care for Portia was true – a truth heightened by the fact that her voluntary wound was replaced by another cause of her 'weak condition': she was pregnant.[6] The elimination of Caius Ligarius meant that Brutus's promise to reveal the charactery of his sad brows to his wife was the last line of the scene, so that they went off together to talk. This also created a nice dovetailing with the following scene between Caesar and Calpurnia, both men in dressing-gowns dealing with their anxious wives, the first with care and compassion, the second with indulgence and bluster.

Georgia Shakespeare came back to *Caesar* eight years later, and again I served as dramaturg. My work on the 2009 production was circumscribed, however, by the fact that I no longer lived in the Atlanta area and could not take time for an extended working visit. Instead, I agreed with the director, Richard Garner, to serve as a consultant, working by phone and e-mail on such matters as script editing, research and concept discussions, then visiting for a sampling of rehearsal early in the process. In the end I was only able to be in the rehearsal room for a few days during table work and initial blocking. I then returned for opening.

Unlike the previous production, Garner never sought to bring an over-arching concept to the play, and even the period choice (roughly First World War or shortly thereafter) was treated lightly and generally, playing simply as 'modern dress.' This less conceptual approach was driven in part by Garner's wanting to create a contrast with the previous production's period specificity, and in part by looking for a more neutral telling of the story which might be better received by high school audiences (or at least their teachers) who would dominate the matinées which are a special feature of Georgia Shakespeare's autumn slot. But the most significant driving force was a commitment which had been made to the casting of the show long before its details took shape. This was to be a small production with a full company of only eleven (including a child Lucius who could not be doubled elsewhere), though a student intern was later added to play Octavius's servant. The casting choice was in part designed to extend the company's ensemble focus, but it was undeniably also a financial one. Though Georgia Shakespeare had weathered the fiscal crisis of 2009 better than most regional companies due to some voluntary cost-cutting the previous year, money was tight. Moreover, as a LORT theatre, they are obligated to maintain a ratio of 12 (higher paying) Equity to every 2 non-Equity contracts.[7] Filling out the company with junior actors was not an option.

The reduced ensemble thus became the show's de facto concept, and the script had to be prepared accordingly. Since the production was to be broadly realist, without the trappings of postmodernism or the conventions of what Grotowski would call 'poor theatre', the director did not want to weaken the importance of character with too much doubling; so we approached the cutting of the script with a view to combining roles where possible and eliminating where necessary. We decided that it was virtually impossible for the actors playing Brutus, Cassius, and Mark Antony to take additional roles, nor could the women playing Portia and Calpurnia play more than members of the crowd without drawing attention to the doubling. The actor playing the soothsayer (Bruce Evers) had very bad knees, resulting in mobility problems which meant he could practically play only Artemidorus, the two roles being combined. We had no one to play Flavius, Marullus, Trebonius, Caius Ligarius or Lepidus, let alone the soldiers who appear only in acts four and five (Pindarus, Strato, Titinius, Varro, Claudius, Messala, Dardanius, Clitus, Cato, Lucillius, Volumnius etc.) The blade on which Brutus ran would be held by the boy Lucius. The conspiracy would be significantly reduced and the crowds would be nonexistent.

We still wanted to present the whole play, though it was immediately clear that the battle scenes would have to be abridged. An initial cutting eliminated Lepidus, for instance, but we missed what Mark Antony's lines about him revealed of Antony himself, so we restructured the proscription scene in such a way that Lepidus could be discussed without actually being on stage.[8] A solution of sorts was found in fully embracing a 'chamber music' approach in which, rather than somehow trying to represent the play's symphonic range, the production focused on the characters and their relationships by combining parts. Flavius and Marullus, for instance, were recast as Decius (who also absorbed Trebonius) and Casca, though we retained the reference to Flavius and Marullus being put to silence, as if they were different people involved in a similar incident to the one played out by Casca and Decius. The device worked well, expanding certain roles and opening up a broader sweep of character arc. When Casca related, for instance, that Flavius and Marullus had been put to silence, the moment got real weight and tension, in part because Casca knew that he could have been apprehended and punished for the same thing.

Casca and Decius were the most expanded roles, and both persisted into the final battle scenes with Casca taking on the (slightly retooled) roles of Pindarus, Messala and Titinius. Rather than vanishing anonymously after the assassination, then, Casca survived long enough to witness their total defeat, to have a hand in Cassius's suicide, and finally to kill himself. The actor got a full trajectory, accumulating experience as he moved towards his final despairing action, instead of having only a few isolated scenes. Though Casca's was an extreme case, similar absorptions were the rule for all but the major actors, and the result was not just parity in role size, but an emotional and intellectual throughline which worked so well that I began to wonder if we had not inadvertently recovered something of what the original audience might have experienced in terms of what Alan Dessen calls 'conceptual casting'.[9] In shedding the rather doggedly accurate historicism of Shakespeare's text (the population of the latter half of the play with new characters in accord with Plutarch's *Lives*), we had stumbled upon something which did more than simplify the story: it created unity out of fragments. If it did so in a somewhat literal or even pedestrian way, I suspect that it approximated (paradoxically) what a less literal-minded audience might have once seen, character arcs implied through the body of the early modern actor playing several parts. Nineteenth-century

13 The conspirators (left to right) Cinna (Eugene H. Russell, IV), Cassius (Joe Knezevich), Casca (Allan Edwards), Brutus (Neal Ghant) and Decius (Brik Berkes) (dir. Richard Garner, 2009).

notions of realist theatre have made it harder for audiences to see those arcs, to ignore the literal differentiation based on character names (Casca is not the same as Pindarus even if the actor's body says otherwise); but in unabashedly blending such roles into one, the production created an analogous effect. The result was seamless, plausible, and largely unnoticed, even by people who knew the play; but the greatest effect may have been less on the audience than on the actors, who were able to commit to fuller roles, and longer and more complex journeys, than they would had they played a collection of smaller, distinct parts. Intriguingly, the effect was not dissimilar to the productions of the eighteenth century whose routine expansion of Casca's role, for instance, has been dismissed as absurd. In fact, we found a deep theatrical logic to such combined roles, one derived from the text as script in spite of the historically punctilious speech prefixes.

To illustrate the point, I want to spend a little more time on Casca or – more accurately – on the Casca created in this production and played by Allan Edwards. This Casca had Casca's assigned text in the first part of the play, but also Flavius's from

1.1, Messala's from 4.3, and Pindarus's and Titinius's from 5.3. This substantially alters the character as written by adding key moments to Casca's stage time, which traditionally ends (in ways that the play leaves unexplained) after the Forum scene. Before this moment he had witnessed the Lupercal events (events he subsequently relayed to Brutus and Cassius), gone through the supernatural storm, and committed to the conspiracy. He was present when Brutus joined them – a scene in which he saw the first strategic disagreements between Cassius and Brutus – and accompanied Caesar to the Capitol. He struck the first blow of the assassination. He then witnessed the second debate over strategy between Brutus and Cassius, but agreed to allow Mark Antony to live, and left the Capitol with blood on his hands. Georgia Shakespeare's expanded Casca continued the character's life as follows. When civil war broke out, Casca (as he continued to be called) went to war as an officer defending the new Brutus-led regime against Mark Antony and Octavius. He was called to a planning session at night where he gave Brutus what he thought was news of Portia's suicide, and watched as Brutus and Cassius argued about the strategy concerning Philippi (the third time he witnessed this tension). He was present at the parley to hear Mark Antony say 'Whilst damned Casca, like a cur, behind / Struck Caesar in the neck ...' During the battle he reported the defeat of Cassius's army and (mistakenly) the capture of Cassius's messenger and the subsequent defeat of Brutus's army. He assisted Cassius's suicide. He then learned of his mistaken reporting and committed suicide himself.[10] Edwards found in this expanded role not just a fuller life, but a core issue to play:

> The 'Casca' I was given to play seemed to me a man desperately searching for a hero to follow. After Caesar fails him, he finds a new hero in Cassius. A crisis occurs for this Casca when Cassius begins to surrender (as Casca thinks) leadership to Brutus.

The resultant through-line created both useful conflict and tragic resolution which bore fruit in the latter half of the production. As Edwards, speaking as Casca, puts it:

> Cassius, my hero, was dismayingly deferential to Brutus. Three times I saw Cassius defer to Brutus, and certainly the last two were mistakes: Cassius, at Brutus' insistence, forbade

recruiting Cicero into the conspiracy. Cassius, at Brutus' insistence, allowed Mark Antony to speak in Caesar's funeral. Cassius, at Brutus' insistence, agreed to attack Mark Antony at Philippi. In each case I took Cassius' advice against my instinct and against Cassius' first impulses. Who is this Brutus to insist with such certainty?

For the actor, the key discovery was his witnessing of the third disagreement between Brutus and Cassius in the tent scene, a moment which formed an insistent pattern, recasting the earlier disagreements and loading them with resonance. The expanded role thus gave new shape retrospectively even to the early scenes which now more clearly seeded issues and ideas resolved later. Since he took Flavius's lines from 1.1, his political loyalties were clear from the outset, so his relaying of the Lupercal events to Brutus and Cassius were critical of Caesar but expressed with caution, the first manifestations of the unease with which he would view Brutus's usurpation of Cassius's leadership.

> I fought in Cassius's – not Brutus's – army. Using Brutus's strategy – the strategy I know is against Cassius's instinct – we lose. We lose because Cassius, from the time Brutus joined the conspiracy, will not lead, but only follow (and the dramatic irony given Casca's own need to follow a hero was particularly rich for me here). I kill Cassius himself out of a sense of loyalty that is quickly shown to be extreme. The whole through-line is now Aristotelian. Casca has as shocking an anagnorisis as any of his heroes. And his pet virtue, loyalty, leads him to self-destruction. 'Alas [we have] misconstrued everything.' And yet: 'See how I regarded Caius Cassius.'

Seen from the vantage point of the production's ending, 'Casca's motivations are,' says Edwards, 'clearer. His crisis is brought on stage. His destruction has meaning.' Furthermore, it draws to the forefront the play's 'critique of loyalty and treason. The consequences of Brutus's certitude are played out in Casca's destruction.' Of course, motivation is not all, and what makes coherence in the mind of the actor may make for confusion or distraction in the audience. I was perhaps too close to the production to assess this particular choice objectively, but my sense of audience response (certainly among my own graduate students) was positive; the change lost little and added a good deal, as was the case for Brik Berkes's Decius.[11] That many audience members did not seem to notice the alteration at all, was – perhaps – another mark of success.

In another tricky doubling, Cinna the poet was played by Cinna the conspirator, which meant, troublingly perhaps, that the mob got it right. In initial rehearsal we struggled with why Cinna revealed his name to them, and we toyed with the idea of their getting hold of his wallet or identity papers during the initial tussle. I liked this idea, because it meant that he couldn't claim not to be Cinna and could only try to suggest he was a *different* Cinna. In the end, the production went with the decision that he blurted out his name in the panic of the moment and then had to try and cover his error. The scene ended with the mob carrying his body up the stairs which scaled the high back wall and casting him over the top.

The biggest problem with a small cast production of this play is negotiating the crowd scenes, particularly the funeral orations and the final battles. The latter were solved first when we realised that we didn't have to demarcate for the audience who was on which side, and that there was value in chaos, particularly since this was a civil war. All troops thus wore versions of the same vaguely 1920s battle dress, and the scenes were staged in low light with explosions, gunfire and aircraft sounds from overhead. We had considered using gas masks extensively to further fudge who was who (as well as to evoke the period and to add an inhuman menace), but they were impossible to speak through and, in the event, were used minimally. There was little attempt to suggest actual combat taking place on stage (always tricky in a period reliant on ballistic rather than melée weapons), and the second half felt a little truncated, though suggestive enough of actual battle.[12]

With so few actors to spare, the funeral orations were always going to be the most difficult part of the production. Various options were considered, including the eliminating of an onstage crowd (replaced by either piped noise or nothing), but the idea which emerged from table work was that a 'crowd' of four should be considered less as the whole than as representatives of the people, and Allan Edwards (who played Casca but was also – suitably disguised – a member of the mob) hit on the image of a labour dispute: the crowd became union leaders who would have to take their verdict back to the people. We even discussed the possibility of having everyone involved sitting around a negotiating table, though that was discarded because it would render the scene too small and static. I would have loved to have seen that idea explored physically, treating the scene as a small-scale interaction between clearly demarcated individuals; but the production as it evolved lost some of its conviction about this moment and became more conventional. The scene worked, up to a point, because those who were present forced both orators to win them over, but reviewers missed the crowds.

Such a chamber production inevitably becomes less about large scale politics than about character dynamics and relationships, and this was foregrounded by Allen O'Reilly's Caesar. In early conversations between the principals and the director, a back story was sketched out, a collection of school ties and shared military service which suggested a strong sense of intimate male community, so that Caesar shared a cameraderie with the senators in spite of his dominance. O'Reilly's Caesar was clubby, avuncular and likeable, raising questions as to the motivations of the conspirators.[13] Joe Knezevich's Cassius was hard, calculating, and personally vindictive – resentful of Caesar's status and the sense that he himself had fallen from favour – but not entirely in control, as was manifested by both the assassination scene (in which he had to be restrained after repeatedly stabbing Caesar's corpse) and the tent scene, where he was badly shaken by Brutus's indifference and hostility.

Early in rehearsals, Neal Ghant insisted that his Brutus was essentially noble and driven only by the public good. This created a problem, because while the audience might see Brutus as merely manipulated by Cassius, it was hard to see what he might fear in this jovial and reasonable Caesar. The director pressed O'Reilly to add some steel beneath the good-fellow surface, and the conspirators began to show more signs of dread (a hasty kneeling if Caesar seemed displeased) which hinted at their knowledge that there was more to the dictator than his pleasant bluster suggested. But it was not until well into the production's run, when Ghant started to darken his Brutus during the 'It must be by his death' speech, that a fitting complexity started to make sense out of the assassination. Even then, his motivation was hard to guess at, because Ghant – a physically imposing African American actor who tended to brood in the role, as if containing some fierce passion which might otherwise lash out – played

Brutus's intellectual stoicism to the hilt.[14] It wasn't that there was no semblance of thought beneath the lines – quite the contrary – but neither his fellow conspirators nor the audience were let in on what those thoughts were. The conspirators as a whole may have had good reason to fear Caesar's rise to power, but their motives were muddied by personal resentments and private ambitions, and the production did not clarify which concerns were dominant.

Not all the critics liked such ambiguity. Curt Holman, writing for *Creative Loafing*, equated the lack of a strong political or conceptual take on the production with not having 'much to say', something he contrasted to the 'stunningly creative' Dillon production (12 October 2009). Though obviously complicated by the company's reputation for strong conceptual approaches and for this production's provocatively early twentieth-century setting (Holman referenced Welles's production in his review), the complaint resonates because so much of the politics of the play is personal rather than reflecting the large-scale social or demographic issues of, say, *Coriolanus*. After Welles, it is difficult to see a production which does not take a strong political angle (often through direct allusion to contemporary issues) as political at all. If we don't see a Yeltsin or a Hitler in the title role, then the play can seem to become merely domestic and personal. Yet Wendell Brock, reviewing for the *Atlanta Journal Constitution*, found something closer to what the director had hoped for, a clearly applicable and contemporary political immediacy facilitated less by a high-concept frame than by clear, character-driven story telling:

> If the tragedy of 'Julius Caesar' seems more eerily prescient than it should, you may attribute that feeling to the heightened tenor of politics in America. An agitated congressman accuses the president of lying in an angry outburst inside the Capitol. Citizens turn up at health-care forums toting guns. A major international accolade is derided as premature and short-sighted.[15]
>
> For better or worse, Georgia Shakespeare's new production of 'Julius Caesar' plays like a cautionary tale – an opulently framed, just-in-time-for-Halloween bloodbath that speaks to the horrors of assassination, mob rule and the torturous inner demons of guilt and grief.
>
> Under Richard Garner's fluent direction, the hell and heartbreak of Caesar's circle of murderers has never felt more

essential and immediate. This admirable production is visually appealing, tautly paced and deliciously gory – a tragic spectacle born more from a sense of unity and ensemble than show-off acting. (16 October 2009)

Brock clearly saw not simply a general political resonance, but a particular echo of the shrill and sometimes alarming rhetoric that marked Obama's first year in the Oval Office, when the president was trying to overhaul health care while battling panicked, incendiary accusations of un-American socialism. As such, Brock treated the production as a kind of nightmare window into a possible future rather than looking to it for an echo of an actual past; and in this, its lack of a more overt conceptual frame surely helped.

Both women were praised for their scenes, though in this boy's club world they felt predictably disconnected from the rest of the play. This might have been otherwise. A visual trope the director came up with early in the process was that the conspirators would wear an identifying mark like a tattoo cut into the inside of their forearms, something which they could reveal by rolling up their sleeves, so that in the orchard scene, Brutus would survey each mark as he resolved to join them and then cut the same into his own flesh. At one point, we considered making this same mark Portia's voluntary wound, a sign of her political complicity which would make her a more active member of the conspiracy. In the end, this fell out of the production, though she still entered the conspiracy scene early enough to overhear some of what was being discussed before accosting Brutus as the others left. The moment, along with the compellingly earnest performance of Susannah Millonzi ensured a strong sense of connection between Brutus and his wife, and gave weight to the announcement of her death, though I couldn't help wishing for the sign of political solidarity which had been considered. Tess Malis Kincade played Calpurnia with a parallel commitment and was given a nicely somber appearance in mourning black during Mark Antony's funeral oration. Her silent vigil over the corpse helped shame the crowd and aided Antony in turning their allegiance. Antony was played with vigour by David Quay, but he had something of the same opaque motivation which characterised the conspirators, and his agenda was open to speculation.

Given that the two Georgia Shakespeare productions were only eight years apart, it is surprising that there was so little overlap in the casting, Brik Berkes (Decius) being the only actor to reprise his (significantly reimagined) role from the earlier show. While there tends to be less continuity between autumn shows from year to year than between the summer repertory seasons, it is striking that the latter production suggests a younger and more racially diverse company. Chris Kayser who played Cassius in 2001, is still a prominent figure in the company but has been, to an extent, replaced by Joe Knezevich (Flavius and ensemble in 2001, Cassius in 2009), who has become central. Bruce Evers, so masterful as Dillon's Huey Long-esque Caesar, had only a few lines in 2009 as the hybrid soothsayer and Artemidorus. None of the other actors from Dillon's production were in Garner's, nor were any of them part of the summer repertory; even the design staff of the two productions were wholly different. Such difference is not the result of individual directorial preference, as it might be at a more major company like the RSC or the National, but an index of changes in Atlanta's performance culture and the structure of Georgia Shakespeare in particular. Had the cast of the 2009 production been twice its actual size, I still doubt there would have been more actors from the earlier show, not so much (diversity aside) because of conscious intent on the part of the company's staff, but because the community itself has evolved.

The material conditions of theatre-making are perhaps more clearly evident in the work of regional companies whose resources, in terms of budget, rehearsal time, actor pool and so on, are considerably more limited than those of companies like the RSC whose work dominates a book such as this. A Georgia Shakespeare production will have only about a month of rehearsal time and a comparable run: about a third of the RSC standard. Their productions will only be star-studded in the most limited local sense; but they tend to be more clearly rooted in their immediate community, and they have a particular freedom which, I think, the RSC generally does not. This chapter notwithstanding, Georgia Shakespeare is generally not playing to the archive. Every RSC *Caesar* immediately becomes part of a global conversation and is, in real terms, always in dialogue with every previous RSC *Caesar*. The downside of such prominence is that it surely constrains directorial approach, particularly to those hot-button issues such as textual editing. Though free from such constraints, most regional companies feel duty bound – perhaps in pursuit of the kind of authority modelled by entities like the RSC – to take a similar approach, and their productions are often thus a shadow of what is being done bigger and better elsewhere. What is worth noting about the two productions I have discussed here is that they found something surprisingly rare in the production history of this play: freshness. Some will deem them gimmicky or transgressive, but to me they were instances of reimagining familiar material, not in ways so radically adaptive that they became new plays, but in fresh and surprising ways that made the play live as a unique art object again.

Notes

1. The other is The Alliance, whose budget is approximately five times as large. The League of Resident Theatres is an organisation which agrees to operate according to guidelines laid by professional theatre unions such as Equity, and which ranks companies based on profile, length of rehearsal periods and production runs, and scale. There are currently only seventy-four member theatres in the United States. Membership is considered an indicator of prestige, it being considerably more difficult to attain membership than it is to attain the Equity Letter of Agreement, under which many more companies operate; and the terms under which the theatre operates are significantly more exacting in matters, for instance, of the ratio of Equity to non-Equity actor contracts.
2. For a full account of what I mean by this, what I consider my work to be and the extent to which I am involved in rehearsals, script preparation etc. see my *Shakespearean Dramaturg* (2005). My work on this production was fairly representative, though it was my first time working with Dillon and I had less involvement in the preparation of the original rehearsal script than was usual with other directors. I have worked at Georgia Shakespeare for a decade-and-a-half and am the only dramaturg who is also an associate artist.
3. Some historians claim that Weiss was unarmed and that Long was killed by a stray bullet fired pre-emptively by one of his bodyguards. Weiss was shot more than sixty times at the scene.
4. Randy Hendricks (an expert on Robert Penn Warren whose *All the King's Men* was based on Long) made the comment.
5. The brand of OP used at the Tavern (which does not include, for instance, all-male casting or natural lighting effects) seems largely about a Folio-centred approach to script, a certain playfully interactive attitude to the audience, a use of period (roughly) dress and music, and an avoidance of 'concept' productions.

6   Such a choice of course loads not just the relationship, but her subsequent suicide, though the production made no overt attempt to get mileage out of this in the tent scene.
7   The summer repertory system is slightly different because of the contracts' duration but is still only 12 Equity to 4 non-Equity.
8   The alterations to the text were surprisingly minimal. We made a few excisions in this scene, altered a few pronouns and had them 'send to' Lepidus since he was not actually present.
9   'Conceptual Casting in the Age of Shakespeare: Evidence from *Mucedorus*', *Shakespeare Quarterly* 43:1 (1992): 67–70.
10 I am indebted to Allan Edwards for his correspondence on the doubling issue and his analysis of the new elements introduced by this production for his character. The quotations in this section are taken from the correspondence.
11 Brik Berkes – one of the few company members who had been in the 2001 production – had similar things to say about the expansion of his role as Decius, an expansion he was acutely aware of because he had also played Decius in the previous production. The new role had less meat than Casca's, however, and much of the effect on the actor actually centred on the expanded Casca who became a clearer mark of the conspirators' new journey and whose miscalculation was emblematic of them all.
12 Though less heavily cut than Dillon's production, the second half (from the proscription scene) still lasted only about forty minutes.
13 Allen O'Reilly is one of the most likeable men I know, and though a brilliant actor in many ways it is the suppression of his essentially pleasant nature which poses the greatest challenge for some roles. We wrestled with it when he played Leontes in *Winter's Tale* and we had similar problems here with finding the danger in the man.
14 I have tried to make a racial point out of the casting of Ghant as Brutus in the context of Obama's presidency without success. I don't think the casting was colour blind, but I also don't think it played a significant part in the production's semantics beyond a general desire to mirror the surrounding community more accurately. In Atlanta, black actors playing Shakespeare suggest a contemporary and democratic approach. Their blackness is neither effaced nor emphasised unless a particular point (as with the black Cinna of the 2001 production) was intended. Since the 2009 production looked largely contemporary, racial diversity in the cast seemed appropriate. If audiences or critics found particular significanse in Brutus's race, I never heard it discussed.
15 The congressman who said 'you lie' to President Obama a month earlier was the Republican from South Carolina, Joe Wilson, and the award in question was Obama's 2009 Nobel Peace Prize.

CHAPTER IX

A strange disposed time: *Caesar* at the millennium

The challenge for *Julius Caesar* in the twentieth century was the negotiation of the play's politics once Welles had demonstrated the triumphs and perils of making explicit comparison with recent or contemporary events. From the Second World War onwards the oratory, heroism and spectacle of the nineteenth century were steadily replaced by more modernist notions of character and totalitarianism. But even when productions escape the charge of gimmickry, the old emblems of 'safe' and easily recognisable dictatorships (Fascism, Nazism and some forms of Communism) have started to feel predictable. As we move into the twenty-first century, productions seem acutely conscious of their place in history, attempting a new – or seemingly new – addressing of the play and its concerns as a distinctly temporal phenomenon. This seems to me perfectly appropriate, and not only as a necessary reassessment of Shakespeare's place in contemporary culture. Perhaps more than for any other Shakespeare play, the legacy of *Julius Caesar* is bound to time and temporality, and not only because of its historical self-consciousness. As a classroom text the play has become a kind of memorial to former educational periods, just as directors have begun to find new urgency and relevance in its political valences. As we move into the new millennium – a little over 2,000 years since the assassination which inspired the play – the negotiation of the play's slippery temporal dimension, the back-and-forth exchange between its long past and the shrill and vibrant insistence of its present, have taken centre stage.

It is fitting that the last conspicuous *Julius Caesar* production of the old millennium took place at the reconstructed Globe theatre in London in Spring 1999. The production, and the debate around it, centred on issues of time, some of which are obviously at work in the play itself, while others have fastened on to it subsequently. One of these, which the production embraced – at least in its programme and shop displays – was Steve Sohmer's thesis about the opening of the Globe theatre and *Caesar*'s arguments about Elizabeth's failure to reform the Julian calendar according to the Gregorian model.[1] This curiously academic bit of historicism surfaced in rehearsals, a fine sketch of which is presented by Jac Bessell on the Globe's website, but reviewers and audiences did not clearly glimpse it in the on-stage action. But time has many aspects and enough of them were in play at the Globe to give the production a singular sense of temporality which might serve to locate the state and direction of *Julius Caesar* as we move forward.

Intriguingly, Mark Rylance, the Globe's artistic director and this production's 'Master of Play', invoked the calendar argument to reinforce a sense of the play's contemporary resonance for the Elizabethan audience, since it connected the Queen to the Roman dictator through popular discontent. Caesar had adjusted the calendar and created a month in his own name, while Elizabeth had failed to bring England into line with Catholic Europe, producing a ten-day discrepancy in dating. The Roman and Elizabethan positions were, it was suggested, indicative of an autocracy which fuelled treachery, albeit one which didn't clearly produce anything theatrically useful in the present except, perhaps, for those inside the production seeking justification for the view that the play was no mere classical history lesson. But the focus on calendar as an issue at the play's heart also facilitated a temporal claim with clearer use value: the argument that the Globe's new season would open on the 400th anniversary of its namesake and with the same play. Immediately the temporal focus became less about calendrical niggling and more about time, timeliness and timelessness. Factor in an all male cast doing an un-cut folio text in quasi-Elizabethan garb on the Globe stage, and temporality became shorthand for authenticity.

'Authenticity' has always been a double-edged sword for the Globe, a term which at once buys one brand of status and authority (the sense of replicating how the plays were originally done in (roughly) the same spot), while sacrificing another (the notion that the liveness of performance demands an immediacy which cannot be found in so-called museum theatre). The Globe's own position has shifted on this issue, not always self-consciously; and even in rehearsal for the 1999 *Julius Caesar* Rylance bolstered the copious Elizabethan dimension of the production, its research, rehearsal and performance practice with the repeated statement that the agenda was experimental, an exploration of what had been forgotten rather than the pursuit of original practices or historical authenticity. Such a framing argument, Bessell notes, came as a considerable relief to the actors (Bessell, 2000: 5).[2]

The production as I recall it was clear in both its verse-speaking and its narrative, solidly acted without significant directorial inflection; and what stands out in my memory were the jig at the end and some clever misdirection at the beginning. As the 'groundlings' gathered before the show I became uncomfortably aware of a man behind me who was manifestly a little the worse for the vast can of beer he had brought in with him, and who soon started attracting attention as he called out for glimpses of Gwyneth Paltrow (who had starred in the recent *Shakespeare in Love*). Though the yard was packed, the audience were clearly trying to give this man (whose accent was, I think, Irish) a wide berth, and there were anxious looks for ushers or security personnel.

He was, of course, Liam Hourican, the cobbler.

The moment this became clear was satisfying: I had been duped, my middle-class assumptions about theatre exploited for the good of the show. But something odd happened as soon as the cobbler climbed up onto the stage to engage the haughty tribunes who had included the entire house in their accusations of senselessness. The spark, the energy, the sense of innovation paled as the audience member revealed his nature as actor and moved inside the script. From that moment on I remembered almost nothing of the show without recourse to notes and reviews.

This is not to say that the rest of the production was dull, but it does suggest a curious feature of the Globe which seems to encourage the chaotic energies of its playing space, and to summon ideas about the original and far less reverential audience, only to contain them. I'm not sure there is a desirable alternative to this. The Globe's first seasons were much criticised for their panto-like encouragement of audience involvement, particularly in the case of serious plays (one thinks of the audience throwing French bread during the 1997 *Henry V*). In the case of *Caesar*, however, there was something pointed about the nature of the containment of the audience, something which became a metaphor for the play.

I have already said that the production was in Elizabethan dress with a few Roman additions, as it is generally thought the Chamberlain's men would have done it. The exception were the crowd (tellingly described in the rehearsal notes as Plebs 1 through 5) including, of course, the cobbler and carpenter who wore casual modern dress in order to blend into the audience. The result was unsettling, seeming to depict a collision of past and present in which the audience's representatives were the jeering, loutish and ultimately brutal mob, while the major players (including Cinna the Poet) look like 'clones of Drake, Raleigh, Leicester and Essex'.[3] What, I wondered, does this mean for the Globe itself if it implies (in some ways rightly) that the audience are the barbarians intruding on a past which would be better without them? Rehearsal reports indicate a real concern for such a dynamic, the following coming from the fourth preview on 15 May:

> This performance took place on a Saturday evening, and many of the groundlings appeared to be quite drunk. These groundlings took an early dislike to Cassius, and booed at him periodically. R[ichard] B[remmer] took all this in his stride, but the effect was a generally disconcerting one for all. Some groundlings had brought playtexts with them, and were able to anticipate several of the Plebeians' lines, shouting them out moments before the 'real Plebeians' could speak.
>
> In general, the performance became a show about the groundlings, rather than for or with the audience as a whole. The actors had to work very hard to bring the audience back to the story, to divert their attentions away from their own reactions *outside* of the story. (Bessell, 2000: 34)

No wonder our modern dress representatives were framed as fools and thugs. The crowd – on and off stage – were the energy of the show, in keeping with the special dynamics of the space, but they had to be contained, hamstrung; and though perfectly understandable, the production as a whole suffered as a result. The audience were only permitted to truly fuse with the fictional crowd before entering the play proper. After that they had to be kept on a tight leash. The curious temporal division in costuming manifested a vexed conflict between past and present, in which the theatre tried to embrace the contemporeity facilitated by the space, while simultaneously drawing part of its authority from a version of the past. As the two collided, the bulk of the show's energies finally seemed to cling to a grounding (not a groundling) in a former age because it was not able to marshal the attention of the present audience. It wanted our engagement, but we had to play by house rules, and when it was clear that wouldn't happen, they went on as if we weren't there at all: the playing of a recording (or rather what was supposed to feel like a recording) which runs regardless of whether anyone is listening. The dangerous dynamic of the space fed in part by previous productions and perhaps even by that carnivalesque opening (the planted cobbler inadvertently facilitating less authorised audience participation) finally created its antithesis, an impulse to retreat from liveness into something safer and more consistent. If a historical theatrical dynamic was being sought to further an exciting and contemporary experience, the inherent paradox proved a sticking point.

A similar rub centred on casting. The women were all played by men, but Brutus was played by a black actor (Danny Sapani), so any historical logic for the casting was badly disrupted and rendered politically suspect. If the casting was color blind (itself a throwback to a former political age) why couldn't the same 'blindness' be applied to gender? Was gender somehow more disruptive than race? To whom? Whatever the answers to such questions, the decision to cast a black Brutus immediately rendered the 'Elizabethan' quality of the production occasional at best, throwing into question the point of investing in all those other historicist claims and methodologies.

These problems are not unique to the Globe. They may, in fact, lie at the heart of the play which wanted to have its historical cake and eat it too even in the sixteenth century. The play's anachronisms are one of those interesting features much loved by classroom teachers – the metatheatrical striking clock and musings on future performance in accents yet unknown – but on stage the play's tendency to shift in its sense of when (and therefore what) it is, produces a distinctly temporal vertigo. Where are we? When are we? If we are seeing the past, which past is it (Roman, Elizabethan or something else entirely) and how does that intersect with our present? As an audience member at the

Globe I seemed to be invited into the play, but the modern dress plebs who seemed to be a bridge between me and the pastness on stage turned out to be not my representatives at all, being scripted, marshalled and finally rendered themselves somehow *past*. This was not a cauldron for spontaneous liveness; and while I didn't want it to be so, I found myself unsure of my temporal footing and therefore of my place as an audience member trying to find meaning in the theatrical present. This was, perhaps, why my favourite moment in the production was the jig which concluded it, in which the version of pastness presented felt paradoxically live and contemporary, partly because there was no script behind it, partly because it demanded nothing of the audience. We clapped along with a spontaneity that was fitting and undisruptive enough to be allowed, and I found (with hindsight) an odd temporal link between myself and Thomas Platter, who seemed similarly struck by the concluding dance.

Critical response was divided, but the division still recorded the temporal as a driving concern for both parties. Anthony Holden in *The Observer* found it 'really quite moving … to see Shakespeare as Shakespeare intended', while John Gross in the Telegraph commended a 'genuine touch of timelessness'.[4] John Peter in *The Sunday Times* found the production refreshingly straightforward but didn't like what he called 'phoney audience involvement', while Roy Shaw in *The Tablet* saw the Elizabethan costuming as giving the production a 'dangerous edge' invoking the Queen's despotism.[5] Individual performances were widely praised, though some found Sapani's Brutus a little flat or hard to hear; others (such as Benedict Nightingale in *The Times*) found the production low on excitement, but many found the programme's claims to Elizabethan topicality sufficiently compelling to assume that that timeliness crossed over into the present.

Michael Billington did not, and having slammed the show in a review (29 May), went on to write a blistering op ed on 2 June which called into question the entire function and future of the Globe. The review began:

> It is time to ask some leading questions about this handsome Southwark playhouse. Is it an artistically ambitious organisation? Or is it content to go on churning out inexpressibly dreary productions, such as this *Julius Caesar*, to restless, inattentive, largely tourist audiences?

The core of Billington's critique hinged on the argument that 'Rylance offers no visible interpretation of the play', an argument since oft repeated by critics of Original Practices (myself included) who contend that in response to 'director's theatre' or 'concept theatre' (both offered as pejoratives) Original Practices offers history, or more simply pastness, as concept. This is, of course, not always the case, but the Globe's *Caesar* was an instance in which directorial inflection, a 'take' on the play and its characters, took a back seat to the larger concept of an Elizabethan frame for an otherwise neutral production. 'Is Brutus,' asked Billington, 'a flawed idealist or a self-righteous bungler? It is impossible to tell from Danny Sapani's noncommittal, and only partly audible, performance.' He concluded that 'Only Sue Lefton's climactic jig lifts it above the level of a humdrum school production.'

Billington's subsequent op-ed made explicit his critique of historical authenticity as neither attainable nor desirable, and challenged the Globe to find its identity as a contemporary performance space for a contemporary audience, rather than hiding in the shadows of the past. Though the *Observer* made a passing remark about the Blair administration turning on itself ('Et tu Gordon [Brown]'), there was strikingly little in the reviews evoking current or recent politics for all their claims to the production's timelessness. The narrative was there, as – for some – were the character issues, but in spite of the daylit and quasi-interactive audience relationship, the production finally felt politically separate: out of time.

The difficulty of such temporal slippage is not reserved solely for the Globe, though that theatre's historicist footprint makes the problem harder to ignore. Elizabethan productions trigger problematic responses ('authenticity' on the positive side, 'museum theatre' on the negative) while echoes of contemporary or near contemporary politics trigger other binaries ('gimicry'/'relevance'). Both approaches are tied to the way we think about Shakespeare more broadly, and the specifics of *Julius Caesar* foreground such concerns because of the play's preoccupation with political history and its contemporary resonance. Thus productions which take the opposite tack to the Globe's find themselves instilling something of the same temporal vertigo, though this can be an asset which gives those productions a resonant sense of depth.

Edward Hall's 2001 production, for instance, which opened at the Royal Shakespeare Theatre before transferring to the Barbican, evoked both the early twentieth century with its black shirts and strutting, jack-booted Caesar, and the Italian present. Several reviewers drew parallels between the actions of the deliberate and uniformed mob with the recent protests at the G8 summit in Genoa, during which hundreds of protesters were beaten and arrested by riot police, and one was shot dead.[6] Some even saw Italian prime minister Silvio Berlusconi (frequently blamed for the harsh behaviour of the Genovese carabinieri and the target of numerous contemporary allegations of widespread corruption[7]) in Hall's Caesar, but with hindsight the temporal vertigo seems most evident in the production's apparent lack of contemporary insistence. The key to this is that Hall's production opened well before the terrorist attacks of 9/11 and ran into the following year, thereby locating the production in assumptions about the geopolitics of the world which seemed to have been suspended during its run. The sense of the present in political and military terms changed, or was perceived to change, the day the Twin Towers came down, and subsequent productions that have chosen not to engage the resultant zeitgeist have done so at their peril. Yet Hall's production did not lose its political edge precisely because it was not located in an actual period and its contemporary intimations were generated by allusion rather than direct parallel, though the world of the play did have sufficient specificity to anchor the production in a compellingly theatrical world. It remains – extraordinarily – one of the most pressing and exciting in the play's history.

Hall's Rome was a deep, broad grey box, largely empty of furnishings but marked with striking visual features for key scenes – a shimmering impluvium for Brutus's orchard which became a bath for Caesar's house, for instance – which relied heavily on brilliant, high-angled lighting to create a hard, stark world. Against the back wall and hanging over the play's action were three huge words in lights: 'Peace', 'Freedom' and 'Liberty'. These provided a song to open the production in place of Shakespeare's first scene, which was cut – a stirring anthem of the republic sung first by a single boy, who was then joined by a woman, and eventually by the whole cast singing in seried ranks while drummers pounded out what became a wall of patriotic sound. The moment was wholly and unsettlingly unironic, leading several reviewers to hear echoes of *Cabaret*'s chilling Nazi hymn, 'Tomorrow belongs to me'. The words were these:

> The love of the Republic in the hearts of the bold,
> Is better than legions,
> Greater than gold.
> We bring forth a new world from the ashes of the old.
>
> Res publica facit nos fortes.
> Res publica!
> Res publica!
> Pax, Concordia, libertas.
> The Republic makes us strong.
> The empire we have conquered is ours alone.
> We laid the foundations stone by stone,
> Ours not to slave in, but master and own.[8]

The Latin was repeated several times, and the final line ('The republic makes us strong') saw the first appearance of Ian Hogg's swaggering Caesar in a blizzard of ticker-tape, arms spread to the

14   A triumphant Caesar (Ian Hogg) greets the crowd after the singing of the rousing republican anthem as Brutus (Greg Hicks) waits upstage centre. (dir. Edward Hall, 2001).

adoring crowd he so clearly needed, a delighted and vainglorious smile on his face. The crowds, far from the usual rag-tag mob, were black-shirted party faithful, many of them wielding lengths of metal pipe like truncheons. This was a Rome unlike Welles's in which Fascism was a dangerously seductive force eating away at the body politic; this was a Republic which had long since morphed into a totalitarian state, something Welles had glimpsed in 1937 but which had become all too familiar in the late twentieth century. Peace, Freedom and Liberty – the watchwords of the conspirators – had already been co-opted as the official slogans of the state, servings as mere propaganda. Brutus and Cassius fought to recapture them as meaningful terms, and did so with principle and selflessness; but the effort was always futile, and as the body count mounted and the faces in charge switched, the machine of the state ground on unchanged.

In ways the English stage had not seen for many years, this was the tragedy of Brutus, played with remarkable intelligence, restraint and suppressed inner turmoil by Greg Hicks, and the production was structured accordingly. With the elimination of the opening scene, the production ran a little over two hours without intermission. Hall cut the final scenes ruthlessly. From the end of 5.1, which cues up the battle sequence, the production eliminated all but 76 of the remaining 230 lines, so the battle was experienced entirely in aftermath, and that briefly. Gone were the misconstrued circumstances of Cassius's death; the capture of Lucilius. and Brutus's repeated quest for someone to aid his suicide. The consequence of this movement from the announcement of the battle directly to its ending in death and tragedy was that it all became postscript to what was – in another curious throwback to a former age – the production's climax: the tent scene.

From the outset, the production had been characterised by a brisk, forthright speaking style which was crisp and urgent, the cast thinking on the line and finding ways to create specificity and thought through pace and emphasis without falling back on pauses and silence. Hall clearly had learned something of this from his father, but there was no pedantry here, and none of the dullness which sometimes characterises Peter Hall's approach. Here energy, urgency, power drove through the line and pushed the story forward. The first scene between Tim Piggott-Smith's Cassius and Hicks's Brutus used that energy to propel their sense of crisis and the need for immediate action. The pace was breathless and the tension close to unbearable. When Casca pointed to the sunrise in the orchard scene, Brutus strayed into his line of sight, and there was a wonderful, hesitant moment in which he tried to withdraw before opting, with a sense of doing something irrevocable, to be the symbol they wanted him to be. Moreover, this Brutus – a man misguided but earnest and deliberate, far from the woolly liberal of Welles – knew immediately after the assassination, perhaps even during it, that he had made the wrong choice. As Caesar gushed blood at the hands of the conspirators, Brutus lingered down-stage, dagger held out in front of him, frozen as if caught between horror and resolution. He began the funeral oration with conviction, but hesitated when the crowd shouted for him to be Caesar, suddenly aware that they didn't understand, that they had got it wrong, and that he couldn't explain himself adequately. When he requested that he be allowed to depart '*alone*' instead of being fêted and crowned, we glimpsed a man who knew even at the height of success, when he had achieved exactly what he had set out to, that all was lost.

The tent scene was the apotheosis of this realisation and the clash between the two men was loaded with things unsaid. Here was the supremely stoic Brutus who had ruminated on Caesar's death over his own reflection in the shimmering impluvium, dressed in a subdued and elegant kimono. He was able to maintain that stoicism at unbearable personal cost until the camp poet's trivialising doggerel finally pushed him over the edge: he threw his wine at the man and shattered a glass at his feet. It was this, not the previous argument about bribery and corruption, that motivated Cassius's amazement that he 'could have been so angry'. The subsequent revelation of Portia's death (given only once, since Varro and Cornelius were cut from the tail of the scene) produced what was without doubt this briskly spoken production's longest silence: an agonised stillness in which language collapsed, and the tortured soul that Brutus had spent the previous two hours concealing was laid bear. It was a breathtaking moment which revealed the extent to which the actions the conspirators had undertaken had eliminated not the capacity to feel, but the capacity to express and to connect. I was forcibly reminded of how much physical distance Brutus had maintained from his wife in their only scene together, and was made to rethink its cautious restraint.[9] After that, the battles with their failure and death were only the inevitable expression of what we already knew, and what Brutus had known since Casca's dagger first struck Caesar.

This gap between the semblance of things and their true workings was a motif of the production. Hogg's grandiose Caesar was only the public version. After the debacle of the Lupercal he slipped into near hysteria and a childish clinging to Mark Antony, while in private we saw the man himself: paunchy, timorous and old, paddling his feet in his bath and muttering about Danger knowing full well that Caesar was more dangerous than he while towelling himself off. With Calpurnia he was patient and affectionate while explaining how right he was, but on Decius's entrance he became haughty and performative, backed into his role – and thus into his death – by his need to play a version of himself for his adoring public. His dismissal of Artemidorus's suit was a PR moment which drew applause, but his 'constant as the Northern star' speech was delivered in a statuesque pose, one hand on his hip, his voice a roar which cowed the senators, though the 'let me show it a little', was self-deprecating, almost a gag. When Mark Antony (played by Tom Mannion as a fumbling opportunist gradually discovering his power and position) revealed Caesar's body in the marketplace, part of the crowd's outrage was in being confronted with the reduction of the Caesar myth to this bloody corpse, shrunken and yet bloated at the same time. This was the ghost which appeared to Brutus, a reduced and bluish geriatric, his wounds washed so that his body made not so much a horrific spectacle as an anatomy.[10]

This Rome boasted only two non-uniformed civilians: the soothsayer, who opened the production by drawing a heart from a trap immediately prior to the anthem, and Cinna the Poet. Everyone else wore either the modern dress and toga accessory of the senate, the armour of a more traditional Rome for the later scenes, or the black shirts and boots of the mob. These last were sprinkled throughout the house for the funeral orations, drumming their metal bars with clangorous menace and swooping down from the house on knotted ropes when invited to gather around the corpse. This was a citizen army, the professional *agents provocateurs* of a single-party state, and their anger – when roused – was cool and deliberate, not ravenous and undisciplined. At the end of Mark Antony's address, they burned Caesar's body in the dark while a solemn rendition of the Res

Publica theme was sung; and when they cornered Cinna, they did so in the surety that he was not one of them. As Michael Dobson (2002) shrewdly observed in *Shakespeare Survey*, 'as a poet he was evidently under suspicion anyway of being a bourgeois intellectual insufficiently committed to the cultural revolution' (307). So they cut out his heart and hung him upside down, after which the proscription scene began immediately, the triumvirate striding in beneath his hanging corpse without even giving him a look.

The heart motif was important throughout the production, and the mob's brutality clearly drew on the interpolated first line of the anthem: 'the love of the republic in the hearts of the bold, is better than legions, better than gold'. If you don't have that love in your heart, best that it be cut out. But the heart, like so many other things in this production, was real, not metaphorical, and cutting it out meant mess, terror, and death. The heart which the soothsayer fished from the trap – the same trap from which Antony daubed himself with blood prior to the Lupercal race – was, at least according to the rehearsal notes, real, as if the director was keen to impress upon the actors the grim and slippery reality which lay beneath all the high-minded talk of sacrifice and liberty. Caesar's refusal to be a beast without a heart was, perversely, supposed to show his contempt for cowardice, but the bloody manner of his death (a splattering, gory affair of blood bags and hidden squeeze bottles) would not allow the metaphor to hold off the grim corporeality of his murder. When Cassius remarked that Brutus had split his heart in twain, Brutus heard something close to truth, that hearts in this world had to be ignored entirely or torn apart, as their mutual suicides – both also bloody – would soon demonstrate. Brutus finally broke down, giving in to the tears he had contained thus far, as he begged Lucilius to kill him with a sword thrust to the chest. Hearts here could stand for nothing – not love, not feeling, nor passion save for the republic itself, and that manifested in a specifically heartless way. This was a hard world lived in a bright and searching glare with room for nothing except political orthodoxy.

Critical response varied widely, many thrilling to the immediacy and briskness of the production, others baulking at the cuts or at what they considered a ham-fisted conceptual approach, in particular the redrawing of the crowd as invested political pawns. Some thought Caesar too obviously fallible, and others found Brutus insufficiently engaging – both of which were, I would say, productively deliberate decisions. Some sought parallels in the politics of the company itself, which was then undergoing a thorough overhaul that worried (and angered) many.[11] The most common response was that the production had caught a generally contemporary ethos, a glimpse of the present in spite of its multi-period costumes, and that a worrying one. The *Sunday Mercury* and *Evening Standard* saw echoes of recent British vigilantism and press-fuelled paedophile witch hunts in the murder of Cinna the Poet.[12] Brian Logan in *The Observer* wrote that the production's defining motif – the civic motto 'Peace, Freedom, Liberty' obscured by the hanging body of a lynched poet – had 'imperishable currency. Don't trust a state's rhetoric, trust its actions.'[13] Pat Ashworth in *The Stage* called it 'savage stuff, all horribly relevant to the times',[14] and Benedict Nightingale in *The Times* called it 'a bold, sometimes spectacular, parable for our own awful era'.[15] For my part, I have seen few productions of Shakespeare which so successfully explored a play's political dimension while beautifully illustrating its personal consequences.

In 2001 the world changed, or was perceived to have done so by those of us in the west. Few successful productions since have evaded entanglement with that new world, and fewer still have worn their temporal insistence on their sleeves as clearly as Deborah Warner's at the Barbican in 2005. Warner, renowned in particular for her 1987 *Titus Andronicus* at the Barbican and her 1995 *Richard II* with a cross-dressed Fiona Shaw in the title role, for her 2001 *Medea* (also with Shaw), and for a controversial *Don Giovanni* at Glyndebourne in 1994, was herself a media magnet. Add a cast of top actors – several with major film credits (particularly Ralph Fiennes) – and the media's salivating before the production opened was perhaps understandable. Not counting reviews, there were no fewer than five major interview-driven features the week of opening (14 April), in *The Independent* (Paul Taylor, 15 April), *The Times* (Benedict Nightingale with the cast, 18 April), *The New Statesman* (Rachel Halliburton, 11 April), *The Observer* (Kate Kellaway, also with the cast, 10 April), and *The Sunday Times* (Patrick Marmion's performance history, 9 April). The feeding frenzy indicated an alignment not just of stars but of issues and a director known for bold strokes. A play many reviews dismissed as 'one of Shakespeare's most dull' had become the 'most eagerly awaited Shakespearean production I can recall in years' and been received as 'one of his [Shakespeare's] very greatest' (Charles Spencer in the *Daily Telegraph*, 21 April). Stellar alignments are as much temporal as they are spatial phenomena, and everything about Warner's production seemed to foreground a particular moment in a very particular time.

The production had what I can only call a hyper-topicality, a sense of temporal embeddedness in the present which is rare in the history of any Shakespeare play, particularly in the history of *Caesar* after Welles. It wasn't just the suits and sand palette combat fatigues which so clearly evoked the military and political world outside the theatre – the US-led war in Iraq, and looming British elections – nor Anton Lesser's agonised Brutus which was (as prompted by the programme) almost universally equated with then prime minister Tony Blair. The production began with a crowd pressing the Lupercal's security barriers, an image which 'looks like a cross between a movie premiere in Leicester Square and the start of the London Marathon' (Paul Taylor, *The Independent*, 22 April), the crowd dotted with socialites and wannabes, homeless people and security guards. The soothsayer was a plummy drunk. John Shrapnel's Caesar was clad in Armani, surrounded by ministers, and working the crowd with a dazzling smile. Ralph Fiennes's Antony was a sporty media star of the David Beckham stripe turned PR consultant *à la* New Labour, and finally the 'cagey temporizer' who would out-manouevre his erstwhile friends.[16] Blocking of the closing combat sequences seemed to have been taken directly from photographs (also included in the programme) of troops aiming rifles in the shell-torn remains of Baghdad. In Fiona Shaw's Portia, the director saw a 'crude parallel' with Janice Kelly, the widow of Dr David Kelly, whose involvement with the dossier on Sadam Hussein's biological weapons programme caused political scandal resulting in his suicide.[17] Simon Russell Beale played Cassius as a fiery Marxist don out of place in the world of high gloss politics and needing someone suitable to take the limelight.[18] That someone was Anton Lesser's Brutus, not the well-meaning liberal of Wellesian yore, but a tortured New Labourite concerned for his own public image, his orchard soliloquy a study in media spin.

There was a particularly heightened sense of the contemporary in the use of famous actors because they were part of the public consciousness already, embedded in the zeitgeist. The issues the production seemed to echo were underscored by the faces known to the audience beyond this play, faces which constantly reminded of the sheer *presentness* of the thing, of the production as a facet of the culture as it was then. History folded in on itself, looped into a Mobius strip in which past and present become inseparable, the journey forward and back a constant locked in the present. Reviewers and audiences alike felt it. Nightingale in the *Times* alluded to the production's temporal hybridity, suggesting it was a throwback to Victorian spectacle (he called it 'anachronistic daring', particularly referencing the 100-strong crowd of supers of which 40 were Equity actors), but championing its detail work, by which he meant the specificity of character according to modernist standards. Others saw in the juxtaposition of past and present – the former in shadows; the latter, hard, clear and unavoidable – the production contextualising itself, nodding back to Rome and Elizabethan England but, unlike the new Globe, keeping the focus squarely on the present. In the words of Carol Rutter,

> Behind, a couple of truncated Roman columns recalled the classical past and cited its survival in postmodernity, a visual prompt, perhaps, for spectators to wonder what else might survive from antiquity: republicanism? democracy? pragmatic political assassination? (2006: 72)

But such gestures to time past recalled one of the prime critiques of the Bush administration and the Labour government which became its ally, a kind of willing amnesia, a blindness to the past's habit of creating the present particularly in international diplomacy, doubly so in the Middle East.[19]

Of course, making topical allusions does not translate into unambiguous meaning, and this was where the production added a further contemporary resonance. *Time Magazine* suggested that the production drew an obvious 'parallel with the perceived misdemeanors of Blair and US President George W. Bush', but the review remained muddy on what the parallel actually was. It tried to make a literal link to Bush as Caesar, which clearly didn't work, and ended smugly (but bafflingly) suggesting that Blair 'may not take heed' of the production's message. Along the way, it made reference to the concurrent Broadway production with Denzel Washington as Brutus to suggest that the story was simply in the air, but ended by lamely implying the transhistoricity of Shakespeare's genius, since the story's truths are 'universal and will ring true for centuries to come' (Jessica Carson, *Time Magazine*, 6 May). The rhetorical move in which the reviewer abandoned her claim to topicality in favour of these platitudes about timelessness was in keeping with the production's temporal slipperiness: it was current, it did engage the present directly and insistently, but not in ways which offered a specific meaning or – better still – a course of action. In an interview by Rachel Halliburton in *The New Statesman*, Deborah Warner made the point *Time* missed explicit:

> 'The play has suffered in the past because people have tried to swing it in one direction or another,' she protests. 'So I'm not, for instance, trying to compare Caesar with Bush – it just wouldn't work. Caesar was a brilliant strategist. Bush rigged a couple of elections.' (11 April)

As a result, the audience felt the insistence of the present but also felt – consciously or otherwise – that whatever modernism the production finally employed was trumped by a postmodern uncertainty about final meaning, rendered not in the abstract, but in the unsettlingly familiar terms of contemporary war, politics and media coverage. The production's clearest contemporary resonance was in its final refusal to be clear, to offer an obvious message, while slickly providing copious evidence of its own political relevance. The experience of watching the production was akin to flicking through cable news channels, each immaculately produced with eye-catching and compelling graphics, each accumulating persuasive sound bites, but each ultimately saying something quite different, so that the viewer feels overwhelmed and, paradoxically, underinformed. As Carol Rutter pointed out, there was even an uncertainty about the mantle which Antony produced in the funeral oration and which produced a troubled ripple through the crowd: they were being offered evidence whose uncertainty recalled the infamous 'dodgy dossier' on Saddam's weapons of mass destruction which persuaded Britain to join the Iraq war (Rutter, 2006: 74). The crowd then decided – as crowds often do – that the evidence was good enough after all, particularly since it gave closure and a clear sense of direction. *You know this story*, Warner seemed to say, *though you don't know what it means*. But then, we never do. In an age of media 'spin', dodgy dossiers and a cadre of generals, pundits, politicians, and voters who seemed to have (in the words of the play and the production's programme) 'misconstrued everything', the most blistering instance of the production's contemporeity was finally about the process of getting things wrong, rather than showing what was, or would have been, right.

> The American-style helmets and battledress at a stunningly staged Philippi suggest we're meant to draw contemporary analogies, but, if so, it's up to us to decide what they are. The complex conflict between democrats with flaws and autocrats with redeeming features? Maybe. (Benedict Nightingale, *The Times*, 21 April 2005)

Paul Taylor offered a more specific reading – 'that the plot to assassinate Caesar was far worse planned than is generally thought and that the disastrous unintended consequences wring the heart because of their cost' – but if such a take on the story might also be applied directly to the Iraq conflict, he did not make it explicitly. The *Curtain Up* review led with the idea that the production was 'unashamedly about the war against Iraq' but made the case for direct parallel through recourse to historical evidence from outside Shakespeare's play or Warner's production, and concluded with a more general statement that the production was 'an anti-war polemic'.[20] Kate Kellaway in the *Observer* tried to make direct parallels but quickly abandoned the exercise as reductive:

> With an election on its way, does the analogy game work in a British version? Is Tony Blair wanting a third term like Julius Caesar? Is Gordon Brown Brutus and Peter Mandelson Mark Antony? You don't have to play this clumsy parlour game for long to see what it reveals. All the men in *Julius Caesar* are ambiguous. Caesar, Mark Antony, Brutus and Cassius may be poured into many moulds, but will never set. (Sunday 10 April)

Charles Spencer in the *Telegraph* (21 April) saw the contemporary references, the crowd 'as the more unlovely citizens of today's Britain, mindless chavs itching for a binge-drinking session and a punch-up', the senators as 'the suavely suited new Labour Cabinet' and saw the assassination and its aftermath as paralleling the Iraq war, but also recognised the production's semantic ambiguity: 'Warner's production ... does not labour the parallels, but allows the audience to draw its own conclusions.' The *Observer*, in one of the few less enthusiastic reviews, extended this response further, saying somewhat perversely, 'There isn't a big idea behind this production, other than magnitude: it's often impressive, seldom moving.' Patrick Marmian, on the other hand, recognised the refusal to offer a 'big idea' for what it was, disturbingly familiar though that might be as one of the derisive watchwords hurled most frequently at New Labour: 'The spin's the thing' (*Sunday Times*, 9 April 2005). Carol Rutter cited the director's claim that it's 'a play for now', and her own unease about the lack of heroic message was couched smartly as itself a temporal factor, a nostalgia for a version of theatre, politics and war which we no longer believe in – in her terms – a 'Trojan horse' which bears a clear directorial message (2006: 85).

It was a mark, perhaps, of that curious temporal location that the production swept away its nineteenth-century heritage in the second half. The crowds and security guards vanished; and while the first half of the play had seen a stage crammed with extras, the battles of the second half were curiously anticlimactic, 'a desultory affair of runnings-about with replica weapons and a few loud bangs' (Dobson, 2006: 330). Much of the drama of the play had evaporated by then, and after the dramatic fashion in which Fiennes's Antony had turned and unleashed a crowd to new heights of stage barbarism (one of the women in the crowd tore Cinna the Poet's genitals away with her teeth), what followed was mundane and unexciting, perhaps deliberately so. Modern high-tech warfare does not easily translate to the alarums and excursions of Elizabethan staging. Furthermore, there is danger in a production providing thrills when it has striven to render an echo of a current and – for many – morally problematic war. This is the danger of making a historical fiction connect with real, weighty, and, most importantly, *current* events. Either the audience is permitted the frisson of exciting staged combat without guilt, or that frisson has to be subverted to reinforce the horror of war, to remind the audience that the urgency of the production is a pale echo of the world it has evoked beyond the theatre where the blood is real, and the corpses pile in the streets.

The kind of heightened contemporeity which Warner used was subsequently expanded to include the mode of presentation itself by Amsterdam's Toneelgroep, whose compellingly acted six-hour Dutch adaptation of 'The Roman Tragedies' combined

Coriolanus, *Julius Caesar* and *Antony and Cleopatra*. The production toured extensively, playing the Wiener Festwochen, the Festival d'Avignon, the Theaterformen, and the Barbican in late 2009 before moving to Montreal in 2010, performing in Dutch with surtitles in modern English. The company approached the plays as a media event, everything being broadcast on screen as it was being performed, the audience being permitted to watch intermittently in between reading newspapers, checking e-mail, getting food and drink, and generally behaving as if the plays were life happening around them. Such a multi-media approach was not new, but the pursuit of such a technique's implications to its logical end was. As Lynn Gardner wrote in *The Guardian*,

> Van Hove's triumph is to create an entire world that fits the technique like a glove: everything is on show here, all life is a performance, a continuous almost operatic soap unfolding in a large conference hall-like setting full of TV screens, pot plants, beige sofas and tables set up for instant press conferences. We the audience are part of this performance. We both watch the play and we are in the play, invited on to the stage to loll on the sofas, check our email on the computers or buy a drink from the on-stage bar.[21]

Tickers streamed across the video screens updating 'historical' details as if they were happening live and in the present, but also warning of coming dramatic moments, counting down to the scene of Caesar's death, for instance. This was history and politics packaged for the 24-hour news channels and structured around the whim of the viewer who could watch, ignore or interrupt the action with text messages of his or her own which would be screened as part of the production. This was deliberately what the Globe production of 1999 sought to avoid, a production ultimately about the audience and – by extension – about the way their casual omniverousness, a buffet approach to news gathering, makes meaning out of event. Most tellingly, perhaps, such an approach doesn't just involve the audience in the conventional way of good theatre; it makes them complicit, reveals the extent to which this is a beast of their own making, in which their attitudes, tastes and prejudices shape not just the coverage of the events, but the events themselves.

Warner seemed to have so definitively tackled the contemporary approach that the Royal Shakespeare Company retreated into other temporal dimensions. David Farr's 2005 touring production fell back on generic modern dress but brought little new or striking to the play, while Sean Holmes in 2006 returned to togas and short swords, augmented by some noisy and unhelpful crowds which looked as though they had spilled out of a Middle Eastern circus, and a wandering ghost of Caesar which, accoutred as it was in the theatrical trappings of a former age, seemed to be searching (unsuccessfully) for something fresh or compelling. Lucy Bailey's 2009 production at the Courtyard, took a different tack on temporality, embracing a revisionist historical perspective on Rome as recently championed by HBO's lurid miniseries of the same name. This was a Rome made squalid, violent and primitive, stripped of its idealism, its nobility and classical aesthetics: a Rome of excess and brutality. The production opened with a fight between two unarmed and largely naked men who – if the projection of the wolf suckling boys overhead was to be trusted – were Romulus and Remus, the fathers of the city. The yelping combat ended when one killed the other with his teeth, thus, it was implied, showing the spirit of the city which grew from them. In an article in the programme written by Jonathan Stamp, the historical consultant for HBO's *Rome*, a series of grotesque events from Roman history are cited to underwrite the statement that 'violence was ubiquitous, its consequences a commonplace, its methods endlessly diversified and reinvented'.[22] To approach the play from this perspective ignores much of what it actually says, and flattens its specific topography.

So Bailey's proscription scene was complete with an illustrative prisoner lashed to a hurdle for torture and a severed head which got tossed around amongst the bloodied triumvirate. The Lupercal was a wild masochistic orgy with wolfish costumes and crowds of revellers augmented, as was the unfortunate pattern throughout, by floor-level projections of people across the rear of the stage. These were used to eke out the crowds for the public scenes, particularly the funeral orations, in which the onstage crowd were obliged to stand in front of the projections and simulate their generic and looping action with gestures of grief and anger. This pretty embarrassing device gave the speakers nothing to work with, all sense of movement in the crowd being supplied by the gratuitous underscoring of musicians above.[23] The use of video projection was another failed gesture towards the temporal, a desire to rewrite the historical Rome in the minds of the audience and to do so in a medium of their own time. When the army of on-stage soldiers squared up against those projected on the back wall, an army looking for all the world like the computer-generated soldiers of recent movies like *300*, the audience saw a clash between past and present in terms of medium.[24] Theatre confronted film and the on-stage soldiers moved through openings in the projection panels and were lost. This was, suggested Bailey, a new kind of theatre which embraced the technology of its long-term rival. The problem, of course, was that the result was a stifling of the core theatrical component of the event – liveness: projections somehow made the production not edgy and immediate, but remote, disconnected from actor and audience alike, a dull and unholy mess that fell between periods and failed to catch that most crucial of temporal categories in the theatre, the compelling *now* of the performative moment.

Not only did the production abandon the politics of the play entirely; it suggested that politics were irrelevant, the actions of conquerors and assassins driven finally by the wolfish hearts of Romulus and Remus. While demonising history, such a perspective simultaneously whitewashed the present, made the audience feel superior to the men who had been so honoured by Kemble and Macready but who were revealed to be little more than savages. So we stepped out of time to find ourselves the better for it, the past conveniently ignored except where it provided the exotically foreign diversion of sex and blood lust *à la* HBO.

Perhaps in response to Bailey's failed attempt to find a new index of temporal immediacy, the most recent RSC production returned to overt contemporary reference, this time African. While much of Gregory Doran's 2012 production used a visual dimension which invoked association with sub-Saharan Africa (including echoes of Yael Farber's *SeZaR* in details like the necklacing of Cinna the Poet), the events of the previous year's Arab Spring suggested other topical resonances. The toppling of Muammar Gaddafi in Libya and Hosni Mubarak in Egypt set the stage for a production which was particularly concerned with what would happen after the assassination, evading the familiar complaint that the play climaxes too early. African Caesars had been seen before, and Farber's *SeZaR* had appeared on various UK stages in 2002, but a 'straight' production of the play (untranslated into African languages as *SeZaR* had been) set in Africa but with a British cast was new in various ways. Jettisoning the politically problematic convention of 'colour blind' casting, Doran's was the first all black production ever mounted by the RSC. One might have expected this (and the setting generally) to have attracted charges of gimmicky, but the press response was almost unanimously enthusiastic, in part because the actors brought such grace and power to their performances, their African accents underscoring a rich musicality in the iambic line which pleased even the most conservative of critics. The dominant response was that the play felt fresh, exciting and relevant in ways RSC *Caesars* had not for over a decade.

The production opened with a colourful and exuberant African market dominated by a colossal bronze Caesar, a familiar element of this play's production history here made fresh by association with the pulling down of the statue of Saddam Hussein seen on television sets all over the world. The soothsayer (Theo Ogundipe) was a clay-daubed witchdoctor, but this was clearly a modern Africa in its dress, its weapons and its politics. Jeffery Kissoon's white-suited Caesar evoked any number of African potentates and demagogues, Paterson Joseph's Brutus regarding him with a mixture of noble principle and delusional arrogance. He beat his breast as he reflected on the pride of his ancestors, and his various tactical errors were met with astonished disbelief by the other conspirators, particularly Cyril Nri's shrewd Cassius who seemed ready to stab Antony even after Brutus's counsel. In a production in which the overall concept might easily have stifled the detail work, character shone through in ways that seemed both specifically African and plausibly contemporary. Adjoa Andoh and Ann Ogbomo as Portia and Calpurnia emblematised such believable modernity in both having the kinds of level-headed realism which their respective husbands could only imagine. The male conspirators, clearly boyhood friends out of their depth as the events of the play ran away with them, became increasingly poignant figures as the production held on to the personally tragic stakes of their larger political actions. That such small-scale, personal and domestic specificity should survive so grand and complete a conceptual approach was surely the production's greatest achievement. Some still carped about the anticlimactic final scenes (the whole was played without an intermission in two hours and fifteen minutes) but Libby Purves, reviewing for *The Times* said the pace was 'faultless, riveting', while Michael Billington approvingly called the production a

15 Caesar (Jeffery Kissoon) is petitioned before the assassination, with the soothsayer above (dir. Gregory Doran 2012).

radical reinvention which gave the play a much-needed shot in the arm, and Kate Bassett called it 'scorchingly reinvigorated' and 'a resounding triumph'.[25] If previous productions had wrestled with the idea of the temporal, Doran's reconsidered the contemporary in global terms unseen before in the UK, simultaneously exploding the RSC's sometimes parochial sensibility in redefining who this most British of companies was and what its concerns may be.

So where will the play go from here? Doran's production suggests there is still mileage in contemporary relevance, doubly so as future political events breathe new detail into the framing idea, and directors' senses of the political landscape globalise. What is clear is that the productions which have generally been the best received have married a sense of political urgency with a specificity of characterisation and a clear and dynamic engagement with the crowd. Ignoring any one of these elements imperils a production, and the best seem to grapple with all three constructively. We have moved beyond oration, and seeing the play simply as an arrangement of set rhetorical pieces underscored by selfless idealism is as close to a seismic shift in the play's production history as we can get. In place of those abstracted heroic virtues, we have found something grubbier, something more clearly marked by self-interest and expediency, but still shot through with a genuine quest to identify and pursue right action. This focus on citizenship, on individual choices which have major effects is likely to endure, as, I suspect, is our interest in news media and how that citizenry is enlisted in political struggle. I doubt we have seen the end of productions which set the play in a resonant historical past such as Fascist Europe, but as such periods become more remote we will see more and more productions seeking more recent or contemporary analogues as a way of focusing the play's political specificity. After all, the word which ghosts the most enthusiastic reviews is nearly always 'relevance': that mild surprise that a play so often dismissed as dull, a classroom exercise whose historical roots anchor it to multiple dusty pasts, can touch something fresh, can echo where and who we are as if the very wounds of Caesar were mouths which spoke the past, present and future.

Notes

1. This aspect of the production was tackled by Lisa Hopkins in her review for *Early Modern Literary Studies* 5.2 (September 1999): 14.1–4, http://purl.oclc.org/emls/05-2/hopkrev.htm, accessed 1 August 2010.
2. The extent to which the Globe (and other Original Practices spaces) manipulate claims to historical authenticity to suit their product and their marketing strategies have been well explored elsewhere. I want to engage the issue here not as a discrete phenomenon about how companies claim authority in production, but as an aspect of this particular play and its twenty-first-century legacy.
3. Benedict Nightingale in *The Times*, 27 May 1999.
4. Both quotations from Sunday 30 May 1999.
5. Saturday 12 June 1999.
6. The Genoa summit took place between 18 and 22 July, so the associated riots were not part of the production's conscious design.
7. In April 2001, for instance, *The Economist* cover bore the headline 'Why Silvio Berlusconi is unfit to lead Italy' citing in particular numerous conflicts of interests including the claim that the prime minister had effective control of 90% of the nation's television stations through a combination of his governmental position and his business properties. This evidence of his unsuitability to lead is in addition to the casual and jocular racism and sexism he has systematically revealed all by himself.
8. The words are taken from the prompt book.

9   In private conversation, Hicks revealed that his mother died at the end of the rehearsal period and that this personal loss helped him to anchor this moment. (Author interview, 11 August 2010.)
10 Rehearsal notes (accessed in the production archive of the Shakespeare Birthplace Trust, Stratford-upon-Avon) from 27 May suggest that the wounds on the ghost should be 'clean, not dripping blood – like an image of Christ' (4), an idea reiterated on 15 June: 'skin to be pale blue with clean dry Christ-like stab holes' (5). I think this loaded terminology was not intended to suggest that Caesar was himself supposed to be Christ-like, but to reduce the power of the ghost, to prevent it from being sensational. If there is a Christological association, I suspect it is because we see the ghost through Brutus's perception of it, so the impression is less about Caesar's sanctity than Brutus's guilt.
11 The RSC, led by Adrian Noble, had recently determined to abandon the Barbican as their London home. They planned to cut more than half of their technical positions as part of a modernisation plan, to tour more, to close The Other Place, and to decenter their base of operations from Stratford, to engage in more speculative commercial production, and to employ actors on shorter contracts. Some of these elements would become central to the ill-fated Project Fleet, whose failure in part led to the resignation of Noble in 2003.
12 Richard Williamson in the *Sunday Mercury* (29 July) and Patrick Marmion, *Evening Standard* (27 July).
13 5 August 2001.
14 2 August 2001.
15 28 July 2001.
16 Rutter (2006: 73). In rehearsal the three core actors – who had all played for the RSC for the first time in 1988 – imagined their characters growing up together as schoolboys.
17 Warner revealed this in her interview with Kate Kellaway in *The Observer*. It was a detail used to anchor Shaw's performance, not one made explicit in the production itself, though audience members may have made the connection themselves.
18 Benedict Nightingale, in *The Times*, 13 May 2010.
19 One of the anthemic 'alternative' political songs of 1998 was Chumbawamba's ironic hymn to New Labour 'Amnesia', whose chorus ran 'Do you suffer from long term memory loss? I can't remember.'
20 Lizzie Loveridge, see www.curtainup.com.
21 21 November 2009.
22 Home Box Office (HBO) is a premium American cable and satellite TV network owned by Time Warner.
23 There was also a vaguely classical image (the Parthenon?) surrounded by computer-generated fire, though why the city was burning before the crowd went on the rampage wasn't clear.

24 There were other odd filmic references which seemed to exist purely for visual associative effect. I was particularly struck by the bizarre appearance of the conspirators at Brutus's house, entering as they did in oversized hooded black cloaks. As they circled him they looked like nothing so much as Nazgul from *The Lord of the Rings* or Dementors from *Harry Potter*. As with most things in the production, the imagery was not what you might call subtle.

25 Purves's piece appeared in *The Times* on 8 June, Billington's in *The Guardian*, on 6 June, and Bassett's in *The Independent* on 10 June 2012.

APPENDIX

Major cast and company staff of select twentieth- and twenty-first-century productions

Stage productions

Mercury Theatre, New York, 1937
Director: Orson Welles. Designer: Jean Rosenthal. Set: Sam Leve. Music: Marc Blitstein. Producers: Orson Welles and John Houseman.
Julius Caesar: Joseph Holland. Brutus: Orson Welles. Cassius: Martin Gabel. Mark Antony: George Coulouris. Cinna the Poet: Norman Lloyd. Octavius: Francis Carpenter. Portia: Muriel Brassler. Calpurnia: Evelyn Allen.

The Staatstheater, Berlin, 1941
Director: Jürgen Fehling. Designer: Traugott Müller.
Julius Caesar: Werner Krauss. Mark Antony: Gustav Knuth.

The Residenztheater, Munich, 1955
Director: Fritz Kortner. Designer: Hans Clarin.
Julius Caesar: Paul Verhoeven. Brutus: Gerd Brüdern. Cassius: Wolfgang Büttner. Casca: Rudolf Rhomberg. Mark Antony: Ernst Ginsberg. Portia: Agnes Fink. Calpurnia: Anne Kersten. Octavius: Stig von Nauckhoff.

The Royal Court, London, 1964
Director: Lindsay Anderson. Designer: Jocelyn Herbert.
Julius Caesar: Paul Curran. Brutus: Ian Bannen. Cassius: T.P. McKenna. Casca: Graham Crowden. Mark Antony: Daniel Massey. Portia: Sheila Allen. Cinna the Poet: Milton Johns. Octavius: Ronald Pickup.

Royal Shakespeare Theatre, Stratford and Aldwych, London, 1968
Director: John Barton. Designer: John Gunter.
Julius Caesar: Brewster Mason. Brutus: Barrie Ingham. Cassius: Ian Richardson. Casca: Derek Smith. Mark Antony: Charles Thomas. Portia: Lynn Farleigh. Calpurnia: Christina Greatrex. Octavius/Cicero: Geoffrey Hutchings. Decius Brutus: Emrys James. Metellus Ciumber: Ron Daniels.

Royal Shakespeare Theatre, Stratford 1972, and Aldwych, London, 1973
Director: Trevor Nunn with Buzz Goodbody, Euan Smith. Designer: Ann Curtis.
Julius Caesar: Mark Dignam. Brutus: John Wood. Cassius: Patrick Stewart. Casca: Gerald James/Philip Locke. Mark Antony: Richard Johnson. Portia: Margaret Tyzack. Calpurnia: Judy Cornwell/Mary Rutherford. Octavius: Corin Redgrave.

Royal Shakespeare Theatre, Stratford, 1983
Director: Ron Daniels. Designer: Farrah.
Julius Caesar: Joseph O'Conor. Brutus: Peter McEnery. Cassius: Emrys James. Casca: John Dicks. Mark Antony: David Schofield. Portia: Gemma Jones. Calpurnia: Lesley Duff. Octavius: Nigel Cooke.

Royal Shakespeare Theatre, Stratford 1987, and The Barbican, London, 1988
Director: Terry Hands, Designer: Farrah.
Julius Caesar: David Waller/Joseph O'Conor. Brutus: Roger Allam. Cassius: Sean Baker. Casca: Geoffrey Freshwater. Mark Antony: Nicholas Farrell/Linus Roache. Portia: Janet Amsbury. Calpurnia: Susan Colverd. Octavius: Gregory Doran.

Royal Shakespeare Theatre, Stratford 1991
Director: Steven Pimlott, Designer: Tobias Hoheisel.
Julius Caesar: Robert Stephens. Brutus: Jonathan Hyde. Cassius: David Bradley. Casca: Bernard Gallagher. Mark Antony: Owen Teale. Portia: Jane Gurnett. Calpurnia: Celia Gregory. Octavius: Scott Ransome.

The Felsenreitschule, Salzburg summer festival, 1992
Director: Peter Stein. Designer: Dionissis Fotopoulos.

The Other Place, Stratford, 1993
Director: David Thacker. Designer: Fran Thompson.
Julius Caesar: David Sumner. Brutus: Jeffrey Kissoon. Cassius: Rob Edwards. Casca: Ken Sabberton. Mark Antony: Barry Lynch. Portia: Francesca Ryan. Calpurnia: Tricia Kelly. Octavius: Andrew Maud.

Societas Raffaello Sanzio, *Giulio Cesare*, 1997–2002 occasional world venues
Director: Romeo Castellucci. Action: Claudio Castellucci. Declamation: Chiara Guidi. Sound composition: Romeo Castellucci. Technical director: Pierre Houben. Stage hand: Flavio Urbinati. Stage assistant: Michele Altana. Metallurgy: Stephan Duve. Taxidermist: Antonio Berardi. Property girl: Carmen Castellucci.
Julius Caesar: Maurizio Carra. Brutus: Silvano Voltolina. Cassius: Sergio Scarlatella. Mark Antony: Dalmazio Massini.

Shakespeare's Globe, London, 1999

Master of Play: Mark Rylance. Master of Verse: Giles Block. Master of Clothing & Properties: Jenny Tiramani. Master of Music: Claire van Kampen. Master of Fights: Terry King. Master of Dance: Sue Lefton. Julius Caesar: Paul Shelley. Brutus: Danny Sapani. Cassius: Richard Bremmer. Casca: Michael Rudko. Mark Antony: Mark Lewis Jones. Portia and Octavius: Toby Cockerell.

Atlanta, Georgia Shakespeare Festival, 2001

Director: John Dillon. Set designer: Paul Owen. Julius Caesar: Bruce Evers. Brutus: Charles Horton. Cassius: Chris Kayser. Casca: Damon Boggess. Mark Antony: Saxon Palmer. Portia: Lisa Paulsen. Calpurnia: Teresa DeBerry. Octavius: Gregory Thomas Isaac.

Royal Shakespeare Theatre, Stratford 2001, and The Barbican, London, 2002

Director: Edward Hall. Designer: Michael Pavelka. Music: Simon Slater. Julius Caesar: Ian Hogg. Brutus: Greg Hicks. Cassius: Tim Pigott-Smith. Casca: Colin McCormack. Mark Antony: Tom Manion. Portia: Claire Cox. Calpurnia: Sian Howard. Octavius: John Hopkins.

SeZaR, Grahamstown National Festival of the Arts, South Africa 2001, and in England at the Oxford Playhouse and at the Theatre Royal, Winchester, 2002.

Director: Yael Farber. SeZaR: Hope Sprinter Sekgobela. Brutus: Menzi Ngubane. Cassius: Tumisho Masha. Mark Anthony: Tony Kgorogi. Porshia: Mmabatho Mogomotsi. Kalphurnia: Keketso Semoko. Njkono (The Soothsayer): Mary Twala.

The Barbican, London, 2005

Director: Deborah Warner. Designer: Tom Pye. Julius Caesar: John Shrapnel. Brutus: Anton Lesser. Cassius: Simon Russell Beale. Casca: Struan Rodger. Mark Antony: Ralph Fiennes. Portia: Fiona Shaw. Calpurnia: Ginny Holder. Cicero: Clifford Rose. Octavius: Oliver Kieran-Jones.

Burgtheater, Vienna, 2007

Director: Falk Richter. Dramaturg: Joachim Lux. Costumes: Martin Kraemer. Set: Katrin Hoffmann. Lighting: Karsten Sander. Video: Bjørn Melhus.
Julius Caesar: Peter Simonischek. Brutus: Ronald Koch. Cassius: Ignaz Kirchner. Casca: Cornelius Obonya. Mark Antony: Michael Maertens. Portia: Myriam Schröder. Calpurnia: Sabine Haupt. Octavius: Moritz Vierboom.

Atlanta, Georgia Shakespeare, 2009

Director: Richard Garner. Designer: Kat Conley. Julius Caesar: Allen O'Reilly. Brutus: Neal Ghant. Cassius: Joe Knezevich. Casca: Allan Edwards. Mark Antony: David Quay. Portia: Susannah Millonzi. Calpurnia: Tess Malis Kincaid. Octavius: Eugene H. Russell IV.

The Courtyard Theatre, Stratford 2009, the Roundhouse, London, 2010, and the Park Avenue Armory, New York, 2011
Director: Lucy Bailey. Designer: William Dudley.
Julius Caesar: Greg Hicks. Brutus: Sam Troughton. Cassius: John Mackay. Casca: Oliver Ryan. Mark Antony: Darrell D'Silva. Portia: Hannah Young. Calpurnia: Noma Dumezweni.

Royal Shakespeare Theatre, Stratford, Noel Coward Theatre, London and on tour in the UK and at the Moscow Arts Theatre, Russia, 2012
Director: Gregory Doran. Design: Michael Vale. Music: Akintayo Akinbode.
Julius Caesar: Jeffery Kissoon. Brutus: Patterson Joseph. Cassius: Cyril Nri. Mark Antony: Ray Fearon. Portia: Adjoa Andoh. Calpurnia: Ann Ogbomo. Octavius: Ivanno Jeremiah. Lucius: Simon Manyonda.

Film and television productions

Independent Feature Film, 1950
Producer and director: David Bradley. Cinematographer: Louis McMahon. Costumes: Katharine Bradley, Music: Chuck Zornig.
Julius Caesar: Harold Tasker. Brutus: David Bradley. Cassius: Grosvenor Glenn. Octavius: Bob Holt. Mark Antony: Charlton Heston. Portia: Mary Sefton Darr. Calpurnia: Helen Ross.

MGM, Feature Film, 1953
Director: Joseph L. Mankiewicz. Producer: John Houseman. Cinematographer: Joseph Ruttenberg. Set: Hugh Hunt and Edwin B. Willis. Costume: Herschel McCoy. Music: Miklos Rozsa.
Julius Caesar: Louis Calhern. Brutus: James Mason. Cassius: John Gielgud. Casca: Edmund O'Brien. Mark Antony: Marlon Brando. Portia: Deborah Kerr. Calpurnia: Greer Garson. Octavius: Douglass Watson.

Commonwealth United Entertainment, Feature Film, 1970
Director: Stuart Burge. Producer: Peter Snell. Cinematography: Ken Higgins. Music: Michael J. Lewis. Costume: Robin Archer. Editing: Eric Boyd-Perkins.
Julius Caesar: John Gielgud. Brutus: Jason Robards. Cassius: Richard Johnson. Casca: Robert Vaughn. Mark Antony: Charlton Heston. Portia: Diana Rigg. Calpurnia: Jill Bennett. Octavius: Richard Chamberlain. Atemidorus: Christopher Lee.

BBC and Time-Life Television Productions, 1979
Director: Herbert Wise. Producer: Cedric Messina. Designer: Tony Abbott. Music: Mike Steer.
Julius Caesar: Charles Grey. Brutus: Richard Pasco. Cassius: David Collings. Casca: Sam Dastor. Mark Antony: Keith Mitchell. Portia: Virginia McKenna. Calpurnia: Elizabeth Spriggs.

Bibliography

Anderegg, Michael T. *Orson Welles, Shakespeare and Popular Culture.* Columbia University Press, New York, 1999.
Anderegg, Michael T. 'Orson Welles and After: *Julius Caesar* and Twentieth Century Totalitarianism', in *Julius Caesar: New Critical Essays*, ed. Horst Zander. Routledge, New York, 2005.
Anderson, Lindsay. *Never Apologise: The Collected Writings*, ed. Paul Ryan. Plexus Publishing, London, 2006.
Baldwin, T.W. *William Shakespeare's Small Latine and Lesse Greeke.* University of Illinois Press, Champaign, IL, 2 vols, 1944.
Beauman, Sally. *The Royal Shakespeare Company: A History of Ten Decades.* Oxford: Oxford University Press, 1982.
Beevor, Antony. *D-Day: The Battle for Normandy.* Viking, London, 2009.
Bessell, Jac. 'Findings from the Globe's 1999 Season', *Shakespeare's Globe Research Bulletin* 15 (March 2000).
Boose, Lynda E. and Richard Burt (eds). *Shakespeare the Movie: Popularizing the Plays on Film, TV, and Video.* Routledge, London and New York, 1997.
Brode, Douglas. *Shakespeare in the Movies.* Oxford University Press, Oxford, 2000.
Burt, Richard. *Shakespeare after Mass Media.* Palgrave, New York, 2001.
Callow, Simon. *Orson Welles: Volume 1. The Road to Xanadu.* Penguin, London and New York, 1995.
Canby, Vincent and Janet Maslin. *The New York Times Guide to the Best 1,000 Films Ever Made*, Three Rivers Press, New York, 1999.
Castellucci, Romeo. 'The Universal. The Simplest Place Possible: Romeo Castellucci, Societas Raffaello Sanzio interviewed by Valentina Valentini and Bonnie Marranca', trans. Jane House, *PAJ: A Journal of Performance and Art* 26.2 (2004).
Chambers, E.K. *The Elizabethan Stage.* Clarendon Press, Oxford, 4 vols, 1923.
Charlton, Kenneth. *Education in Renaissance England.* Routledge and Kegan Paul, London, 1965.

Jean Chothia. *'Julius Caesar* in Interesting Times', in *Remaking Shakespeare: Performance Across Media, Genres and Cultures*, eds Pascale Aebischer, Edward J. Esche and Nigel Wheale. Palgrave, London, 2003.

Cibber, Colly. *An Apology for the Life of Colley Cibber, With an Historical View of the Stage During His own Time: Written by Himself*, eds R. Byrne and S. Fone. Courier Dover, Mineola, NY, 2000.

Cook, Matt. *A Gay History of Britain: Love and Sex Between Men Since the Middle Ages*. Greenwood World Publishing, Oxford, 2007.

Daniel, David (ed.). *Julius Caesar*. Arden Third Series, A. & C. Black Publishers, London, 1999.

Dauth, Brian (ed.). *Joseph L. Mankiewicz Interviews*. Mississippi University Press, Jackson, MS, 2008.

Desai, A. *The Tragedy of Julius Caesar*. Orient Longman, Hyderabad, 2001.

Dobson, Michael. 'Accents yet Unknown: Canonisation and the Claiming of Julius Caesar', in *The Appropriation of Shakespeare: Post-Renaissance Reconstructions of the Works and the Myth*, ed. Jean I. Marsden. St. Martin's Press, New York, 1991.

Dobson, Michael. *The Making of the National Poet: Shakespeare, Adaptation and Authorship, 1660–1769*. Oxford University Press, Oxford, 1995.

Dobson, Michael. 'Shakespeare Performances in England, 2001', *Shakespeare Survey* 55 (2002): 285–321.

Dobson, Michael. 'Shakespeare Performances in England, 2005', *Shakespeare Survey* 59 (2006): 298–337.

Doherty, Thomas. *Cold War, Cool Medium: Television, McCarthyism, and American Culture*. Columbia University Press, New York, 2003.

Gadberry, Glen. 'The History Plays of the Third Reich', in *Theatre under the Nazis*, ed. John London, Manchester University Press, Manchester, 2000.

Geist, Kenneth L. *Pictures Will Talk: The Life and Films of Joseph L. Mankiewicz*. Charles Scribner's Sons, New York, 1978.

Grindon, Leger. *Shadows on the Past: Studies in the Historical Film*. Temple University Press, Philadelphia, 1994.

Hall, Peter. 'J'Accuse', *Plays and Players Magazine* 379 (April 1985).

Halpern, Richard. *Shakespeare Among the Moderns*. Cornell University Press, Ithaca, NY, 1997.

Hartley, Andrew James. 'Discovering Space: Shakespeare and the Material Theatre', in *The Edinburgh Companion to Shakespeare and the Arts*, eds Mark Thornton Burnett, Adrian Streete and Ramona Wray. Edinburgh University Press, Edinburgh, 2011.

Hartley, Andrew James. *The Shakespearean Dramaturg: A Theoretical and Practical Guide*, Palgrave, New York, 2005.

Hatchuel, Sarah (ed.). *The Tragedy of Julius Caesar*, New Kittredge edition. Focus Publishing, Newburyport, MA, 2008.

Hatchuel, Sarah. *Shakespeare, from Stage to Screen*, Cambridge University Press, Cambridge, 2004.
Holland, Peter. 'Shakespeare Performances in England 1990-91', *Shakespeare Survey* 45 (1992).
Holland, Peter. 'Shakespeare Performances in England 1992-93', *Shakespeare Survey* 47 (1994).
Hortmann, Wilhelm. *Shakespeare on the German Stage: The Twentieth Century*. Cambridge University Press, Cambridge, 1998.
Houseman, John. 'Filming Julius Caesar', *Sight and Sound* (July–September 1953).
James, Clive. *Visions Before Midnight*. Pan, London, 1981.
Kennedy, Dennis. *Looking at Shakespeare: A Visual History of Twentieth Century Performance*. Cambridge University Press, Cambridge, 2002.
Knortz, Karl. *Shakespeare in America*. Berlin, Theodore Hoffman, 1882.
Krutnik, Frank, Steve Neale, Brian Neve and Brian Stanfield (eds). *'Un-American' Hollywood: Politics and Film in the Blacklist Era*. Rutgers University Press, New Brunswick, 2007.
London, John. 'Non-German Drama in the Third Reich', in *Theatre under the Nazis*, ed. John London, Manchester University Press, Manchester, 2000.
Manvell, Roger. *Shakespeare and Film*, Praeger Publishers, New York and Washington, 1971.
Marr, Andrew. *A History of Modern Britain*. Pan Macmillan, Basingstoke and Oxford, 2007.
Matheson, Tom. 'Royal Caesar', in *Julius Caesar, New Critical Essays*, ed. Horst Zander. Routledge, New York, 2005.
Navasky, Victor S. *Naming Names*. Viking, New York, 1980.
Orme, Nicholas. *Medieval Schools from Roman Britain to Renaissance England*. Yale University Press, New Haven, CT and London, 2006.
Parrish, Michael E. *Anxious Decades: America in Prosperity and Depression, 1920–1941*, W.W. Norton & Company, 1994.
Peacock, D. Keith. *Thatcher's Theatre: British Theatre and Drama in the Eighties*. Greenwood, 1999.
Quince, Roland. *Shakespeare in South Africa: Stage Productions during the Apartheid Era*. Peter Lang, New York, 2000.
Ripley, John. *Julius Caesar on Stage in England and America, 1599–1973*. Cambridge University Press, Cambridge, 1980.
Rothwell, Kenneth S. and Annabelle Henkin Melzer. *Shakespeare on Screen*. Neal-Schuman Publishers, Inc., New York and London, 1990.
Rovit, Rebecca. 'Jewish Theatre', in *Theatre under the Nazis*, ed. John London. Manchester University Press, Manchester, 2000.
Rutter, Carol. 'Facing History, Facing Now: Deborah Warners' Julius Caesar at the Barbican Theatre', *Shakespeare Quarterly* 57: 1 (2006).

Schwartz, Richard A. 'How the Film and Television Blacklists Worked'. Florida International University, 1999, http://comptalk.fiu.edu/blacklist.htm, accessed 18 June 2011.

Sheffield, John, Duke of Buckingham. *Poems on Several Occasions to which are added the Tragedies of Julius Caesar and Marcus Brutus*. Robert and Andrew Foulis, Glasgow, 1722.

Sohmer, Steve. *Shakespeare's Mystery Play: The Opening of the Globe Theatre 1599*. Manchester University Press, Manchester, 1999.

Sorlin, Pierre. *The Film in History: Restaging the Past*. Barnes and Noble, Totowa, NJ, 1980.

Trivedi, Poonam and Dennis Bartholomeusz (eds). *India's Shakespeare: Translation, Interpretation and Performance*. Delaware University Press, Newark, 2005.

Vaughan, Virginia Mason. 'Making Shakespeare American: Shakespeare's Dissemination in Nineteenth Century America', in *Shakespeare in American Life*, eds Vaughan, Virginia Mason and Alden T. Vaughan. Folger Shakespeare Library, Washington DC, 2007.

Welles, Orson and Richard France. *Orson Welles on Shakespeare: The WPA and Mercury Theatre Playscripts*. Routledge, New York, 2001.

Wells, Stanley. 'Shakespeare Performances in London and Stratford-Upon-Avon 1986–87', *Shakespeare Survey* 41 (1994).

Willis, Susan. *The BBC Shakespeare Plays: Making the Televised Canon*, University of North Carolina Press, Chapel Hill, NC, 2002.

Wright, L.S. 'Shakespeare in South Africa: Alpha and "Omega"', *Postcolonial Studies* 7: 1 (2004).

Wyke, Maria. *Projecting the Past: Ancient Rome, Cinema and History*, New York/London, Routledge, 1997.

Wyke, Maria. *Caesar, a Life in Western Culture*. University of Chicago Press, Chicago and London, 2008.

Zander, Horst. *Julius Caesar: New Critical Essays*. Routledge, London, 2004.

Index

Note productions are listed by director rather than venue. Italicised page numbers refer to illustrations.

Adler, Stella 61
Alkzai, Ebrahim 180
Allam, Roger 142
Anderegg, Michael 35n.22, 51, 53, 55n.1
Anderson, Lindsay 84–94 *passim*, 98, 120
Animated Tales 124, 132n.7
Anne (Queen) 15
Astor Place Riots 34 n.10

Bailey, Lucy 237–8
Baker, Sean 142
Bannen, Ian *87*, 90, 93
Barnay, Ludwig 25
Barons Court Theatre 137, 158
Barrett, Lawrence 20
Barrymore, John 61, 63, 80n.1
Bart, Lionel 99
Barton, John 84, 94–9
battle scenes 41–3, 65, 76, 114, 118, 130, 139, 141, 154, 171, 187, 210, 234
BBC 111, 124–41 *passim*, 235
beau ideal 21–2
Benson, F.R. 28–9, 31, 35n.20, 52

Berlusconi, Silvio 174, 223, 241n.7
Bessell, Jaq 218–20
Betterton, Thomas 13, 15
Bhardwaj, Vishal 182
Billington, Michael 222–3, 239
Blair, Tony 231, 234
Blatchley, John 83–4
Blitz! 99
Blitzstein, Marc 38–9
Bogdanov, Michael 149
Booth, Barton 18
Booth, Edwin 20–1, 23, 51
Booth, John Wilkes 20–1
Booth, Junius Brutus 20
Bower, Dallas 124
Bradley, David 112
Brando, Marlon 56–7, 61–5, 115, 121
Brecht, Bertolt 91, 168, 170
Brenton, Howard 149
Brett, Leonard 124
Bridges-Adams, William 29–31, 35n.21, 39, 51, 52
Brighton bombing 136–8
Brode, Douglas 122–3
Brook, Peter 53, 83

[253]

Burge, Stuart 111, 116, 124, 131
Burns, Ken 198
Burton, Richard 62
Bush, George W. 174, 232–3

Caesar, Julius (historical figure) 8–10
Calhern, Louis 65
Callow, Simon 47, 53
Calpurnia's dream 113, 132n.5
Castellucci, Romeo 176–8, 191
Chamberlain, Richard 116
Charles I 12–13
Chothia, Jean 81n.6, 81n.9
Cibber, Colley 13
Cinna the Poet, murder of 14, 16, 23, 26, 30, 33n.5, 35n.21, 41, 43–7, 73, 93, 105, 114, 119, 129, 143, 147, 151, 170, *174*, 186–7, 197, 200, 210, 228–30, 235, 238
Collinge, David 127
Communism, 66, 69–74, 78, 135, 163, 217
Cooper, Thomas Abthorpe, 19
Copeland, Aaron 38
crowd scenes 16, 22–5, 27, 43–6, 77–80, 105, 113, 129, 139, 147, 152–3, 156, 226, 237–8, 240

Daniels, David 127
Daniels, Ron 135, 137–44, 151, 160
Davenant, William 15
Davenport, Edward Loomis, 19, 20
Dawson, Anthony 34n.15
Dead Poets Society 80n.3
Decker, Thomas 183
Delaware Federal Theatre 53
DeMille, Cecil B. 65, 70–7, 79, 80, 115
Desai, A 180

Digges, Leonard 11
Dignam, Mark 105
Dillon, John 196–204
Dobson, Michael 18–19, 33n.8, 229, 235
Doran, Gregory 238
doubling 205–7
Dryden, John 15
Dutt, Utpal 178–9

Ebrahim, Carter 184
Edwards, Allan 207–9
Egerton, Daniel 22
Elizabeth I 9–10
Evers, Bruce 198, *199*, 203, 205, 214

Falkland Islands war 135
Farber, Yael 187–91, 238
Farr, David 237
Farrah (designer) 142
Fascism 36, 39, 48, 50, 54, 57, 67, 73, 78, 104, 143, 160, 163, 168, 174–5, 217, 226
Federal Theatre, 44
Fehling, Jürgen 164, 167–9
Fiennes, Ralph 230–1
Ford, John 72
Forrest, Edwin 34n.10
forum scene 23, 26, 27–8, 63–4, 73–4, 78, 115, 120–1, 141, 143, 210–11
Fox News 174–5
funeral oration scene, *see* forum scene

Gaddafi Muammar, 238
Gandhi, Indira 179
Garner, Richard 194, 204, 212
Garrick, David 19
Garson, Greer 65
Geist, Kenneth L. 81n.8, 81n.10
George I 15
George II Duke of Saxe-Meiningen, 25, 170

Georgia Shakespeare 194–216 *passim*
Ghost of Caesar 66–7, 81n.5, 96, 133n.11, 144, 198, 228, 242n.10
Gielgud, John 56–7, 58–61, 62, 87–8, 92, 97, 104, 106, 116, 120
Globe Theatre (reconstructed) 217–23
Granville-Barker, Harvey 29
Gray, Charles 127

Hall, Edward 224
Hall, Peter 87–9, 91, 92, 94, 149–51, 156–8, 226
Halpern, Richard 20
Hamblin, Thomas, 19
Hands, Terry 142–4, 151
Hart, Charles 13
Hayden, Sterling 69
Heston, Charlton 111–23 *passim*
Hicks, Greg 225, 226–8
Hitler, Adolf 37, 39, 40, 50, 135, 169–73
Hogg, Ian 225, 228
Holland, Peter 134, 147–8, 156–7
Hollywood
  Blacklist 69, 75
  changes during the 1960s and 1970s 110–11, 116–18
Holmes, Sean 237
Hortmann, Wilhelm 165, 168–9
House Committee on Un-American Activities (HUAC) 69–76
Housemann, John 38, 49–50, 56, 67, 73
Howells, Roger 108n.14
Hussein, Saddam 231, 239
Huston, John 69, 70
Hutchings, Geoffrey 97

I, Claudius 111, 131
India 163
Ingham, Barry 97
Iraq (war in) 174, 231–5

Jackson, Barry 52
James I 12
James, Emrys 140, 142
Japan 163
Jesus Christ Superstar 99
Johnson, Richard 116
Joseph, Patterson 239
Julius Caesar (the play)
  doubling 14–15
  education 18, 110, 125, 131, 163
  in India 178
  in South Africa 182–3, 185
  lack of theatricality 4–5
  politics 1–4, 134–5
  textual history 10–11, 14, 15, 18

Kapadia, Vikram 180–1
Kathakali, 181–2, 191
Kayser, Chris 199, 203, 214
Kemble, Charles 22
Kemble, John Phillip 15, 21–3, 31, 46, 238
Kennedy, Dennis 176–8
Kerr, Deborah 65, 80n.4
Kissoon Jeffery, 239
Knezevich, Joe 214
Kortner, Fritz 170–2
Kynaston, Edward 13

Langham, Michael 59
Leavis, F.R. 88
Lee, Christopher 116
Lesser, Anton 231
Long, Huey 196–204
Losey, Joseph 70, 77
Lynch, Barry 155

McCarthy, Joseph 69
McEnery, Peter *139*, 140
Mac Liammoir, Micheal 39
Macready, William Charles 23, 238
Mandela, Nelson 183–4, 190
Mankiewicz, Hermann 56
Mankiewicz, Joseph 56–82 *passim*, 115
Marr, Andrew 136
Mason, Brewster 96
Mason, James 56–7, 58–61, 62
Massey, Daniel 90
Meiningen *see* George II Duke of Saxe-Meiningen
Mercury Theatre *see* Welles, Orson
Messina, Cedric 125
Method (acting technique) 61, 63, 87–8
MGM (Metro-Goldwyn-Mayer) 68
Mitchell, Keith 128–9
Mohr, Robert 185
Mohun, Michael 13
Morley, Christopher 100
Mubarak, Hosni 238
Muldoon, Roland 150
Murdoch, Rupert 174
Mussolini, Benito 37, 39, 50, 52

Nazi attitude to Shakespeare 165–7, 172–3
Neyerere, Julius 183
Noble, Adrian 242n.11
Nri, Cyril 239
Nunn, Trevor 84, 99–107
Nuremberg effect 39–40, 50, 142

O'Brien, Edward 65
O'Conor, Joseph *139*, 140, 142
Olivier, Laurence 61, 65, 87
orchard scene 48, 86, 142, 144, 231

Other Place, The (Stratford) 151–4

Padamsee, Alyque 179–80
Palmer, Saxon 201–4
Parks, Larry 75
Pasco, Richard 127–8
Peacock, D. Keith, 161n.8
Pepys, Samuel 13
Phelps, Samuel 23
Phillips, Ron 158–60
Pimlott, Steven 144–8, 151
Pinter, Karoly 186–7
Platter, Thomas 11–12, 221
Poel, William 29, 31, 39, 51, 52
Pope, Alexander 18
popular culture 110–11, 131
Portia's death 15, 22, 60, 81n.4, 86, 97, 104, 142, 148, 154, 227
projected images and video 138, *139*
proscription scene 15, 26, 30, 41, 63, 73–4, 76, 105, 114, 121–3, 129, 148, 229, 237
Purkey, Malcom 185–6

quarrel scene *see* tent scene
Quayle, Anthony 59
Quo Vadis, 65

Ramones, The 131
Reagan, Ronald 122
Reinhardt, Max 164
Reynolds, Joshua 21
RKO Pictures 69
Richardson, Ian 97
Richter, Falk 173–5, 191
Rigg, Diana 116
Ripley, John 14, 15, 30, 32 n5
Robards, Jason 116, 118, 132n.4
Romans in Britain, The 149–50
Rome (HBO miniseries) 237

Romeo and Juliet (dir. Zeffirelli) 116–17
Rosenthal, Jean 40, 50
Rothwell, Kenneth 123
Royal Court Theatre 85
Rutter, Carol 232–5
Rylance, Mark 218

Sapani, Danny 221
Scaparro, Maurizio 175
Schary, Dore 69, 73
Schiller, Leon 52, 170
Schlesinger, John 92
Schofield, David 140–1
Schofield, Paul 62
Screen Directors Guild (SDG) 70–1, 75, 76
September eleventh terrorist attacks 200–1, 224
Sex Pistols, The 131
SeZaR see Farber, Yael
Shah, Naseeruddin 180–1
Shakespeare Memorial Theatre, Stratford-upon-Avon 28–31, 100–2
Shaw, George Bernard 28, 89
Sheffield, Edmund 16–17
Siddons, Mrs. Sarah 22
Smith, William 13
Snell, Peter 115
Sohmer, Steve 9–10, 218
soothsayer 66
South Africa 163
Soviet Union 163
Stander, Lionel 75
Stanivlavski, Constantin 61, 87–8
Stauffenberg, Claus von 95, 169, 172, 184, 192n.7
Stein, Peter 171–2
Stephens, Robert 145, *146*, 147, 151
Stewart, Patrick 104, 106
storm scene 66–7, 95–6, 119

television 110–11
tent scene 15, 16, 24, 26, 60, 80n.1, 115, 128, 140, 142, 148, 209, 226–7
Thacker, David 134, 151–6
Thatcher, Margaret 135–7, 138, 143, 145–8
representation as Caesar at Barons Court 158–60
theatre funding and censorship under 148–51
theatricality in *Julius Caesar* lack thereof 4–5
politics 1–4
Thomas, Charles 97
Toneelgroep 235–6
Tree, Sir Herbert Beerbohm 25–8, 31, 51, 89

Up Pompeii 111

Vaughn, Robert 116
verse speaking 29, 59, 61, 86–91, 95
Verwoerd, Hendrik 185
Volankis, Minos 83–4
Voodoo Macbeth 37, 40

Waller, David 142
Walpole, Robert 15, 19
War on Terror 175
Warner, Deborah 230–6
Washington, Denzel 232
Welles, Orson 36–55 *passim*, 56–7, 61, 73, 76, 80 n1, 93, 94, 99, 115–16, 135, 160, 167, 179, 212, 217, 226–7, 231
Wells, Stanley 144
Whigs 15–19
Whitehouse, Mary 149
Wilder, Billy 70
Wilks, Robert 18
Willis, Susan 124, 126

Wise, Herbert 111, 124–41
 passim
Wood, John 103–4
World War II 37, 42–3, 66, 76,
 110

Wright, Laurence 184–9
Wyke, Maria 9–10

Young, Charles Mayne, 22

EU authorised representative for GPSR:
Easy Access System Europe, Mustamäe tee 50,
10621 Tallinn, Estonia
gpsr.requests@easproject.com

www.ingramcontent.com/pod-product-compliance
Lightning Source LLC
Chambersburg PA
CBHW070236240426
43673CB00044B/1813